THE
BARGAIN HUNTER'S
GUIDE TO
ART COLLECTING

THE
BARGAIN HUNTER'S
GUIDE TO
ART COLLECTING

STEVEN NAIFEH

with the assistance of
Gregory White Smith

QUILL

New York   1982

Library of Congress Cataloging in Publication Data

Naifeh, Steven W., 1952–
  The bargain hunter's guide to art collecting.

  Includes index.
  1. Art as an investment.   2. Art—Collectors and
collecting.   I. Smith, Gregory White.   II. Title.
[N8600.N34   1982b]   332.63   81-19275
ISBN 0-688-00815-1   AACR2
ISBN 0-688-00801-1 (pbk.)

Printed in the United States of America

First Quill Edition

1 2 3 4 5 6 7 8 9 10

BOOK DESIGN BY MICHAEL MAUCERI
          & BERNARD SCHLEIFER

For Hume and Nancy Horan

Acknowledgments

Without the help of dealers and auction officials, I could not have written this book. Most were contacted during my research on it; others were contacted several years ago, when I was researching a book on the New York art world. The various individuals helped with extraordinary generosity. They let me interview them, provided me with the photographs used as illustrations, and reviewed sections for completeness and accuracy. In particular, my thanks go to two dealers and friends in Boston, D. Roger Howlett of Childs Gallery and Barbara Krakow of the Harcus Krakow Gallery. In this book, I say that a dealer is the beginning collector's best teacher. Roger and Barbara were certainly mine.

My thanks to Jack Banning, Poster America/Yesterday, New York; J. H. Beal, Littleton, New Hampshire; Lee Beshar, A. Beshar & Co., New York; Doris Leslie Blau, Doris Leslie Blau Gallery, New York; Diane Brown, Diane Brown Gallery, Washington, D.C.; Francis A. Caro, Frank Caro & Co., New York; Edward Lee Cave, Sotheby Parke Bernet, New York; Allan S. Chait, Ralph M. Chait Gallery, New York; Charles Cleland, Pueblo One, Scottsdale, Arizona; Ted Cooper, Adams Davidson Galleries, Inc., Washington, D.C.; Carl Crossman, Childs Gallery, Boston; André Emmerich, André Emmerich Gallery, New York; Esther Fitzgerald, Edward H. Merrin Gallery, Inc., New York; Mary Gera,

Sotheby Parke Bernet, New York; Lucien Goldschmidt, Lucien Goldschmidt, Inc., New York; Portia Harcus, Harcus Krakow Gallery, Boston; Jem Hom, Hom Gallery, Washington, D.C.; Ivan C. Karp, O.K. Harris Fine Arts, New York; Klaus Kertess, Bykert Gallery, New York; Leland La Ganke, La Ganke & Co., New York; Arline Lanphear, Stair & Co., New York; Robert Mann, Harry Lunn Gallery, Washington, D.C.; Missy McHugh, Christie Manson & Woods, New York; Nancy McIntosh, McIntosh/Drysdale Gallery, Washington, D.C.; Edward H. Merrin, Edward H. Merrin Gallery, Inc., New York; Chris Middendorf, Middendorf/Lane Gallery, Washington, D.C.; Donald Morris, Donald Morris Gallery, Inc., Birmingham, Michigan; Chip Nourse, Nourse Gallery, Washington, D.C.; Carolyn Owerka, Pace Editions Inc., New York; Betty Parsons, Betty Parsons Gallery, New York; Angus Percival, Stair & Co., New York; Perry Rathbone, Christie Manson & Woods, New York; Susan Reinhold, Reinhold Brown, New York; Sydney Rosenblatt, Minna Rosenblatt Ltd., New York; Brent Sikkema, Vision Gallery, Boston; Holly Solomon, Holly Solomon Gallery, New York; Richard H. Soloman, Pace Editions Inc., New York; Alastair A. Stair, Stair & Co., New York; John Stair, Jr., Sotheby Parke Bernet, New York; Gerald Stiebel, Rosenberg & Stiebel, New York; Paul Vandekar, Earle D. Vandekar of Knightsbridge, Los Angeles; Christine Vining, Christine Vining Antiques, Marblehead, Massachusetts; Abbot W. Vose, Vose Galleries of Boston Inc.; Ann. P. Vose, Vose Galleries of Boston Inc.; Robert Vose, Vose Galleries of Boston Inc.; Terry Vose, Vose Galleries of Boston Inc.; Angus Whyte, Angus Whyte Gallery, Washington, D.C.; Marjolaine Williams, Christie Manson & Woods, New York; Lee D. Witkin, The Whitkin Gallery, Inc., New York; Robert C. Woolley, Sotheby Parke Bernet, New York.

In addition, I would like to convey my appreciation to the many other individuals who have shared their knowledge of collecting and the art market, especially Co de Koning, a Dutch management consultant and collector who first excited my imagination about the possibilities of collecting. Thanks also to Marie Adams, professor, Harvard University; Will Ameringer, Cultural Media Associates, New York; Jean Sutherland Boggs, director, The Philadelphia Art Museum; James K. Chiu, collector; Jerry Cohn, conservator, the Fogg Art Museum, Cambridge, Massachusetts; Robert Judson Clark, professor, Princeton University; Gene Davis, artist, Washington, D.C.; Walter B. Denny, professor, University of Massachusetts, Amherst; Martin Eidelberg, professor, Rutgers University, New Brunswick, New Jersey; Sydney Freedberg, professor, Harvard University; Henry Geldzahler, commissioner of the arts, New York; Bonnie Naifeh Hill, collector; Sam Hunter, professor, Princeton University; Robert Koch, professor, Princeton University; Hilton

Kramer, arts editor, *New York Times;* Mary Lanier, arts consultant, New York; Benny Naifeh, collector; Cynthia Packert, student, Harvard University; William Rubin, director of the Department of Painting and Sculpture, the Museum of Modern Art, New York; Seymour Slive, director, the Fogg Art Museum, Cambridge, Massachusetts; Colin Streeter, consultant in English furniture, New York; Diane Upright, professor, Harvard University; S. Cary Welch, consultative chairman, Islamic Art, the Metropolitan Museum of Art, New York.

My agent, Connie Clausen, was, as usual, thoughtful and supportive. Elizabeth Frost Knappman, my editor at William Morrow and Co., helped determine the focus of the book and shape its contents. I am grateful for her enthusiastic cooperation. My partner and frequent co-author, Gregory White Smith, generously edited the book; his eloquent ear and patient care are responsible for much of its quality. Finally, as always, my family provided me with unstinting support.

Contents

The Pleasures and Profits of Collecting Art

ART FOR EVERYONE

Everyone collects something. Whether it's beer cans, recipes, friends, or money, the urge to acquire is a basic part of the human personality. And throughout history, nothing has been more avidly sought after or more proudly possessed than art. From the caves of Lascaux to the galleries of Madison Avenue, works of art have been the crowning fulfillment of the urge to acquire: the collector's grail.

Then why don't more people collect art?

The problem is that most people don't understand what collecting is all about. They're afraid that it's too expensive. (Aren't all art collectors Rockefellers or Fords?) They think that you have to be an expert to collect intelligently. (How else can you make the subtle distinctions between the worthy and the worthless?) Or they think that art collecting has to be a full-time affair. (Aren't there dealers to visit, auctions to attend, and books to read?)

If any of these considerations has kept *you* from collecting art in the past, now is the time to reconsider.

Art Collecting Doesn't Have to Be Expensive. Certainly, any collector envies the lucky few who can bid millions of dollars for paintings by old masters and Impressionists. Who would turn down a Rembrandt? But there's a crowded world of great art works that *anyone* can afford: a world where everything costs between $10 and $10,000. And don't feel that buying art on a budget will make you a second-class collector. Whether you plan to spend large sums or small, you're embarking on the same compelling adventure.

You Don't Have to Be an Expert to Collect Art. In collecting art, as in anything, knowledge is the key to success. That doesn't mean, however, that you have to become a professional art historian or curator in order to buy art intelligently. Anyone can develop an "eye"—the term used by experts to describe a person's ability to see quality in art. In fact, some of the major experts in the art world today trained themselves, simply by looking at art in their spare time.

Collecting Doesn't Have to Be a Full-Time Affair. While there are a *few* professional collectors who spend their entire lives buying art, most people turn to art as a diversion. Politicians, businessmen, and housewives have all found time to explore the pleasures and rewards of collecting art on weekends and after work.

ART BARGAINS AND INVESTMENT BARGAINS

Another common misimpression is that the art market is a place to "get rich quick." No wonder: Newspapers and magazines report only the big winners. Someone buys a painting by Jasper Johns in 1959 for $950, then sells it twenty years later for a cool $1,000,000. An undistinguished Renaissance panel that sold at auction for several hundred turns out to be a Raphael worth millions.

In fact, these exceptions prove the rule: For every work of art that goes up in price, there are hundreds that never budge—and hundreds more that go down. Your chances of winning big on the art market are no better than they are at the racetrack.

Art Bargains. I can't tell you how to find the exceptional work that will make you rich overnight—be suspicious of anyone who tries. But I *can* do almost as much. First, I can tell you how to purchase extremely fine and relatively inexpensive works of art. They may not bring you a quick, dramatic return on your investment, but they will bring you a lifetime of pleasure and pride. I call these works *art bargains.*

Investment Bargains. Second, I can offer advice to help you safeguard the investment you make in art. Of course, I can't *guarantee* you a certain profit on the works you buy. But I can tell you how to identify works that are likely to increase in value at a steady rate. Although such works are seldom cheap, I'll point out the ones that are relatively inexpensive. I call these works *investment bargains*. Obviously, the best bargains are those rare works that combine exceptional quality and low price with likely investment potential.

BECOMING YOUR OWN EXPERT

Whether you want art bargains or investment bargains, whether you want to spend a lot of money or a little, you will be competing in a highly sophisticated market. How do you begin the search for objects worthy of your collection? How do you know what kinds of objects you might like? Where can you find them? To answer these questions, you need expert information. That's what this book is for. It will tell you how to avoid buying the wrong object, *and* how to avoid paying too much for the right one.

The issues are many. Should you buy from a dealer or an auction house? How do you find a good one? How can you make sure you get the best deal? What about alternative sources? How do you acquire works directly from the artist, at garage sales, flea markets, and other less glamorous outlets? How do you sell a work you no longer want—and why you should consider giving it away to a museum.

Once you've bought a work, how should you mat and frame it? How can you frame works yourself—or locate a suitable shop to do it for you? Finally, and most importantly, how do you care for your collection to maintain both its beauty and its investment value?

Art collecting is a challenging and exciting activity. By giving you the answers to these and other important questions, this book will make it pleasurable and profitable as well.

THERE IS NO TYPICAL COLLECTOR

There is no such thing as a "typical" art collector. Some collectors are young people just beginning their careers and decorating their first homes; some are ending their careers and looking for a new activity to engage their retirements. Some are professional art historians or curators; some have just begun to look at art for the first time. Some are wealthy enough to spend funds almost at will; some buy on a strict budget. The only thing art collectors have in common is the passion to own and enjoy great works of art.

Thus, there are as many different kinds of collectors as there are different budgets and different tastes. To show you the many possibilities, here is a portrait gallery of the collecting community: profiles of a collector on a comfortable income, a collector on a strict budget, and a collector in the grand style.

Collecting on a Comfortable Budget

From the age of five, Diane Reinert knew she would become a politician one day. She debated her way from high school in Ames, Iowa, to a national championship in her senior year. She went on to become valedictorian at Drake University, winning a scholarship to Yale University Law School. Graduating from law school in 1975, she went west again, not to Iowa but to Denver, and became one of three women in the largest corporate law firm in that city. Today, only five years later, she has married a lawyer in another Denver firm, developed a reputation as an effective litigator, joined several Colorado political groups, "made partner," and begun to contemplate running for elective office.

Left, Robert Motherwell. *Africa Suite #3.* 1970. Silkscreen. 40¾" x 28¼". Courtesy Harcus Krakow Gallery, Boston.

Right, Andy Warhol. *Marilyn Monroe.* 1967. Silkscreen. 36" x 36". Courtesy Leo Castelli Gallery, New York.

However satisfying these activities may be for her, Reinert recognized early on the need for an activity that could take her mind off the law from time to time. She chose to become a collector. Even while still in law school, she took some of her earnings as a summer law clerk, went to New York, and after looking through the galleries, decided that she liked contemporary art best. She liked the boldness, she liked the wit, she liked the energy. It was immediately apparent, however, that she could not afford paintings by the major contemporary artists, and she therefore determined to buy their prints instead. After six hours of intense scrutiny, she settled on two small *Homages to the Square* by Josef Albers that a prominent dealer recommended to her, then took them back to her law school dormitory.

Since Reinert moved to Denver, she has continued to collect on the same modest scale. At least once a year, she goes to Chicago, San Francisco, New York, or some other city with a leading gallery of contemporary art. The visit is the occasion of an annual purchase. Each year, a new work enters her collection. One by one, the walls of Reinert's Denver home have filled with prints by Helen Frankenthaler, Ellsworth Kelly, Robert Motherwell, Claes Oldenburg, Robert Rauschenberg, and the other superstars of the contemporary art "scene."

When a curator from the Denver Art Museum recently saw the collection, he was astonished by its uniformly high quality. Simply by reading as much as she can about contemporary art, and by visiting as many exhibitions as possible, Reinert has developed her eye to the point where she can distinguish an artist's best works in the print medium.

Collecting on a Strict Budget

Benny Smith is an unlikely collector. As a high school student, he struggled his way to an Oklahoma state wrestling championship in the heavyweight division. And in Oklahoma that means something. Long after he graduated from school and bought a supermarket in Tulsa, friends and customers would know better than to pick a fight with Smith.

The first thing Smith collected was records. A rock fan like most of his generation, he assembled over three hundred albums. As the years passed, he found that he prized the jackets as much as the records themselves. He liked their visual forms. Soon he was trading jackets, first with other record collectors in Tulsa, then by mail.

Trading record jackets soon led Smith to another form of popular art on paper: movie posters. This should not have come as a surprise. His enthusiasm for movies, especially old movies, was equalled only by his continuing love for rock music. He began by collecting posters of movies with his favorite actor, Humphrey Bogart. He began subscribing to all the

J. Bonneaud. *Le Faucon Maltais.* c. 1946. 47⅛" x 62⅝". Courtesy Phillips, New York.

film magazines, meeting other poster collectors, and going to all the flea markets in hopes of finding the gold among the dross. Within a few years, Smith has become one of the leading movie-poster experts in the city of Tulsa. He has also become a part-time dealer, selling some posters at a large profit to finance purchases of even more desirable items.

Smith is now less interested in the subjects of the posters and more interested in their esthetic qualities. He speaks with particular enthusiasm about those with innovative designs and good graphics. Not that he has ever completely lost interest in the movies themselves: His two favorite posters are still the widely sought-after "one-sheets" of Bogart's two blockbusters, *Casablanca* and *African Queen*.

Collecting in the Grand Style

Everett Saunders was born wealthy. His grandfather, who owned a newspaper chain in northern California, sold it before the Depression, then made a series of astute investments. By the time Saunders arrived at Stanford University on the eve of World War II, he was reputed to be one of the richest men in America.

At Stanford, Saunders majored in art (like his father who preceded him there and his son who followed him). In the mid-1940s, the typical Stanford freshman was still so well-heeled that a fine arts professor could instruct his class, as a homework assignment, to buy an original work of art. From this compulsory beginning, Saunders went on to acquire other objects solely for his own pleasure. Among his purchases at the time was a group of seventeen American Indian masks (everyone else thought they were props for a John Wayne western). It was also while a student that Saunders developed a fascination with Islamic art: ceramics, metalwork, and, most of all, illuminated manuscripts.

Instead of setting out on a business career, Saunders decided to make a career out of what he was already doing. He stayed on at Stanford as a part-time lecturer and curator—and full-time collector. To this day, he travels each year to some part of the Middle East acquiring art objects the way other tourists buy postcards. The quality of his choices is legendary. Over the years, item by item, he has built a comprehensive collection of Islamic miniature paintings that rivals the holdings of the great museums.

Without letting it detract from his preoccupation with collecting, Saunders has made ample time to teach, curate exhibitions, and write about Islamic art. In fact, by the time he was fifty, he had already written more than twenty superb books and exhibition catalogues. When one of the country's leading museums recently began a search for a new curator of Islamic art, it was no surprise that the museum turned first to Everett Saunders.

Mughal. *A Prince & Companions Hunting Blackbuck.* c. 1670–80. 13⅞" x 9½". Courtesy Christie's, New York.

Traveling around the world buying beautiful objects, then writing books, assembling museum shows, and teaching seminars to help others see with the same joy: It is a life that most collectors envy.

You will undoubtedly define your own style of collecting, but these three profiles, each based on a real collector, demonstrate how different that style can be.

BETTER THAN BEER CANS AND BASEBALL CARDS

This is a guide to collecting *art*. Not matchbooks covers, baseball cards, or beer cans. Not just curious objects, but objects of enduring beauty. The distinction must be made from the outset because, in recent years, the word "art" has been much abused.

Auction houses are partly to blame. Traditionally the clearing-house of the fine arts, they now traffic in anything anyone will buy and sell, regardless of artistic value. Sotheby's, the world's greatest auction firm, has sold Rembrandt's *Aristotle Contemplating the Bust of Homer*—but Sotheby's has also marketed a $10,000,000 estate in St. Croix, the U.S. Virgin Islands; an autograph signature by President Lincoln; and two stuffed gorillas from *The Planet of the Apes*.

Hollywoodiana. That's right: stuffed gorillas. They're examples of *Hollywoodiana,* or memorabilia from Hollywood, a term coined at the end of the 1960s. If stuffed gorillas don't interest you, another sale of Hollywoodiana in 1970 featured Judy Garland's ruby-red slippers from *The Wizard of Oz* (they sold for $15,000). If your taste runs to the kinky or the bizarre, you could have bid instead on a pink tutu worn by Doris Day's male double in *Jumbo*.

Collectibles. Hollywoodiana is only one kind of *collectible,* a catchall term coined in the art market for objects that don't fit—or belong—in any of the accepted categories of art. Among the many collectibles now popular are baseball cards, comic books, and dolls. There is nothing wrong with collecting any of these—only with bringing them into the art market and charging incredibly high prices for them. Certain dolls made by a French firm called Bru now sell for more than $20,000. (For the connoisseur: Bru dolls with closed mouths, the ones made before 1895, are worth substantially more than Bru dolls with open mouths, made thereafter.) Collectibles are often of personal interest, occasionally of historical interest, but rarely of artistic interest.

Fine Arts **and** *Decorative Arts.*   Don't get the wrong idea. Paintings and sculptures are not the only objects worthy of being called "art." Any object of extraordinary esthetic merit deserves the label: an object that is "crafted"—a work of *decorative* art—as well as one that is "created"—a work of *fine* art. In 1965, J. Paul Getty, a notable collector, said, "To my way of thinking, a rug or carpet or a piece of furniture can be as beautiful, possess as much artistic merit, and reflect as much creative genius as a painting or a statue."

But few collectibles reflect much in the way of creative genius. It's conceivable that a doll, a baseball card, or some other popular object might be so well-designed that, a hundred years from now, people will still admire its visual accomplishment. At that point, it might be a candidate for serious collections. This book, however, deals with more conventional—and safer—categories: paintings, sculptures, carpets, posters, porcelain, and other objects of recognized artistic worth.

WHY DO PEOPLE COLLECT ART?

There are many reasons to collect art. Some reasons are more laudable than others. Most collectors are motivated by more than one:

Investment.   First, of course, people buy art because it is a tangible item that appreciates with time. In other words, art is an investment. This idea is more complicated than it sounds. Richard H. Rush, the investment expert, has said that the appreciation "provides not only a real reason for investing in art, but at the same time a splendid excuse for a person to buy what he loves."

Decoration.   "Most people approach art as interior decoration," says André Emmerich, the New York dealer. Robert C. Woolley, vice president of Sotheby's, adds that the "serious collection doesn't begin until after the home has been created"—that is, until after all the walls have been filled.

Status.   Basil Goulandris, the shipping magnate, reportedly said that buying an expensive Gauguin still life in 1957 was the publicity coup of his career: "Having that picture knocked down to me has made my name known everywhere. I'm praised for my courage and respected for my taste. In terms of advertising, the articles the press has published about me are worth easily double the sum I spent that afternoon." Even more modest collectors find that collecting earns them the respect of their acquaintances.

Hobby. For some, collecting is enjoyable primarily for the activity it generates. "There are people who take it up as a hobby," one dealer said. "It leads to meeting people, going to museum openings and having something to do on Saturday." Even the most modest collector occasionally experiences the feeling described by J. Paul Getty: "Excitement, romance, drama, a sense of accomplishment and even of triumph are all present in collecting."

Creativity. For some collectors, buying art allows them to participate in the creative process. "The urge to collect art is part of the urge to create art," says William Copley, an artist and collector. "Creating a good collection is like making a good painting." Patronizing young, unknown artists gives the collector an especially acute sense of participation in their work.

Instinct. "I am not a nibbler but a glutton," said Catherine the Great; "I have a madman's rage for art," said Joseph Hirshhorn. In the end, the true collector collects because he can't help it. For him, collecting is an instinct.

COLLECTING AND YOU

To many beginners, the art market seems like a closed and forbidding community. Collectors and dealers wage million-dollar bidding wars against each other. If you ask them why a particular object is worth so much, they mumble some jargon about its "quality"—something they can neither define nor demonstrate. If the high prices—or the jargon—have kept you away from art collecting in the past, this book can provide you with the information you need to understand the prices, penetrate the jargon, and finally beat the experts at their own game.

The Facts about Investment

The art world has mixed feelings about the relationship between art and investment. True, investors bring money into the market, but they also tend to disrupt it, often confusing esthetic worth with financial worth. Their speculations generate a land-office mentality that distorts prices and discourages serious collectors. What are the facts about investment? Is art a good investment? Is investment good for art? What are the best investment strategies?

Many art-world people condemn those who buy art as an investment. "Using art as an investment scares the hell out of me," David Bathurst, president of Christie's, said in 1979. "There's going to be a flood of money in and out, leaving a market devastated because of people who shouldn't have been there in the first place." "We at Christie's don't believe in art as an investment," adds Perry Rathbone, also of Christie's, expressing a sentiment that is common among auction officials and dealers everywhere.

Yet James Elliott of the Wadsworth Atheneum in Hartford, Connecticut, admits that if you spend substantial sums on art "you have to begin thinking of investment; if you spend $100,000 and you make a botch of it, you've really wasted something." And while dealers speak scathingly of investment-minded collectors who buy works over the telephone, they admit that such collectors are good for business. Investors not only spend large sums, they also sell works frequently, giving dealers a second profit on the same object.

Whether or not investment is good for the art market, its influence can't be ignored. Some art is an excellent investment. "Try and argue with people that art's not a good investment when they see a Man Ray painting selling for $750,000," one dealer has said. In the past few years, leading investment counselors such as Merrill Lynch, Pierce, Fenner & Smith and Salomon Brothers have advised their clients to diversify their holdings to include tangibles such as art.

The trouble is that art is a highly speculative investment; you can make money in the art market, but you can just as easily—in fact, more easily—lose it. "As far as buying art for investment goes," says Virginia Zabriskie, the New York dealer, "it still remains the least liquid and most speculative investment of all. The people who make money are those who make good choices in the first place, buy a lot of them, and hold on to them for a long time."

Barbara Krakow of the Harcus Krakow Gallery in Boston says, "There's no doubt that art is a good investment; the problem is knowing what art to invest in." The key to making money in the art market is knowledge: knowledge about art and knowledge about the market itself. But the people who make the *most* money in the art market are those who buy only what they like. Knowledgeable collectors who follow their own intuition and buy what they like generally do better than cold-blooded investors who follow elaborate investment strategies.

NO QUICK RICHES

Because the art market is so highly speculative, investors occasionally make a great deal of money. These few spectacular successes, however, are the exceptions, not the rule. "It is almost trite to accuse the press of distorting the general perspective in the art market," says a museum curator. "The six- and seven-figure quotations on the front page are quite misleading. They make headlines but do not represent the nitty-gritty facts."

Inflation more than any other factor distorts the investment value of art. When you read in a newspaper that a painting has doubled in value in ten years, it may actually have lost value in *real* dollars. According to Gerald Rietlinger, an economic historian, "The real peak of the art market was somewhere about 1912. Works of art which became established in the course of the past century as the highest achievement of their kind, have often failed to maintain the level of 1912 in real money terms and sometimes they have failed to maintain it even in paper figures."

Winning Big: The Art Lottery

The few people who do make big money in the art market do so by buying dirt cheap an object that turns out (sometimes immediately, sometimes eventually) to be very valuable. Perhaps it's an unattributed bust that is later revealed to be the work of a great sculptor; perhaps it's the work of a young, unknown artist who develops into a recognized master. In almost every case, the investment value of the object is coincidental. The collector bought it because he liked it, not because he thought the purchase might one day earn him a handsome profit.

Bargain-Basement Bernini. In 1979, an English bookdealer named Nicolas Meinertzhagen visited the antiques section of London, looking for a work of art to decorate his apartment. In one store, he saw a marble sculpture labeled, simply, "bust of a pope." Meinertzhagen, who liked both the bust and the $525 price tag, took the work home with him.

Not long afterwards, Meinertzhagen went to the library of the Victoria and Albert Museum to identify the pope represented in the sculpture. He was amazed at what he found: an illustration of a bronze sculpture exactly like his marble bust. The subject of the bronze was Pope Gregory XV; the artist was Giovanni Lorenzo Bernini, the greatest sculptor of the Baroque period, and one of the greatest sculptors of all time.

It turned out that Bernini had in fact made a marble bust along with two bronze casts of Gregory XV in 1621, the year of his election to the papacy. A third bronze was cast the following year at the request of Scipione Cardinal Borghese. The whereabouts of all three bronzes were known; the marble, however, had been lost since the seventeenth century. Meinertzhagen immediately showed the bust to the curators at the Victoria and Albert who confirmed that it was probably the lost Bernini.

How had it ended up in a London antique shop? The Earl of Lanesborough had sold it in 1978, along with the other contents of his home, at Christie's. The auction house listed the sculpture as an anonymous bust of a pope, and the antique dealer bought it for a mere $200. That is what it was worth as an anonymous work. As the work of Bernini, however, it was worth considerably more. In fact, Meinertzhagen sold it along with its new attribution at Sotheby's in 1980 for $280,800.

Scull's Angels. Discovering young unknown masters is just as rare as discovering lost works by acknowledged masters. At least 120,000 people in this country think of themselves as serious artists; of that number, fewer than 500 will ever see their works appreciate in value, and most of these are already either extremely well-known (and extremely expensive) or reasonably well-known (and reasonably expensive).

When a collector *does* "discover" an artist, or a group of artists, it's not because he is looking for a good investment. The investment is an unexpected bonus. Consider the example of Robert C. Scull, the owner of a taxi fleet in New York called Scull's Angels. During the early 1960s, Scull assembled once of the finest collections of recent art—especially Pop Art. He bought works by then unknown artists such as Jasper Johns, Robert Rauschenberg, Andy Warhol, Claes Oldenburg, and Frank Stella for only a few hundred or a few thousand apiece. He also bought in quantity. If he liked an artist's show, he didn't just buy a work or two; he bought the entire show.

Although Scull bought these works for very little money, he sold them for a lot. In 1965, he auctioned twelve works for $197,500. In 1973, he sold another fifty for $2,200,000. Larry Poons's *Enforcer,* which cost him $1,000, sold for $25,000; Andy Warhol's *Flowers,* which cost him $3,500, sold for $135,000; Jasper Johns's *Double White Map,* which cost him $10,500, sold for $240,000. The profit margin was impressive by any standard.

But Scull didn't buy the works as an investment. If he and his wife Ethel had an ulterior motive in buying contemporary art, it was to acquire instant status as patrons of the arts. They wanted media exposure, and they got it: newspapers, magazines, gossip columns, even a lengthy piece by Tom Wolfe called "Bob and Spike." But Scull also bought the works because he liked them: "From a financial point of view my art purchases were fairly ridiculous. . . . I bought because I cared for them as experience—not as an investment." The profit was an unexpected pleasure.

Losing Big

Although profits are rare in the art market, losses are not. In recent times, the two schools that have suffered the most devastating losses in the art market are eighteenth-century English portraitists and nineteenth-century academic painters. The prices for eighteenth-century English painters peaked just before the Great Depression. In 1929, a work by Sir Henry Raeburn sold for $75,000. In 1969, four decades of inflation later, the same work had to be bought in at a reserve price of only $17,640. *The Roses of Elagabalus* by the prominent nineteenth-century academician, Sir Lawrence Alma-Tadema, sold for $20,000 in 1888, $480 in 1934, and $250 in 1960. Both Raeburn and Alma-Tadema have rebounded in popularity and in price, but their works are still not worth what they once were. Barbizon landscapes, Renaissance art, tapestries, and Italian majolica are also worth significantly less today than they were in 1929.

The worst losses generally come when an artist or style goes out of fashion, when a highly speculative market collapses, or when economic conditions are unfavorable. During the early 1970s, Japanese collectors bid the prices of works by Foujita and Kuniyoshi, two expatriate Japanese artists, from about $40,000 to as high as $220,000 within two years. In 1973, however, an economic downturn in Japan and the United States weakened the yen and forced Japanese collectors out of the Western art market. Prices plummeted.

But collectors sometimes lose money even on the most enduringly fashionable artists in the best of years. A collector bought a Picasso called *Mother and Child* for $185,000 in 1957, then sold it the following year for $152,000—a loss of $33,000. The moral is clear. Gambling in the art market is like gambling in Las Vegas: For every winner, there are a thousand losers.

THE ART MARKET AND THE STOCK MARKET

Investing in the art market is not like investing in the stock market. There are some superficial similarities, of course. During the 1950s, *Fortune* magazine even divided the art market into "gilt-edged securities" (old masters), "blue-chip stocks" (modern masters), and "speculative or 'growth' issues" (everything else). But this is where the similarities end, and the differences begin:

No Set Price. On any given day, stocks have a set price. If you decide to buy or sell that day, you know how much the stock is worth. A work of art, by contrast, is ultimately worth only what someone is willing to pay for it. You don't know the work's value until it's sold.

Poor Liquidity. Selling an object quickly is both difficult and foolish. Art should be a long-term investment. You have to keep it five to fifteen years, preferably longer, to reap the best returns on your investment.

Never invest money in art that you can't afford to have tied up for a long time. Jeremy Eckstein, art-market analyst at Sotheby's says, "The art market is not like the stock market. Sudden price moves are not frequent and complete liquidity is nonexistent as it is with options or commodities. One usually must have patience with art, even though cycles are shortening."

Maintenance Expenses. A stock certificate requires very little maintenance: You simply put it in a safe place and forget about it. A work of art can also be hidden away, but generally at much greater expense. If you keep it at home, there are security, insurance, and other maintenance costs. There also may be substantial conservation costs to consider. All these expenses must be deducted from any profits you realize in selling an object.

Buying Retail, Selling Wholesale. The commission paid to a dealer or auctioneer is much larger than the commission paid to a stockbroker. The difference is so dramatic that the seller sometimes receives only two thirds of the sale price. "The nature of the [art] transaction is to buy at retail and sell at wholesale," says Frederick H. Sandstrom, vice president of the United States Trust Company.

Art Looks Better Than Stocks. The final difference, of course, weighs in favor of art. Art, unlike stocks, pays a daily "dividend" in viewing pleasure.

Relationship Between the Art Market and the Stock Market

Traditionally, the art market, like the stock market, has followed the economy as a whole. "If you can tell me what will happen to the stock market," New York dealer Andrew Kagan has said, "I can tell you what will happen to the art market."

When there was more money, people had more to invest—whether it was in art or in stocks. In times of recession, both suffered. There was, for example, a marked fall in art sales following the recession of 1973. As a rule, however, art prices tended to hold their own somewhat better than stock prices, and to resist the recessionary effects somewhat longer. "The normal pattern," Peregrine Pollen of Sotheby's noted in 1973, "is that if the stock market drops precipitously, the art market goes up. When there is a long decline, the art market follows, but less sharply."

Art Over Stocks. By 1980, however, the traditional relationship between the stock market and the economy appeared to be reversed. Nineteen seventy-nine was a bad year for the economy and for stock prices, but a terrific year for the prices of art. Leo Castelli, the contemporary dealer, noted a 30 percent increase in business over the previous year. Within three months, Pace Gallery, another leading contemporary art gallery, had already set new sales records. "We've already done more than last year's entire volume," said owner Arnold Glimcher, "and last year was our biggest."

Why the boom? First, art looked like a good hedge against double-digit inflation. Virginia Zabriskie made the point emphatically: "There's no question that it all relates to inflation." But art also looked like a good refuge from the sluggish equities market. Jeremy Eckstein, the Sotheby's expert, says that if an investor had put $1,000 into Dow Jones stocks in

1975, his investment would have been worth only $1,333 at the end of 1979. If the same amount had been invested in European nineteenth-century paintings, it would have been worth $2,230; in Chinese ceramics, $3,020; and in American paintings, $3,100.

Always Buy Quality.   In bad times and in good, quality is the key to investment. The best items appreciate most when the market is flourishing, and they hold their value best when recession sets in. "We've always advised people to collect the very best quality pieces they can afford," adds Eckstein. "But in a recession, one must be especially careful, because second-rate items weaken before first-rate ones." In fact, since the recession of 1979, some dealers have detected the evolution of a two-tier market: First-quality works continue to sell briskly; more modest works bear the brunt of the economic slowdown. At auction, for example, distinguished items have continued to set record prices while lesser examples have failed even to meet their reserve prices.

Never More Than 10 Percent.   Most experts also agree that art investors should never invest more than 10 percent of their assets in the art market. Art should be one element in a carefully devised investment portfolio. Robert Schoenfield of Sotheby's says art should always be a "complementary" investment.

The Long Range.   Asked about the long-range prospects of the art market, Ted Cooper, the Washington, D.C., dealer, sounds an unguardedly optimistic note. "The art market is just beginning to rise," Cooper says. "I'm totally convinced of it. Simply add to the supply and demand, world-wide inflation and the increasing scarcity of fine pictures and increasing devaluation of currency. If you don't think the market is going to keep on booming in nineteenth-century American pictures, which is all I can speak for, then you have to believe that loads of American paintings are suddenly going to flood the market."

KNOWLEDGE IS EVERYTHING

Successful investment in art requires knowledge. You should pick a field and learn as much as you can about it. For information on the different fields, see the chapter, "What to Collect." The next step is to learn why one work of art is worth more than another. For information on how to price an object, see the chapter of that title.

There are basically three ways to keep up with what is happening in the art market:

1. *Visit dealers.* You wouldn't buy a stereo without first shopping for the best price. You should approach buying a work of art with the same care. Before you purchase a work, price comparable items in the holdings of different dealers. You'll be amazed, for example, how often two examples of the same print, in the same condition, have different prices.

2. *Attend auctions.* Dealers normally set their prices according to current auction prices. Suppose a dealer has a Jasper Johns print and he's asking $2,000 for it. If, in two successive sales, similar impressions of the same print sell for $2,200 and $2,500, the dealer knows he can raise his price to $2,500, and perhaps even a few hundred dollars higher. You can maintain your competitive edge with dealers by attending the auctions yourself.

Of course, few collectors or dealers have the time or energy to attend every major auction. The solution is to subscribe to the auction catalogues. At the end of each year, the two major houses, Sotheby's and Christie's, publish lists of the major items sold at auction that year and the prices they brought.

The year's print prices are assembled for you in a critically useful guide, *Gordon's Print Price Annual* (New York: Martin Gordon, Inc.). International auction prices are listed in *E. Mayer International Auction Records* (Paris: Éditions Mayer). There are also numerous published price lists for antiques. The most complete listing is *The Official Price Guide to Antiques and Other Collectibles*, third edition, by Grace McFarland (Orlando, Fla.: The House of Collectibles, Inc., 1981). For a more up-to-date list, see *The Antique Trader: Price Guide to Antiques and Collectors' Items*, published quarterly (100 Bryant Street, Dubuque, Ia. 52001). For specialized price lists in your field of interest, contact Edmonds Book Sales (P. O. Box 143-T, Ledbetter, Ky. 42058).

3. *Subscribe to the guides.* In addition to auction catalogues, there are numerous guides to the art market for anyone who wants to keep up with current market values and art world tips. Here are a few recommended ones:

The Art Investment Report
(54 Wall Street, New York, N.Y. 10005).

The ARTnewsletter
(122 East 42nd Street, New York, N.Y. 10017).

The Collector-Investor
(740 Rush Street, Chicago, Ill. 60611).

International Art Market
(850 Third Avenue, New York, N.Y. 10022).

The Photograph Collectors Newsletter
(127 East 59th Street, New York, N.Y. 10022).

The Print Collector's Newsletter
(205 East 78th Street, New York, N.Y. 10021).

Although the information in these guides is useful, the investment advice is fallible. Before you confidently follow anyone's advice, consider the following: The first issue of *The Currency of Art*, published in 1959, recommended buying the paintings of Bernard Buffet. A major book on art investment published in 1961 recommended *against* buying Abstract Expressionist paintings. The successful collector was clearly the one who ignored both these tips, avoided Buffet, and bought Jackson Pollock.

Art Experts

If you don't know a field well, you should never make a major purchase without consulting an expert. In fact, even the most educated and experienced collectors continue to rely on outside opinions. "The cost of having an independent authority expertize a work of art before he buys is the cheapest insurance any collector can obtain," J. Paul Getty wrote. Getty certainly followed his own advice. Despite his own long-standing involvment in the art market, he regularly consulted more then twenty experts, including Bernard Berenson, Julius Held, and W. Valentiner.

Most experts are scholars, curators, or dealers who have specialized in the art of a particular period—or even a particular artist. For a major artist, the expert is generally a scholar, curator, or dealer who wrote a book about the artist or edited a *catalogue raisonné* of his works. Curators and dealers tend to see a much broader range of material than scholars, and are therefore generally more helpful in assessing the works of less recognized artists.

Some experts are more expert than others. John Wilmerding, for example, curator of American painting at the National Gallery of Art, is the acknowledged expert on Fitz Hugh Lane, the American marine painter. But the curator of American art at your local museum can probably tell you what you need to know.

Some experts are also more accessible than others. But most are willing to provide free advice concerning a specific work. For a dealer, it's good business: Helping a collector is cultivating a client. For a scholar or curator, it can also be good business, since the gratified collector may one day become a generous donor. Some museums, such as the Houston Museum of Fine Arts, have even established clubs to cultivate collecting.

SOME GROUND RULES FOR INVESTMENT

If you want to buy art primarily as an investment, here are some ground rules:

1. Pick a field and develop some expertise.

2. Never rely solely on your own expertise, however; always check your reactions with an expert or an appraiser.

3. Buy only the best objects.

4. Spend as much as possible, but spend it on a single superior work rather than several lesser items.

5. Hold a work for a long time, at least five years, preferably fifteen or more.

6. Watch the market carefully, keep up with current prices in your field, and be prepared to sell at the best moment.

7. Only buy works with a secondary market. Before you buy a work, think about where you'll sell it.

8. Sell works as carefully as you buy them, using the best dealer or auction house and keeping the tax consequences in mind.

9. Protect and preserve your collection with the necessary conservation, proper maintenance, adequate insurance, and appropriate security.

10. Never put more than 10 percent of your assets into art.

11. Don't have unrealistic expectations. Always factor in the expenses of owning a work, the costs of disposing of it, and the inflation rate.

12. Never buy anything you don't like. That's the best way to ensure that you never lose.

How to Price an Object

THE TWENTY MOST IMPORTANT FACTORS

A work of art has no set value. It's worth whatever someone is willing to pay for it, and the only way to find that out is to sell it. Of course, successful dealers and astute collectors have learned to estimate the value of a work *before* they buy or sell it. To help you develop this important skill for yourself, I've listed below the twenty most important factors in pricing a work of art.

1. Quality
2. Style
3. Artist
4. Typicality
5. Rarity
6. Historical Importance
7. Certainty of Attribution
8. Authenticity
9. Provenance
10. Condition
11. Medium
12. Subject
13. Size
14. Signature and Date
15. Seller
16. Time of Sale
17. Site of Sale
18. Laws Governing Sale
19. Publicity
20. Chance

Quality

"Quality. Quality. Quality. Quality is everything," says Seymour Slive, director of the Fogg Art Museum of Harvard University.

Quality is the key factor at every level of the art market. In 1980, for example, two Van Gogh paintings were sold at auction: *Le Jardin du Poète, Arles* for a record-breaking $5,200,000 and *Portrait of Adeline Ravoux* for a "mere" $1,800,000. Both were oil paintings in the artist's mature style. Both came from superb collections. What is the difference between the two works?

The difference is quality. The portrait of Ravoux is a fine painting, but it has neither the commanding presence of Van Gogh's other portraits, nor the intensity of his famous self-portraits. *Le Jardin,* by contrast, is not only one of the artist's landscape masterpieces, but also arguably one of his finest works in any genre.

Quality determines liquidity as well as price. "Dealers have no trouble finding buyers for the very best items," says Barbara Krakow, of the

Vincent van Gogh. *Le Jardin du Poète, Arles.* 1888. Oil on canvas. 28¾" x 36¼". Courtesy Christie's, New York.

Harcus Krakow Gallery in Boston. But while there is usually a short turn-around time on a superb work, a modest work will stay in a dealer's show-room for months or even years.

Style

People pay for what they like. And what they like changes from one decade to another. Works of art go up and down in price as they go in and out of fashion.

Vincent van Gogh and Sir Lawrence Alma-Tadema, a Victorian academic painter, both worked during the late nineteenth century. At the time, people considered Van Gogh a madman—if they considered him at all. He did not sell a single work during his lifetime and was forced to subsist on handouts from his brother Theo. Alma-Tadema, who painted historical subjects in a precise, academic style, ranked as one of the most popular artists of the day. He sold his works as quickly as he painted them, and for handsome prices. At the height of his fame, a work by Alma-Tadema called *Roman Picture Gallery* sold for 10,000 pounds, or $300,000 in today's dollars.

What Goes Up Comes Down, and Vice Versa. Of course, the times and public tastes eventually changed. After World War II, Van Gogh and the other Post-Impressionists became the darlings of curators and collectors. Their paintings regularly brought prices in six figures. By 1980, a work by Van Gogh fetched the third highest price ever paid for a work at auction. Alma-Tadema and the other academicians, however, didn't fare so well. Collectors gradually lost interest in their sentimental subjects and precious techniques. Prices plummeted. In 1960, a work by Alma-Tadema called *The Roses of Elagabalus* sold for $250.

But the academicians were not down for long. In 1957, when the taste for academic painting reached its low ebb, *A Girl Feeding Peacocks* by Lord Leighton, the prominent English Victorian artist, sold for only $75. In 1980, the same work sold in San Francisco for an astounding $67,500. In 1981, a work by Alma-Tadema called *A Corner of My Studio* sold at Christie's in New York for $95,000. The clever collector avoids the currently stylish and searches instead for the soon-to-be stylish. It may be too late to "rediscover" academic painting, but it's still early enough to buy superb examples at relatively low prices.

Artist

Rembrandt van Rijn was a painter from the Dutch Baroque period. So was Govaert Flinck. The difference is that Rembrandt was a great painter,

Sir Lawrence Alma-Tadema. *A Corner of My Studio*. c. 1893. Oil on canvas. 24″ x 18″. Courtesy Christie's, New York.

Govaert Flinck. *Portrait of a Girl*. Oil on canvas. 26¼″ x 20½″. Courtesy Christie's, New York.

perhaps the greatest of all time. His name is known to anyone who has ever taken an art course or visited a museum. Flinck was a competent painter, known only to a few dusty scholars of the Dutch Baroque. A great painting by Rembrandt will bring $5,000,000 or more; a great painting by Flinck, only $200,000—if that. The point is simple: The art market functions according to the star system; big prices are paid only for big names.

Westerners since the Renaissance have been especially guilty of establishing personality cults around great masters. We have tended, more often than people from other cultures or other ages, to think of individual artists as geniuses who transcend mortality, rather than as craftsmen who simply adorn mortality. As a result, works by famous Western artists bring exaggerated prices, while works by somewhat lesser ones bring comparatively little, and unattributed works almost nothing.

By contrast, the beauty of an Attic Greek vase, a Chinese porcelain from the Ming dynasty, or a Bambara antelope headdress from Mali is often appreciated without reference to the artist who made it. Unlike recent works of Western art, works from other periods and other cultures are not penalized for their lack of attribution. High prices are often paid for totally anonymous works. Of course, when a piece *can* be attributed to a specific artist or craftsman, the price soars. The Metropolitan Museum of Art paid $1,000,000 for a single Attic vase in 1972; the record price was justified in part because it was signed by a potter named Euphronius.

Typicality

Every artist passes through stages, or "styles," in the evolution of his work. The style that the experts and collectors like best becomes the artist's "typical" style. It is the style that carries an artist to prominence and is permanently linked to his name.

Most often, an artist's typical style emerges from his late mature works, rather than from his early exploratory ones: Jackson Pollock's classic drip paintings, for example, rather than his earlier figurative ones. Occasionally, however, an artist develops his mature style early, then passes on to styles that prove less popular. The most valuable works by Picasso, for example, are the ones he did before the 1940s: the works from his Blue, Rose, Cubist, Classical, and Surrealist periods. Only a few artists, such as Henri Matisse, have been able to develop one significant—and typical—style after another.

Sometimes an artist has a typical subject as well as a typical style. Albert Bierstadt, for example, is best-known for his panoramic landscapes of the American West, notably the Rocky Mountains and Yosemite National Park. Equally beautiful, though less well-known and therefore less expensive, are the landscapes Bierstadt painted during trips to Switzerland and Italy.

Rarity

The art market is, after all, a market, and the laws of supply and demand apply. Works are expensive if they're in heavy demand *or* if they're in short supply. By "supply," I mean not just the overall number of the artist's works in existence, but the much smaller number of high quality works still in private hands and therefore potentially available to collectors. More than five thousand paintings are currently attributed to Renoir. His major works still command prices in the millions, however, because so many of them have already entered public collections.

John Russell has written that the rare becomes rarer every day: "It would only be logical," he wrote in *Art in America* in 1966, "to forecast a gradual but consistent decline, since the number of top-class works of art in private hands is already small and is bound to get smaller. Where they do remain, quite exceptionally, in private hands, it is a sure bet that the tax man and the museum director between them will see to it that they never reach the open market."

The strongest complaint among collectors today is the scarcity of "top-class" works. Barbara Krakow, the Boston dealer, says, "All the dealers go to the same auctions and bid on the same works. The difficult part of being a dealer today is finding good works. Selling them is no problem."

Exceptions to the Rule. There is a small caveat to the rule that rare equals expensive. Some works are actually too rare for their own good. If works in a certain style come up for auction too infrequently, collectors sometimes begin to lose interest. An example is American Pilgrim furniture: furniture made in this country between 1640 and 1710. Avidly collected during the 1920s, the small supply soon dried up. Within a decade, collectors demonstrated how fickle they can be and switched to more readily available styles. The prices of Pilgrim furniture fell precipitously.

In a similar way, availability has actually *increased* the value of some works. *Le Repas Frugal,* a famous aquatint by Picasso, was issued in a small edition in 1904, the year the plate was etched. In 1912, the plate was steel-faced and an additional 250 impressions were pulled. Because it came up for auction so often, the print became a familiar favorite. Every serious Picasso print collector had to have a copy. By 1973, an early impression of *Le Repas* sold for a remarkable $154,000. Before you begin to question the importance of rarity in valuing a work of art, however, note that this was one of the earlier, better, and *rarer* impressions.

Historical Importance

A few masterpieces are used so often as illustrations in standard reference books that they're practically synonymous with the artists: the self-portraits of Rembrandt, Monet's *Cathedrals,* the *Sunflowers* of Van Gogh. These historically important works are exceptionally valuable—more valuable, even, than other works of comparable quality by the same artist. With a historically important work, you are not only getting a fine work of art; you are also getting a piece of history. You have to pay for the difference, of course.

Although few collectors are in a position to buy a historically famous painting or sculpture, most can benefit indirectly from the premium on historical importance. Keep your eye out for drawings that are studies for famous works or prints based on them. These drawings and prints are worth more than other works by the same artist that lack the historical cachet.

Certainty of Attribution

In 1901, J. Pierpont Morgan bought a portrait for $100,000. He was under the impression that the sitter was Anne of Austria and the painter was Peter Paul Rubens. The Metropolitan Museum, to which Morgan later gave the work, recently began to doubt the attribution to Rubens. In 1980, the museum sold the painting, attributing it to the School of Sir Peter Paul Rubens, meaning that it *may* have been by an assistant or student, but certainly was *not* by the master himself. No longer a Rubens, the work brought only $22,000.

How do you know for sure who created a specific work? After all, the artist is no longer alive to authenticate it. Even if he were alive, he might not be able to identify his own work. Maurice Utrillo, the modern French painter, for example, often found it impossible to distinguish his own early works from skillful forgeries.

Sometimes the confusion over attribution is bona fide: No one really knows who created it. Sometimes, however, the confusion is intentional. A dishonest dealer or collector will deliberately attribute a work by a minor artist to a master in order to inflate its value. Occasionally, the artist himself is the guilty party. More than one master has signed the works of other artists to help them out financially. Jean-Baptiste-Camille Corot, the French Barbizon painter, for example, frequently signed works by students, admirers, and others. It is often said in jest that Corot painted two thousand works of which five thousand are in the United States. The joke is not far from the truth.

Catalogues Raisonnés. In deciding whether a work should be attributed to a master, the principal guide is the artist's *catalogue raisonné*. This is a complete listing by a noted scholar of all works attributed to the artist, including detailed information about each of the listed works. If the artist was prolific, the *catalogue raisonné* can consist of dozens of volumes and thousands of pages. The *catalogue raisonné* of Picasso's works, for example, compiled by Christian Zervos over a period of several decades, has thirty-three volumes.

The first *catalogue raisonné* of Rembrandt's drawings was edited by Otto Benesch during the 1950s. Benesch decided to include in the catalogue four drawings that had been sold at the beginning of the 1950s but had not been attributed to Rembrandt. Christie's in London sold three of the drawings, attributing them to the School of Rembrandt, for a combined price of 100 pounds—about $280 at the time. The fourth drawing was attributed to a lesser Dutch Baroque artist. The price: $25. After Benesch attributed the works to the master, their value shot up to $28,000 or more. In the art market, a Rembrandt by any other name is not a Rembrandt.

Authenticity

Sometimes, misattribution is planned. One artist will intentionally create a work in the style of a more prominent artist. At the first sign that a work might not be authentic—that it might not be what it's supposed to be—the price plummets. Fakes and forgeries are every collector's nightmare.

Fakes.   Fakes are not necessarily meant to deceive. They often start out as honest, straightforward copies. A student in an artist's workshop, for example, will make a copy of the master's work. Later, long after it has passed from one collector to another, it will end up on the market as the work of the master himself. The "copy" will have become a "fake." Several of the many *Mona Lisa*s by "Leonardo" originated this way.

Forgeries.   Several other *Mona Lisa*s, however, were undoubtedly made by artists with fraud rather than flattery in their hearts. Their only intention was to sell them to unwitting collectors as Leonardo's own work—at a considerable profit. These are not just fakes, but *forgeries,* because the artists *intended* to deceive.

Forgery has a long, but not entirely dishonorable history. Forgeries are recorded as early as ancient Rome, where there was a heavy traffic in Roman-made "Greek" antiquities. During the Renaissance, the young Michelangelo was commissioned by Lorenzo de Medici to forge an antique cupid in marble. The cupid was aged artificially, then offered as a genuine antiquity to Cardinal Riario, a prominent collector of the day.

Fakes and Forgeries Today.   With time, it has become more and more difficult to produce a successful forgery. First, *catalogues raisonnés* now permit a buyer to detect copies by verifying the existence and whereabouts of originals. Second, scientific and technical advances permit the buyer to test the authenticity of a work's materials and construction.

The very best forgers, however, have adapted to advances in scholarship and science. Instead of copying a master's originals, they simply fashion "new" compositions by combining elements from different known works. Forgers have also learned to use scientific methods to their own advantage. Today, a good forger has to know as much about chemistry as any of the experts who may scrutinize his creations.

Hans van Meegeren.   Consider the most famous forger of modern times: Hans van Meegeren. An unsuccessful artist himself, Van Meegeren became so frustrated that he began forging the works of Dutch Baroque masters, especially Vermeer. Instead of copying existing works, Van Meegeren always invented his own images. He painted over old canvases, ground his own pigments using old recipes, then developed new methods of simulating the consistency and crackelure of centuries-old paint. His masterful forgeries were never detected. Van Meegeren revealed them himself only after he was charged with the war crime of selling national treasures (supposedly Vermeers but, in fact, Van Meegerens) to Hermann Goering during World War II.

Are forgers still at work today? No doubt—and no doubt getting away with it. In 1979, a conservator at a leading museum was asked if he could forge an antique bronze that would dupe his fellow experts. The conservator responded with an emphatic yes: "If you bring me an ancient bronze statue missing an arm, for example, I could replace it in such a way that the new limb would never be suspected as anything but the original. Come to think of it, give me an arm and I could provide you with an entire 'original' body!"

Provenance

The *provenance* of a work is its pedigree: It lists all of the work's previous owners;—ideally, all the way back to the artist himself. A work with this kind of complete provenance is far more valuable than an "orphan" work—a work whose origins are obscured. This is not just a matter of snob appeal (although snob appeal undoubtedly enters in). Scholars use a provenance, along with scientific and visual data, to attribute a work to the appropriate artist. A work with a complete provenance is of more certain authenticity than a work without.

It also increases the value of a work if one of its previous owners is well-known: either because the collection he formed is historically important or because he himself is historically important. This *is* a matter of snob appeal. Collectors who bid on porcelains from the Nelson Rockefeller collection at Sotheby's in 1980 undoubtedly recognized that they were bidding on objects previously owned by one of the most illustrious and discriminating collectors of the twentieth century.

Condition

In the art market, quality is everything—and so is condition.

Condition is especially important where the collector has a choice between several examples of the same object: prints and photographs, for instance. If the collector can hold out for an example in pristine condition, he doesn't have to settle for one that's torn, creased, stained, foxed, bleached, or damaged in any way. What if the choice is between a *superb* impression of a print in *poor* condition and a *poor* impression of a print in *superb* condition? In that case, the decision is more complicated.

And what if the decision is between an object in poor condition and no object at all? In certain fields, pristine examples are so rare that even the most discriminating collectors must settle for less than perfection. Posters, for example, were generally made to be hung out of doors. After a short period of time, they were bleached by the sun, marked with graffiti, covered over by another poster, and eventually thrown away. Collectors search for posters in the best condition possible, but that's rarely mint.

Pristine items are also rare in Chinese porcelains. In fact, they're so rare that collectors now pay high prices for damaged pieces. For example, a rare Yueyao jar sold at Sotheby's in 1980 for $55,000 despite a flaking glaze and some restoration.

Medium

The unofficial record price for a work of art is $12,000,000, the amount reputedly paid in 1980 for a work by the German Renaissance artist, Albrecht Altdorfer. It's no coincidence that this record was set by a painting in oils; in today's art market, oil painting is the favored medium.

This hasn't always been the case. Until World War II, the highest prices were generally paid, not for paintings or for any other works of fine art, but for decorative objects. At the turn of the century, a good piece of majolica (a kind of intricately decorated earthenware) would routinely command a higher price than an old-master painting. Although the decorative arts no longer dominate the art market in the West, they continue to be the favored form in other cultures. The highest prices in Oriental art, for example, are paid not for paintings but for porcelains.

Painting, the Preferred Medium.   Among the fine arts, painting is preferred to sculpture or drawing. This is a generalization, of course; certain old-master drawings, especially from Renaissance Italy and eighteenth-century France, are expensive indeed. A brown-ink drawing of three saints by Andrea Mantegna sold in 1980 for $363,000. And if a Michelangelo sculpture ever came up for sale (something that hasn't happened for centuries), it would send shock waves through the art market and rewrite the record books. Until that happens, however, sculptures and drawings will continue to play supporting roles.

The reason has more to do with logistics than esthetics. Drawings are too small for decoration and too fragile for constant display. Sculptures are usually too large and cumbersome to be transported easily: It would take a crane to install even a medium-size bronze in your back yard. Paintings, on the other hand, are large enough to be decorative and light enough to be moved around. They can fit comfortably into the decorative scheme of any collector's home.

It is precisely because drawings and sculptures are less practical than paintings that they are often better bargains. In fact, drawings by an artist often bring even less than his prints.

Subject

Most collectors shy away from any subject that might give offense. They want their art to be pleasant and decorative. Favorite subjects have traditionally been landscapes and still lifes, especially floral pieces, and prices are correspondingly high. Among the less popular and less expensive subjects (bargain hunters take note):

Portraits: Other People's Ancestors. As a rule, people have no interest in other people's ancestors. Of course, if the alien ancestor is historically noteworthy, they'll reconsider. No one would turn down a portrait of George Washington by Gilbert Stuart simply because he or she was not a descendant. Among anonymous sitters, women sell better than men. And looks definitely count: A prominent dealer recently said, "You can't sell an ugly lady."

Animals: Cows, Cows, and More Cows. Animals have frequently been a favorite subject of painter and patron alike. This was especially true during the nineteenth century, when certain artists *specialized* in "animal pictures." Ambroise Vollard, the Impressionists' dealer, writes in his memoirs of an artist who "painted cows to perfection" but who told the dealer that, "to suit the taste of his customers, he would be equally pleased to paint horses, donkeys, sheep, or even poultry." Today, you can buy a lot of poultry for very little money: The average collector is simply not interested in farmyard fowl.

Religious Subjects: Render Unto . . . Until the seventeenth century, the church was the primary patron of the arts. Artists would have starved if it hadn't been for altarpieces and devotional images. Today, most patrons are private individuals, and they don't want religious paintings in their homes.

Violent Subjects: Blood and Gore. Collectors looking for household decoration don't want pictures of murder and mayhem—or even anything mildly disagreeable. The prints of mutilated bodies in Goya's series "The Disasters of War" would be all but unmarketable, regardless of their quality, if they weren't by Goya. The same is true of a Rembrandt print with a dog defecating in the foreground.

Obviously, in some cases, a work of art is valuable whatever its subject matter. Many of Rembrandt's paintings are portraits of anonymous, fat, and happy burghers. But no sane collector would turn one down.

Attributed to Thomas Gainsborough. *A Rocky Wooded Landscape with a Horse and Cattle and Figures Beyond*. Oil on canvas. 32¼″ x 39¼″. Courtesy Christie's, New York.

School of Guercino. *The Flagellation*. Oil on canvas. 45″ x 54″. Courtesy Christie's, New York.

Size

Although serious paintings are never sold by the square inch, size is a major factor in determining value. Collectors want works that are small enough to fit comfortably into a house or apartment, but also large enough to justify the price. The optimum size for an oil painting has traditionally been two to three feet by three to four feet. Works of that size are generally more expensive (per square inch) than smaller or larger works of comparable quality.

But tastes in size, as in everything, change with time. As the typical collector's home has gotten smaller and smaller, he paradoxically has been acquiring larger and larger paintings. Wall-size paintings, once unmarketable, are now actively sought after.

Signature and Date

A work that's signed and dated is worth more than one that's not—assuming, of course, that the signature and date are both authentic.

A signature and date are more important in some cases than in others. Because Dutch artists of the seventeenth century routinely signed their paintings, collectors pay less for Dutch Baroque paintings that are unsigned. By contrast, because Italian artists of the same period did not make it a practice to sign their works, collectors pay a premium for the rare signed ones.

Signatures are especially important for prints and photographs. Because the plate of a print and the negative of a photograph can yield hundreds of images, both authorized and unauthorized, a signature is often the only way to distinguish an original from a copy. Even here, however, the importance of the signature depends to some extent on the practice of the individual artist.

Collectors prefer signed and dated works primarily because they are more verifiably authentic. By putting his name on a work, the artist certifies that he created it and that he's proud of what he has created. But a signature is desirable for another reason: It creates a special bond between the person who owns the object and the personality who stands behind it.

Seller

As a general rule, collectors prefer to buy works of art from prominent dealers or through prestigious auction houses. It isn't just the guarantee of authenticity implied by the seller's reputation that attracts them, it's also the simple snob appeal.

There are other advantages, of course, in dealing with the largest and most reputable firms. Wildenstein, for example, the largest United States dealer in old-master paintings, and Hirschl & Adler, the largest dealer in *American* paintings, are both unequaled in the range and quality of their stock. Only at Wildenstein Hirschl & Adler could you ask to see works by Claude Monet or Childe Hassam and have a dozen or more works brought out for your consideration.

Time of Sale

Most collecting is done during the nine months from September through May each year. The activity peaks during the months before Christmas. Auction prices are lowest during the summer, therefore, and highest during the fall. It's no coincidence that smart sellers try to get their objects into an October or November time slot at an auction house, or that smart buyers keep a close eye on the block in June and July.

Site of Sale

The price of a work of art depends, to some extent, on *where* it is sold. Some works of art have international appeal: modern French painting, for example. Two of the highest bidders at the Garbisch auction at Sotheby's in 1979 were a Japanese museum and a wealthy Argentine collector. The Bridgestone Museum in Tokyo purchased Picasso's *Saltimbanque Seated with Folded Arms* for $3,000,000; Amalia Le Croze de Fortabat of Buenos Aires purchased Gauguin's *Tahitian Women Under the Palms* for $1,800,000. Although New York and London are the preferred locations, it doesn't really matter where modern French paintings are sold.

Other kinds of objects have a less international audience. As a rule, Japanese Imari ceramics will sell best in Tokyo; Italian Capo di Monte porcelain figurines in Milan. Mexican paintings sell best in Mexico City; Canadian paintings sell best in Toronto and Montreal. Those looking for bargains should look for regional works being sold outside their region.

Laws Governing Sale

If you plan to buy works of art outside the United States, you should be aware of the laws that apply to their sale and export. The time has long since passed when Lord Elgin could transport the Parthenon friezes to the British Museum or Napoleon could transport the *Laocoön* to the Louvre without hearing a murmur of protest. In fact, many American museums now voluntarily return works that have been illegally imported into this country. And to deal with those who are less scrupulous, or would like to be, the United States government also regularly cooperates with foreign governments in enforcing their art exportation laws. Even when those laws don't actually prohibit the export of a work, they may significantly affect its price.

Italy. Consider the example of Italy. In accordance with Italian law, all significant works are listed with the Soprintendenza delle Antichità e Belle Arti. A painting can be sold only if the government refuses to match the offering price, and exported only if the government grants a special export license. Even if a license is granted, the foreign collector must pay an export tax which can easily rise to 30 percent of the value of the work depending on the price.

Italian collectors and dealers prefer to keep their works off the Soprintendenza's lists because unlisted works are easier and cheaper to export (or smuggle) out of the country. Italians also prefer to buy and sell unlisted works because they draw less government attention. Dodging taxes is a national sport in Italy, and it's more difficult to dodge them if the Soprintendenza knows of a collector's activity in the art market. In Italy, therefore, works listed with the Soprintendenza are worth significantly less than unlisted works.

France. In France, there is a sales tax on all works of art bought at auction. As a result, auction prices are at least 10 percent lower in France than in England, where there is no tax on auction sales. French law also provides that the country's national museums have the right to preempt any sale simply by matching the highest bid. In addition, the government may refuse an export license for any work, even if the state has no intention of purchasing it. These regulations make sale prices in France lower than elsewhere, but they also make it more difficult to get works out of the country.

England. In England, the Reviewing Committee on the Export of Works of Art can hold up the export of any work more than a hundred years old that has been in the country for more than fifty and is worth 2,000 pounds or more. If, however, within three months, no museum is capable of raising a matching price, the sale and export are allowed. As a result, foreigners can buy works in England much more easily than on the Continent. Because of these relatively liberal export laws and tax-free sales, England has long outpaced France, Italy, and other European countries in attracting foreigners to auction. Since World War II, only the auction houses in New York have set more record prices than those in London, and even the most important New York houses are now largely English-owned.

Publicity

The price of an artist's work can be affected by the publicity it has received. Did it appear in a museum show? Has it been mentioned in books, newspapers, or magazines? Was it featured in a gallery advertisement? Was it listed in an auction catalogue? Was it illustrated there? Was the illustration in black and white or color? Each of these factors can substantially affect the price of a work.

Major Sales.   Sometimes the effects are immediate. When *Icebergs* by Frederic E. Church sold for a remarkable $2,500,000, it raised the value of all other works by the American landscape master. "Works by Church are very much in demand," says dealer Warren Adelson of the Coe Kerr Gallery in New York. "They were expensive before *Icebergs* sold, but they're probably more so now because of the publicity surrounding the sale." Robert Graham, Jr., of the New York gallery bearing that name, agrees: "The Church market in general was improved substantially by the drama surrounding *Icebergs.*"

Retrospective Exhibitions.   Sometimes, however, the effects of publicity are more ambiguous. Although a retrospective exhibition at one of the country's leading art museums usually boosts an artist's reputation, it doesn't always work out that way. William Rubin, curator of the Museum of Modern Art, points out that the value of an artist's retrospective depends on the character of the artist and the quality of the retrospective.

"You could have a series of pictures," Rubin says, "which, taken together, don't do anything for one another. But, on the other hand, you could have a series of pictures in which the whole is greater than the sum of the parts. It depends on what kind of painter is involved. It also depends on whether the retrospective is well done—whether it is well chosen, whether it is well hung. History shows that the reputations of artists have fared very differently after retrospectives." In particular, Rubin notes that the second Georges Rouault exhibition at the Modern may actually have depressed the market for the artist's work. It created "a feeling that Rouault wasn't as good as people had thought and there was a definite slump in the market for his works."

But if you have to follow a single rule, take it from show business: Any publicity is good publicity.

Chance

When all is said and done, there are times when the price of a work of art simply can't be rationally explained. A Paul Jenkins painting, for example, was recently sold at auction for $36,000, about twice its true value. Two collectors both wanted it and, as the saying goes, each had more money than brains. Of course, irrationality can also work to the buyer's benefit: A collector buys a sculpture now attributed to Bernini for $525 simply because the seller didn't know what it was.

Research and careful analysis will take you a long way in assessing the value of a work of art, but they won't take you the full distance. In the end, a work is still worth whatever someone's willing to pay for it.

PUTTING IT ALL TOGETHER

It's one thing to know the twenty factors that affect the price of a work of art; it's quite another to put them to use.

The **Three Flags** *of Jasper Johns.* The most prominent contemporary artist today is probably Jasper Johns. His painting, *Three Flags,* sold in 1980 for $1,000,000, the highest price ever paid for the work of a living artist. Many of the factors listed above contributed to the astonishing sum. First, there was the *artist.* Johns was recently listed in the *Saturday*

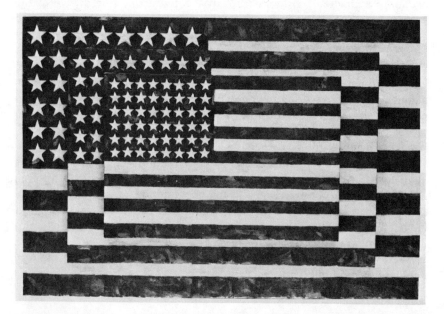

Jasper Johns, *Three Flags*. Encaustic on canvas. 1958. 30⅞″ x 45½″ x 5″. Collection Whitney Museum of American Art, New York. Courtesy Leo Castelli Gallery, New York.

Review as the number-one "Blue Chip" artist in the country. *Three Flags* also features one of the artist's most *typical* images, the American flag. The work was well *publicized:* It was included in a retrospective exhibition of Johns's work at the Whitney Museum in 1979 and was illustrated in countless places, including the cover of a leading history of twentieth-century American art, giving it considerable *historical importance. Three Flags,* which is in superb *condition,* was also extremely *rare* since it was one of the last early Johns masterpieces still in private hands. The *sellers* of the work were the prominent contemporary collectors, Mr. and Mrs. Burton Tremaine. The Tremaines bought the work directly from Leo Castelli, Johns's dealer, in 1959, so it had a complete and sterling *provenance.* The *attribution* to Johns was unassailable.

What if the *medium* had been lithography, rather than oil paints and encaustic on canvas? What if several other versions of the flag exactly like it had been floating around in private hands or if, for some reason, there had been some doubt as to its *authenticity?* What if the painting had come from one of the artist's more recent and less fashionable *styles?* Finally, what if the painting had not been of such singular *quality?* In fact, if anything had been different, the price might not have been so high. It takes a lot to make a million-dollar painting.

BARGAINS

The factors listed in this chapter can be especially helpful when you're trying to decide whether or not to buy a new work. Of course, how you *weigh* each of these factors will depend on why you're buying. If investment is your primary motive, these factors will probably be controlling. If you're in it simply for the enjoyment, however, your knowledge of the rules can help you find works that are both enjoyable *and* inexpensive.

There are certain factors you should take into consideration whether you're buying for pleasure or profit. First and foremost is quality: The most pleasurable *and* the most profitable art is art of recognized quality. In addition, it is always advisable to buy from a reputable dealer during an off-season.

How much importance you ascribe to the other factors—authenticity, condition, subject, medium, etc.—will depend on what you're looking for: investment bargains or art bargains.

Investment Bargains

David Dalva, president of the Art Dealers & Antique Dealers League of America, recently said that "multiple increases in value" can be found only "in the mainstream" of the art market, not in its "obscure corners." If you want an investment bargain, you want to look, within your price range, for:

1. Works that are now securely fashionable, or soon will be.
2. Works by artists of historical significance.
3. Works that are in the artist's mature style.
4. Works that are rare without being esoteric.
5. Works that are historically important, or related to works that are historically important.
6. Works attributed with certainty to the named artist, unless most of the works in the field are unattributed.
7. Works that are indisputably authentic.
8. Works with a complete provenance, preferably a prestigious one.
9. Works in the best possible condition.
10. Works in the most sought-after medium (e.g., oils in Western art, porcelains in Oriental art).
11. Works with desirable subjects.
12. Works large enough to be impressive but small enough to fit comfortably in a home.
13. Works that are signed and dated, unless the artist never made it a practice to sign and date his works.
14. Works that have been discussed and illustrated in books or articles.

Art Bargains

What if you want a terrific work of art and you're only mildly concerned with maintaining its financial value? What if you want an art bargain, not an investment bargain? Then, by all means, take advantage of the peculiarities of the market to get the most for your money. In particular, look for:

1. Works from periods that are currently out of fashion.
2. Works by second- and third-tier artists.
3. Works that are not typical of the artist's mature style.
4. Works that are relatively common, or else too esoteric to generate widespread popularity.
5. Works of uncertain attribution.
6. Works of uncertain authenticity.
7. Works without a complete provenance.
8. Works in less-than-perfect condition.
9. Works in the less-popular media (e.g., an artist's drawings instead of his oils; Oriental ivories instead of Oriental porcelains).

10. Works with unpopular subjects (e.g., portraits of anonymous sitters, animals, religious images, violence or other unpleasantries).

11. Works that are larger—or smaller—than collectors generally prefer.

12. Works that are not signed or dated.

13. Works that have not been well-publicized.

You should be willing to make these concessions, however, *only* if they are reflected in the price. For example, you should never buy a work of uncertain attribution unless the seller acknowledges the flaw and sets the price accordingly. There's no better way to put together a good collection on a small budget than by sacrificing the likelihood that your collection will appreciate dramatically.

Of course, there is always the possibility that works bought only for enjoyment will prove to be good investments. Given the unpredictability of the art market, collectors who buy what they like often do better in the art market than collectors who follow careful investment strategies. The Burton Tremaines did not buy Jasper Johns's *Three Flags* as an investment. Nicolas Meinertzhagen did not discover a long-lost Bernini sculpture by looking for a quick return. If you only buy what you like, and you only like first-quality works, your art bargains may one day become the best of all investment bargains.

QUALITY

Throughout this book, the same advice appears again and again: Buy what you like, but buy quality.

Suppose you have a thousand dollars to spend on art. What do you do? Do you buy five works at $200 each? Or do you spend it all on a single item?

It's hard to generalize. Superior examples of the art you like best may cost only $200 each. You may like reproductive engravings, for example (engravings based on the paintings of the old masters). These engravings are relatively inexpensive, especially if they were made by someone other than the master himself. If they're your favorites, go ahead and buy five.

On the other hand, you may like photographs by the best twentieth-century photographers. If you find two prints by your favorite for $500 each and a single print for $1,000, what should you buy? Again, it depends. Although the *best* art is often the most *expensive,* it's not always so. The $500 images could actually be superior to the $1,000 image. They could be cheaper only because they are smaller or because they were printed in a larger edition. Of course, if the $1,000 print *is* of superior quality, buy it instead. Remember, your collection will be judged by the quality of each item, not by its size.

So the rule is this: First, decide what you like; then buy the very best example of it you can find. If this means waiting until you can afford it, be patient—or buy the best of something else. Even collectors on the most limited budgets shouldn't have to be satisfied with second-best.

Improving Your "Eye"

What is quality? How do you know it when you see it? Isn't it all a matter of subjective taste? It doesn't help much to have an art expert tell you the Miró print you always loved is mediocre, or that Andy Warhol's portrait of Marilyn Monroe, which you never took too seriously, is a fine work of art. At first, it all may seem like a mystery, or even a hoax. Yet it's a mystery you need to unravel—or a hoax you need to unveil—if you are ever to make astute purchases in the art market.

A Matter of Consensus. During an artist's life, and for decades thereafter, no one can be sure about the quality of his work. A general consensus emerges only with the passage of time. This consensus is as close as we can come to a notion of absolute quality. Five hundred years later, no one is going to quibble about the quality of Michelangelo's *Pietà*. Unfortunately, few collectors enjoy the privilege of buying works of undisputed greatness. Most collectors, however, accept this as a challenge rather than a disappointment. In fact, the true measure of a good collector is his ability to find quality in unexpected places. He recognizes the greatness in an object *before* everyone else does—and before the price begins to rise.

How Do You Know Quality When You See It? How does a collector acquire an ability to detect quality in art—or, as members of the art world refer to it, a "good eye"? Is he born with it, or is it the product of experience? Although a few people have a remarkable ability to recognize a good work of art when they see it, even they weren't born with that ability. Like any skill, it is a slow labor of love.

Training Your Eye. The best way to train your own "eye" is to look at as much great art as possible. Take a course in art appreciation at your local college or university. Read the standard books on art history and make it a regular practice to skim through the art journals. Finally, visit galleries and museums. There is nothing that will sharpen your powers of discrimination more than exposure to actual works of art. No amount of reading can substitute for the experience of holding a Chinese porcelain in your hands. Minutes spent looking at a painting by Rembrandt will do more for your eye than hours spent reading about it.

Making an Acquisition.   Eventually, you will want to test your newly educated eye by acquiring a work. There is no reason to wait until you feel entirely secure in your selection; many dealers recommend buying right from the start. (Although patently self-interested, the advice is valid.) André Emmerich, a leading New York dealer, says, "A funny thing happens to people when they spend serious money on art—and serious money is serious money to *them*. It can be a hundred-dollar print or a hundred-thousand-dollar painting depending on the financial bracket. The same situation applies in psychoanalysis: You must pay the analyst a meaningful sum or you don't seem to work at it. When people spend meaningful sums of money to acquire art, they make a commitment, and they start to look harder."

Some Cautions.   No doubt, owning a work creates a stronger bond than is possible just by looking at it in a museum—indeed, the strength and magic of that bond is one of the main reasons for collecting art. I would sound two cautionary notes, however. First, don't spend too much. The sum should be meaningful, but not so meaningful that it breaks your bank account. Second, deal only with a reputable dealer, preferably one who will take a work back in trade. Then, if your tastes should change, you won't live to regret your early impetuosity.

CONDITION

There are many things that can happen to a work of art after it leaves the artist's studio—most of them bad. Collectors have been known to cut paintings down to make them fit a particular spot on the wall. Ceramics and glassware break or crack with unsettling ease. Works on paper are particularly fragile: Exposed to the sun, they bleach; exposed to acidic materials, they stain. They are easily torn, creased, blistered, warped, or otherwise damaged through careless treatment. A successful collector must know how to distinguish a work in good condition from one in bad—and also a work in irreparable condition from one that can be repaired.

How Do You Assess the Condition of a Work?   Fortunately, many imperfections are visible to the naked eye. Are the colors in a watercolor so badly bleached they're no longer recognizable? Does the glaze in a porcelain bowl lose its lustre along a repaired crack? Is the canvas torn, or does it show signs of restoration? Is the paint flaking, or does it look newer is some areas than in others? Many signs of poor condition are obvious to anyone who bothers to look.

Look at It Under a Raking Light—and from Behind. Other imperfections, however, are more difficult to detect. Always examine the work under a "raking" light (a light that strikes the surface at an oblique angle). Raking light is more revealing than direct light. Also, you can usually tell more about the condition of a work from the back than from the front. Knowledgeable collectors refuse to buy a work until they have had an opportunity to study the reverse side, even if they have to demand that the dealer remove the work from its frame. For example, a torn canvas may have been carelessly sewn together—something a clever restorer can mask from the front with a little deceptive brushwork but is readily apparent from the back.

Remove It from the Frame. Perhaps a drawing or print has been framed for years against a cheap piece of acidic cardboard. More than one collector has purchased a Picasso print, taken it to a framer for reframing, and discovered that the work must be pealed away from its acidic cardboard backing. Acid has already seeped from the cardboard onto the back of the paper, leaving it stained yellow. It's only a matter of years before the acid will work its way through to the front of the print and destroy the image. This nightmare could easily have been avoided if the collector had taken the precaution of removing the print from its frame *before* buying it.

Removing a work from the frame is also one of the best ways to tell if it's been cropped. Few painters work right up to the edge of a canvas, so there should be a complete, narrow border of unpainted canvas concealed under the frame. If there is no such border, a collector is alerted to the possibility that the original work is not there in its entirety.

Don't Hesitate to Ask. You may feel awkward at first asking a dealer to remove a work from its frame or take it off the wall so you can examine it more carefully under the appropriate light. Just be aware that any reputable dealer will accommodate your request, and respect you the more for making it. If a dealer refuses, or even hesitates, perhaps you should look for another dealer.

Train Your Eye. All of these signs of poor condition are visible to the unaided eye. It helps, however, if the unaided eye also happens to be an educated eye. The more you look at works in every state of repair and disrepair, the better you'll be able to assess the condition of a work you contemplate buying. Everyone knows enough to avoid a painting with a big gash in it; but many collectors will let flaking paint or a cropped canvas pass unnoticed. Jerry Cohn, conservator at the Fogg Art Museum of Harvard University, cautions collectors to "be sure to examine authentic works in good condition so that they will be familiar with how they are supposed to look before trying to spot problems."

Tools of the Trade

An educated eye is the key to assessing the condition of an object. But even the most educated expert wouldn't look at objects without the help of certain tools. The first and most basic one is a magnifying glass. Many collectors carry one at all times. For most works, a magnification factor of three or five is sufficient; for prints and drawings, a factor of ten or fifteen is preferable. In any case, the magnifying glass should have a battery-operated light.

The second most common tool among collectors is the ultraviolet, or UV light. In the dark, the ultraviolet rays make the different pigments and glazes of an oil painting fluoresce—or glow—at different levels. The simplest way to see if an old painting has been substantially repainted is to examine it under a UV light. The pigments in the newer paint will fluoresce differently from the pigments in the older paint. The newer portions will show up as dark blotches. If you don't want to carry an ultraviolet light around with you, most reputable dealers will lend you one.

Nothing's Perfect

One last point: In assessing the condition of a work of art, don't be too hard on it. Even an item in "superb" condition will rarely look "factory-new." In fact, if you find a painting by an old master that looks as if it were made yesterday, it probably was. Works without the telltale network of cracks—or *crackelure*—that comes with age should always put you on your guard. According to Jerry Cohn, "Beginning collectors are too accustomed to reproductions. They object to the 'physicalness' of the real thing."

What do you do if a work appears to be in poor condition? Do you reject it out of hand? If you like a work despite its physical flaws, and if the price reflects those flaws, don't let the condition stand in your way. You can simplify your decision by factoring in the one-time cost of having the work cared for by a competent conservator. Does the price still seem reasonable?

Deal with Good Dealers

Many new collectors have not yet had the opportunity to immerse themselves in a particular field, or to learn the technical aspects of a particular medium. The best solution for newcomers is to deal only with reputable dealers. Jem Hom, the Washington, D.C., print dealer, for example, sells only works that are in mint condition. If a dealer is selling a work in less than mint condition, he should detail its defects to you.

If you have some reason to think a dealer isn't giving you the full story, or if you're buying at auction, you may want to resort to a higher authority. In that case, get an expert opinion. It's worth the cost to have a disinterested dealer or conservator look at the object you are considering for purchase. If it's being auctioned, have the expert look at it during the presale period. If it's being sold by a dealer, take the work on approval, then take it to the expert; or else purchase the work with a buy-back guarantee, then take it to the expert, secure in the knowledge that if his verdict is negative you can always take it back.

AUTHENTICITY

In assessing the *condition* of a work of art, you examine it with an educated eye aided by advanced scientific techniques. In determining the *authenticity* of a work, you should use the same process in reverse: employ scientific methods of analysis and apply them with an educated eye.

Structural Properties. The more you know about the chemical and structural properties of a work of art, the more easily you can assess its authenticity. Consider, for example, the paper used to make a drawing or print. There are basically two kinds of paper, *laid* and *wove,* the difference being in the kind of screen used to make them. Laid paper, held up to a light, shows a watermarklike pattern of close parallel lines; wove paper, on the other hand, is smooth and unpatterned. Wove paper wasn't invented until the eighteenth century. Therefore, if you find a "seventeenth-century" drawing on wove paper, you know you've found a fake.

Scientific Techniques. The best collectors also take advantage of advanced scientific techniques to ferret out fakes and forgeries. An ultraviolet light, for example, can be used not only to identify areas of over-painting but also to discern a new signature on an old work. Serious collectors occasionally avail themselves of other, more sophisticated scientific tools—X-ray radiography, infrared photography, pigment analysis, radiocarbon dating, neutron activation, autoradiography, and thermoluminescence—but these require the equipment, knowledge, and skill of a trained conservator.

An Educated Eye. Despite the space-age technology, most collectors don't put their ultimate faith in science. The final judgment of whether a work is authentic—whether it is, in the language of the art market, "right"—is a human judgment. In 1979, Charles Kelekian, a New York dealer in antiquities, said, "I am not crazy about these techniques, because forgers can use their own methods to bypass them. My eye is better than any thermoluminescence test. It's a question of instinct and experience."

Hindsight, the Best Test. Of course, most competent forgers don't just copy existing works: This would put the careful collector on his guard. More often, they synthesize elements from several works by the imitated artist into new compositions. The less they borrow, however, the more they have to create. With the passage of time, experts are able to see with increasing clarity the forger's interpolations. Hans Tietze, an expert on forgery, has written that a forger "reproduces somebody else's emotion . . . If he follows his model slavishly the constraint will be very strong; if he allows himself some freedom he runs the risk of making mistakes."

Olga Raggio, a curator at the Metropolitan Museum of Art, adds, "No matter how good, the forger will eventually demonstrate some of the sensibility of his own time. We look at fakes made 50 years ago and we simply cannot understand how anyone was fooled—to us they look pure 1920s." In the end, the collector's most useful tool in assessing the authenticity, condition, and quality of a work is his own educated eye.

A Checklist

In order to avoid fakes and forgeries, experts recommend the following:

1. Always ask for documentation when you buy an object.
2. Don't trust auction house descriptions.
3. Deal only with reputable dealers.
4. Don't trust signatures.
5. Avoid works by artists with a history of fakes.
6. Exercise special care when buying antiquities and primitive art.

Where to Buy
and Sell Art

Most works of art are bought and sold in private galleries and auction houses. Either way, the process can intimidate the beginning collector. Unlike most consumer goods, art works don't come with price tags. What you pay depends on your skill at manipulating the market. What are dealer discounts? What is a reserve bid? What warranties are commonly made and what do they mean? What breaks do dealers give their best customers? What is the psychology of an auction? Unless you can answer these questions, you may end up paying too much.

DEALERS: MERCHANTS OF ART

A reputable dealer is the new collector's best friend. In fact, as a rule, new collectors should avoid auction houses altogether and put their trust in a carefully selected dealer.

Selection: What You Want, When You Want It. If you're determined to buy a work by a specific artist at auction, you may have a long wait: A month, a year, even a decade could pass before the right work shows up on the block. A tour of appropriate galleries, on the other hand, is almost

Harcus Krakow Gallery, Boston. Photograph by Christopher James. Courtesy Harcus Krakow Gallery.

certain to produce a selection of suitable examples available for immediate purchase. For example, if you want a painting by Thomas Sully, the nineteenth-century American portraitist, Hirschl & Adler in New York can show you a dozen or more fine works. If you prefer the paintings of Frank Stella, the contemporary American abstract artist, both the Leo Castelli Gallery and M. Knoedler & Co., also in New York, can offer you several dozen to choose from.

Deliberation: Time to Reflect.   When and if the right work comes up at auction, you won't have much time to think about buying it. You can read about it in a catalogue several months in advance, but you can't actually see it until a few days before the auction takes place. The auction itself is very brief. In a moment, the object you've waited so long for can be sold to the highest bidder before you can make up your mind how much it's worth to you.

At a private gallery, by contrast, you can look at the object several times before making a decision, knowing there's only a small chance that someone else will buy it in the meantime. In fact, if you have a good relationship with the dealer, he might be willing to hold the object for you while you make up your mind. He might even be willing to let you take the work home on approval, although, if you're a new client, you may be required to put down a substantial deposit.

Preselection: Distinguishing the Worthy from the Worthless. A dealer's reputation is based, in part, on the quality of his merchandise. Many dealers employ "runners" or "pickers" who scavenge small galleries, rural antique shops, country auctions, and flea markets in search of those few objects that might be of interest to the serious collector. In other words, the dealers do the sorting you'd otherwise have to do yourself. At the best galleries, you can be sure that *anything* you buy is worth buying, a fact that should inspire confidence in neophyte collectors.

In contrast, even the best auction houses are sometimes forced to market worthless objects alongside worthier ones. If a house knows that a certain estate has a single genuine old-master painting set amidst rooms of third-rate copies, it will usually agree to auction the entire estate, dross and all. A good dealer would accept only the real thing—and sell the copies at auction.

Guarantees: You Get What You Pay For. A good dealer stands behind what he sells. If he inadvertently sells you a work attributed to the wrong artist, you can return it and get your money back. Only the very best auction houses guarantee the authenticity of what they sell, and even then the guarantees are limited. Dealers are also much more conscientious about revealing the details of an object's condition. While auction catalogues mention condition only occasionally, a reputable dealer will bring every imperfection and restoration to your attention.

Returns: Good Dealers Often Take Works Back. Many dealers will let you return in exchange for another object, or in some cases for cash, *any* object, for *any* reason—even if you simply decide that you like something else better. No auction house, no matter how reputable, offers such a liberal exchange policy.

Education: A Good Dealer Is a Good Teacher. A good dealer is really an evangelist: His mission is to win converts. He will take the time to teach you the rudiments of collecting. He will discuss market trends, help you decide what to collect, give you a selection of works to choose from, and note their good and bad points. In other words, he will begin to train your "eye." Auction officials can rarely devote this much time to an individual buyer.

These are the advantages of buying from a dealer: varied and high quality merchandise, time to decide on a purchase, broad guarantees, a liberal buy-back policy, and generous assistance. Against these advantages you should weigh the single major disadvantage: Although the situation varies from object to object, items often *cost* more at a gallery than at an auction house.

What Is a Good Dealer?

The first thing you should know is the difference between art galleries and art "stores." The difference is that art galleries sell serious art; art stores sell decoration—usually bad decoration.

Sometimes the difference is obvious. No one would mistake a hole in the wall crammed with paintings on black velvet for a serious gallery. But sometimes an art store looks deceptively like the real thing. It's *called* a "gallery"; it has the same white walls and the same good lighting; it's located on the same street; it advertises in the same art magazines; and it charges the same high prices. The "only" difference is in the quality of the art.

"Why would anyone ever go into an art 'store'?" a prominent dealer recently asked. "They might have some good pictures, but you'd have to *hunt* for them. There are tons of galleries like that. Just look in the Sunday papers and you'll see ads for hundreds of artists you've never heard of—and you'll never hear of again." The problem is that for every serious art gallery there are dozens of art stores.

Even among the genuine galleries, some are more reputable than others. Here are some things to look for:

Selection: Quality, Breadth, Depth.   First, you want a dealer who carries a large selection of the kind of works you want to acquire. But more important, you want a dealer who sells only items of indisputable quality. If you're going to rely on a dealer's eye, be sure his eye is better than yours.

Honesty: A Word You Can Trust.   If a dealer tells you that a work is by a certain artist or that it's in good condition, you should be able to take him at his word. If you discover that a dealer hasn't been giving you the full story, take your business elsewhere.

Helpfulness: A Willingness to Talk.   One of the principal advantages of a dealer is that he can help train your eye. Obviously, he can only do this if he takes the time to talk with you. To expect this kind of assistance, you shouldn't feel obliged to make a purchase, even a minor one. Helping collectors is considered part of a dealer's duty. If a dealer refuses to answer your questions, look for another dealer. Superior knowledge and expertise don't justify snobbery.

Cost: Comparison Shopping. Some dealers charge more than others for the same item. This is especially obvious if you're buying multiple art forms like prints and photographs. It's not uncommon to find two dealers charging different prices for the same print in the same condition. Before you settle on a dealer, shop around.

These criteria are easy to state but difficult to apply. It's especially difficult to find a single dealer who meets all four requirements. For example, some of the most honest dealers with the finest merchandise are known to charge more and help less than other dealers. Sometimes, you may have to settle for less than all four.

How to Find a Good Dealer

If you know a collector and trust his judgment, ask him to recommend a gallery. Or ask a dealer in one field to recommend a colleague in another field. Your best source, however, is generally a curator at your local museum. Most museums keep lists of recommended dealers and are happy to share them with you.

You should also be aware of the two principal professional associations, The Art Dealers Association of America (575 Madison Avenue, New York, N.Y. 10022) and The National Antique & Art Dealers Association of America (59 East 57th Street, New York, N.Y. 10022). Membership in these organizations is limited to reputable firms, and the membership lists are available upon request. You should be aware, however, that some of the finest firms don't belong to either of these associations. Even Wildenstein, the leading old-master gallery, is not a member. Therefore, whether or not a particular dealer belongs to an association is only one factor in assessing that dealer's reputability.

For further assistance, you should consult the lists of dealers in the chapter "What to Collect." Although inevitably incomplete, they were compiled with considerable care. The dealers have been selected primarily for the quality of what they sell and the strength of their reputations, not for their competitive prices. Even if you can't afford to buy at the more expensive galleries, however, you should still visit them so you can train your eye. The dealers who own the galleries can also lead you to other dealers with less expensive items.

Dealers' Shows

From time to time, prominent dealers from throughout the country travel to the same city and set up booths for a week or two. These fancy variations on the common flea market are called "dealers' shows." Their principal advantage is that they allow collectors to sample the offerings of galleries nationwide—without having to travel nationwide.

Many of the finest antique shows are organized by charitable associations to raise funds for worthy causes; several of them are also supervised by two individuals, Russell Carrell and Richard Field. The shows are listed, with dates and locations, in the antiques magazines. Among the best-known are:

Mint Museum Antiques Show
Charlotte, North Carolina
(September)

Cincinnati Antiques Festival
Cincinnati, Ohio
(October)

Ellis Memorial Antiques Show
Boston, Massachusetts
(October)

Theta Charity Show
Houston, Texas
(October)

Western Reserve Antiques Show
Cleveland, Ohio
(October–November)

Connecticut Antiques Show
Hartford, Connecticut
(October and March)

Delaware Antiques Show
Wilmington, Delaware
(November)

Los Angeles Antiques Show
Los Angeles, California
(November)

Washington Antiques Show
Washington, D.C.
(January)

Winter Antiques Show
New York, New York
(January)

Maryland Historical
    Society Antiques Show
Baltimore, Maryland
(February)

Tri-Delta Show
Dallas, Texas
(March)

University Hospital
    Antiques Show
Philadelphia, Pennsylvania
(April)

Lake Forest Academy Show
Lake Forest, Illinois
(June)

How to Deal with a Dealer

Even if you're working with a reputable dealer, there are certain steps you can take to make the dealer-client relationship more rewarding.

Discounts: It Can't Hurt to Ask. Most collectors don't realize that the dealer's asking price isn't the only price. Many dealers give their best clients a discount of 10 percent or more. Even if you've never bought at a particular gallery, however, you can sometimes obtain a discount simply by asking. Although such discounts are common, they're not standard. The only way you can find out is to ask.

Bargaining: A Bazaar Mentality. A surprising amount of bargaining goes on at art galleries. Instead of asking for a dealer's discount, make a counteroffer: Twenty percent off the asking price is reasonable. Offer more and you might end up paying more than you should. Offer less and the dealer might be insulted. If a reputable dealer tells you he doesn't accept counteroffers, don't press the point. Many dealers *don't* bargain, even with their best customers.

Barter: More Bazaar Mentality. Not all deals in the art market are straight cash transactions. You may want to offer a dealer something besides money in exchange for the item you want. Although exchanges usually involve other works of art, jewelry, real estate, and other assets are sometimes part of the bargain.

Payments: Buying on Time. Buying an expensive work of art can create a serious cash-flow problem. A collector may be able to afford the work, but not all at once. To ease the burden of major purchases, many dealers allow collectors to pay for them over time. Although dealers don't normally charge interest, they do require at least a third of the price in advance and full repayment within three to six months. Also, unless you're a regular client, you probably won't be able to take the work home until the dealer's been paid in full.

Good Clients Get Good Deals. A dealer doesn't have to show every item in his showroom to every customer; only his best clients may get to see a particularly good new work. Dealers cultivate good collectors just as collectors should cultivate good dealers.

AUCTIONS: ART TO THE HIGHEST BIDDER

When people think of art auctions, they think first of the two main auction houses, Sotheby Parke Bernet (Sotheby's) and Christie Manson & Woods (Christie's). Sotheby's is the larger and more aggressive of these two giants, with offices in forty-eight cities in nineteen countries. Christie's prides itself on more exclusive merchandise and a higher profit margin. Although both firms are British-based, Christie's retains more of the British character, even in its New York office (where even the Americans speak with a proper British accent).

There is an open rivalry between the two houses. David Bathurst, president of Christie's in America, says, "They call us timid, but the opposite of that is foolhardy. We see ourselves as cautious and sensible. We are expanding slowly, and while we appreciate volume, we prefer quality to quantity." Officials at Sotheby's, on the other hand, bristle at Christie's officials who pose as gentlemen but operate as entrepreneurs. One journalist has cleverly likened the feud to a war of words between Rolls-Royce and General Motors.

Sotheby's and Christie's are the undisputed leaders of the art auction business in America. A dozen other houses follow close behind, from Barridorff in Portland, Maine, to Butterfield & Butterfield in San Francisco. Some of these regional auction houses are no less distinguished

Auction at Christie's, New York. Photograph by Helaine Messer. Courtesy Christie's, New York.

than Sotheby's or Christie's, only smaller. Bringing up the rear are hundreds of other auction businesses, many of them small country enterprises that lack even a showroom. As a rule, the "merchandise" at these smaller establishments is not up to the standards of the leading houses, but occasionally gold emerges from the dross.

Although this discussion of auctions refers often to the two main houses, Sotheby's and Christie's, most of the principles hold true at every level of the auction trade.

A Booming Business.   During the past decade, the focus of activity in the art market has shifted from the private gallery to the auction house. Consider the statistics. During its 1979–1980 season, Sotheby's had worldwide sales of $573,000,000, almost half in North America. The United States sales figure alone increased by more than 65 percent over the previous year. Christie's prospered, too, with worldwide sales of $363,000,000. In fact, so many works of art are now sold on the auction block that dealers are afraid of being edged out of the business.

The auction houses boosted their sales by attracting more record-price items—the ones you read about in the newspaper—and by offering more items at moderate prices. Although most people don't realize it, the vast majority of items sold at auction—even at Sotheby's and Christie's—are relatively inexpensive. Eighty-five percent of the objects sold at Sotheby's, for example, bring less than $500. Both Sotheby's and Christie's have divisions (the Arcade Auctions at Sotheby's York Avenue Galleries and Christie's East) that specialize in objects for the collector of modest means.

The Auction House vs. the Dealer

Just as there are advantages to buying from a dealer, there are advantages to buying at auction:

Quantity and Objectivity.   According to Perry Rathbone, a senior official at Christie's, "The auction house makes known to the collector more material than he could ever find in the galleries of private dealers. Can you imagine how many dealers you would have to visit in order to see as many things as you can see in the auction house? The other point one has to keep in mind is that a sale at an auction house is much more objective than a dealer sale. A dealer has a lot of money wrapped up in the object and wants to liquidate it at the highest price possible as soon as possible."

Of course, quantity is an advantage only when combined with quality. Some auction houses attract exceptional items from time to time, but the proportion of quality to quantity is usually very low. There is truth as well as professional jealousy in many dealers' references to auctions as "dealer's dumping grounds." As for the superior objectivity of auction houses, most auction houses do not exercise Christie's restraint in buying objects for resale rather than taking them on consignment. William Doyle Galleries, for example, owns many of the objects it sells. Even Sotheby's sometimes engages in the practice. In other words, many auction houses are not more objective than dealers because they *are* dealers.

Lower Prices. The main advantage of buying at auction is not larger volume or greater objectivity but lower prices. Collectors of all means turn to auctions in search of bargains—or at least better prices than they could find at private galleries. After all, the most active auctiongoers are the dealers themselves. What they buy, they turn around and sell at a substantial profit. By bidding against dealers for the same object, the collector can avoid paying the dealer's markup—ranging from 5 to 50 percent, depending on the cost of the item.

Auctions and the Beginning Collector

Despite the advantages of buying at auction, the beginning collector should enter the auction house with caution. Since knowledge is essential for wise bidding, an auction is no place for amateurs. If you can't assess the real value of a piece, you could easily end up paying too much for it. Know the quality, know the value, know the authenticity and the condition, or stay out of the bidding.

Go for the Education. That doesn't mean you should stay out of auction houses altogether, even if you're a beginner. Auctions can provide a first-rate education for new collectors at no expense—so long as you look and don't buy. According to David Redden, vice president of Sotheby's, 25 to 50 percent of the people who attend auctions "are there just to watch." Study the objects being sold and see which ones attract the most interest. Talk to auction officials. Strike up conversations with dealers and other collectors. Try to learn why some objects bring more than others.

Hire an Expert. What if you see an object you want to buy, but you still don't feel confident enough in your expertise to make a bid? The solution is to hire the expertise you don't have. Even auction officials recommend that beginning collectors consult an expert to help them bid wisely. Robert C. Woolley, vice president of Sotheby's, says, "Any time you're going to spend a lot of money on something, whether it's soybeans, or stocks, or art, you need expert advice." Ask a dealer or art consultant to take a look at the object you like. For a modest fee, he will assess its quality, attribution, and condition; help you determine a reasonable bid; and then, if you want, do the bidding.

The Ins and Outs of Auctions

To bid wisely at auction, you should be familiar with both the objects you're bidding on and the bidding process. While it may take years to learn about the art, you can become an expert on the bidding process almost overnight. Here are the ground rules for buying at auction.

Newsletters and Catalogues. Most auction houses publish newsletters. At a nominal cost (Sotheby's charges $3 annually), you can receive, every month or so, detailed information about auction schedules, specific objects of interest, and the operations of the auction house.

If you're interested in an upcoming auction, the next step is to order the catalogue. (Catalogue order forms are usually included in the newsletter.) Most auctions and their catalogues are referred to by number, although Christie's follows the amusing practice of giving each auction a person's name as if it were a hurricane. Catalogues are not cheap. You can buy them one at a time for $5 to $15, or you can sign up for a year's subscription to all the catalogues in a particular field for between $25 and $75. Despite the expense, you *must* order a catalogue if you plan to participate in an auction. You can't bid intelligently without one.

The catalogues list each item included in the upcoming auction. The amount of information varies depending on the importance—and anticipated price—of the object. For an important object, the entry will include a description, a brief discussion of both the object and the artist, a provenance, an exhibition history, and a full bibliography. There might also be an illustration, usually in black and white but occasionally in color.

Limited Warranties. The catalogues prepared by the major auction houses are remarkable publications. Herds of well-dressed but impoverished art history graduates spend hours researching each element. You should be aware, however, that the houses rarely stand behind the information they offer. Although generally accurate, it should never be treated as more than a starting point for your own research.

To see how little responsibility auction houses accept for the accuracy of their descriptions, all you have to do is read the disclaimer at the beginning of every catalogue: "All property is sold *as is*." Sotheby's, for example, takes responsibility only for the limited information printed in bold type—and even the boldface information isn't warranted for works that date from before 1870. The house does guarantee attributions of pre-1870 works, but only against the possibility that they're outright fakes. The moral: When you're thinking of buying at auction, you should always look *first* at the conditions of sale and the terms of guarantee.

Attributions. The form of an attribution often indicates how much credence the auction house places in it. At the beginning of every catalogue is a list of "authorship codes" to help you interpret the attribution. Christie's, for example, has seven different levels of attribution:

1. FRANCESCO GUARDI (In our opinion a work by the artist.)
2. Attributed to FRANCESCO GUARDI (In our qualified opinion a work of the period of the artist which may be in whole or part the work of the artist.)
3. Circle of FRANCESCO GUARDI (In our qualified opinion a work of the period of the artist and closely related in style.)
4. Studio of/Workshop of FRANCESCO GUARDI (In our qualified opinion a work possibly executed under the supervision of the artist.)
5. School of FRANCESCO GUARDI (In our qualified opinion a work by a pupil or follower of the artist.)
6. Manner of FRANCESCO GUARDI (In our qualified opinion a work in the style of the artist, possibly of a later period.)
7. After FRANCESCO GUARDI (In our qualified opinion a copy of the work of the artist.)

In my qualified opinion, there is a great deal of equivocation going on here. The only work that might be by Guardi himself is probably the one labeled simply FRANCESCO GUARDI.

There are two other tricks of the trade you should be aware of. If the auction house indicates a work is "signed," the signature is, in the qualified opinion of the house, the artist's own signature. A work that "bears the signature" of the artist could have been signed by anyone. A work that's "dated" simply bears the date—it could have been dated by anyone, anytime.

Catalogue Estimates. Another important part of the catalogue is the list of estimated prices at the back. An entry that reads "55 1200/1800" means the auction house expects that lot 55 will sell for between $1200 and $1800. Such estimates are provided only as a guide to potential buyers, not gospel, and you should treat them the same way you treat all the information provided by auction houses—with some skepticism. Their crystal ball is generally no clearer than your own.

The Presale Exhibition. For a week or so before every auction, the auction house exhibits the objects listed in the catalogue. You should never bid on an object unless you've had a chance to touch, see, and study it at one of these presale exhibitions.

If you've never attended a presale exhibition before, don't be intimidated. The exhibition has been mounted specifically for collectors like yourself. If you need help, ask for a customer service representative. Some houses, such as Christie's, will even lend you an ultraviolet light to check for overpainting. If you want additional information, ask to see someone who was involved in preparing the catalogue. Auction officials are generally too busy to give you the kind of personal attention you might expect from a dealer, but a little persistence can work wonders.

The Auction

Sales normally take place in three sessions beginning at 10:15 A.M., 2:00 P.M., and 8:00 P.M. As a rule, you should arrive thirty to forty-five minutes early. This isn't just to ensure a good seat; it's to register for the sale. You will be issued both a registration card and a plastic bidding paddle with your registration number on it. Although cards and paddles are by no means universal requirements, many of the newer auction houses won't let you bid without them. Don't forget to bring identification.

Where you sit is entirely a matter of taste. Many bidders prefer to sit close to the front; others favor the sides. At an important sale, you may not have a choice, since the front seats will probably be reserved for well-known collectors. At a *very* important sale, you may not even be able to find a seat anywhere. You may have to sit in a side room and follow the bidding on closed-circuit television. This may reduce your feeling of participation but it won't reduce your competitive edge. Successful bids can come from anywhere inside or outside the salesroom.

Bidding. For new collectors, the most surprising thing about an auction is the rapid pace: Objects come and go, huge amounts of money are spent, all in a matter of seconds.

The auctioneer begins by announcing the lot number and reading a short description of the item up for bid. He opens the bidding at a predetermined minimum, then calls for bids from the floor. The amount of increase between bids is determined by the auctioneer and varies with the intensity of the bidding. For an item that opens at $1,000, the auctioneer might ask for bids in $100 increments. If bidding is still active at $2,000, he might begin to call out $200 increments. At Sotheby's, bids are simultaneously recorded in five currencies on an electric "scoreboard" above the auctioneer's podium. The final bid is repeated, the auctioneer gives "fair warning," the object is "hammered down," and the sale is consummated.

Bidding Signals.   You've probably heard stories about unusual bidding signals: One collector scratches his ear, another crooks his finger, taps on a notebook, or pats a handkerchief. Louis Marion, father of Sotheby's president, John Marion, once said, "Women who use their catalogues to salute late-coming friends do so at their peril."

Some well-known dealers and collectors do indeed arrange with the auctioneer to bid using some private signal. For example, comedian Bill Cosby, who is an active collector, bids by removing his cigar from his mouth. James Rorimer, director of the Metropolitan, bought Rembrandt's *Aristotle Contemplating the Bust of Homer* with a crook of the thumb and a wink of the eye. Most auctiongoers, however, simply hold up their paddles. This is easier for the auctioneer and safer for the collector. Whatever method you choose, don't worry that a stray scratch may buy you some object you don't want. Even if a mistake is made (which is rare), the mistaken bid can later be withdrawn and the object awarded to the last legitimate bidder.

Decide on Your Maximum Bid in Advance.   The most important part of bidding is deciding how much to bid. It is especially important for new collectors to decide *in advance* how much they're willing to spend and, under no circumstances, should they bid a penny more. When other people are competing heatedly for an object you want, it's altogether too easy to be swept along in a wave of enthusiastic bidding. Auction fever is an ever-present danger. "The greatest barrier to wise buying is allowing yourself to get caught up in the excitement," says Eunice S. Carroll, vice president of special services at Sotheby's. "Set your limit and stay with it. Always feel that if you miss the piece you wanted, another will come along."

The simplest and safest way to bid is to decide on your maximum bid, then pencil it in the margins of your catalogue. When the object you want comes up for sale, keep lifting your paddle—or keep it lifted—until the auctioneer has passed that amount. Although it's painful to lose an object you want badly, it's even more painful to buy an object you can't pay for.

When you decide on a maximum bid, be sure to factor in the hidden costs: A 10 percent buyer's premium (now charged by most American auction houses); state sales tax, if any; and the cost of shipping and insurance. Remember, you can avoid the sales tax by having the object shipped to an out-of-state residence.

Reserve Prices.   Even if you're lucky enough to be the only person bidding on an object, don't count on paying much less than the low estimate. Auction houses have developed a mechanism for protecting the seller against a drastic loss: He can set a "reserve price" on the item. If the bidding fails to meet the reserve price, the item is "bought in." The auction house, standing in for the owner, buys the work. A reserve price is always lower than the high estimate, and generally lower than the low estimate. As a general rule, you can assume it's about 60 to 80 percent of the low estimate. Although auction houses never reveal the reserve price (for obvious reasons), they do indicate in the catalogue which items have a reserve price.

Mail Bids. During some sales, the auctioneer may continue to call out bids even though you don't see anyone signaling. The reason is that the auctioneer is "picking bids off the wall." He isn't inventing the bids; he's simply recognizing bids that were mailed in prior to the sale.

It is very easy to bid by mail. Most auction houses provide a form at the back of the catalogue. All you do is fill out the necessary information, specify the lots you're interested in, and indicate your maximum bid for each lot. If the bidding falls short of your maximum, the house won't charge you the full amount. It will give you the object at the bid following the highest bid at the auction. For example, if you tell the house your maximum bid is $2,000, and the last bid from the floor is $1,400, the object will go to you for $1,500 (assuming that the bidding proceeds in $100 increments). To make sure that you don't lose an object by a single bid, you can instruct the house to increase your maximum bid by a single increment. That way, if another collector bids $2,000, you get the object for $2,100.

Mail bids can be helpful, but they can also be risky. Auctioneers are known to misplace or forget mail bids from time to time. It's advisable, therefore, to telephone the auction house on the day of the sale to make sure that your mail bid has been processed properly. You may also want to telephone the house at the conclusion of the sale to find out if your bid was successful. Otherwise, you may have to wait a week or more to learn the results of your mail bid by mail.

Telephone Bids. It is even possible to bid for an object by telephone. You simply arrange with the auction house in advance to have someone call you a few minutes before an object comes up for bidding. You then place your bids over the phone. Although you should be aware of telephone bids, they're of little import to the common collector. Despite the obvious advantages, they're generally available only to the wealthiest collectors bidding on the most expensive items.

Ignored Bids. What happens if the auctioneer inadvertently ignores your bid and awards an object to another bidder? If the hammer has fallen, it's a *fait accompli.* Nothing you say or do can reopen the bidding.

This policy may seem draconian, but the auction houses really have little choice. They're auctioning tens of thousands of items each year, all at breakneck speed. If they reopened the bidding at every complaint, they'd be hostage to every collector who has second thoughts about what an object is worth.

Payment. If you make the winning bid, you should go immediately to the accounting office after the auction is over and pay for your new acquisition. Auction houses accept several forms of payment. Preferred payment is in the form of cash or certified check. If you have already established your credit (a months-long process in which the auction house investigates your bank references), you can write a check. If you haven't yet established credit, you can still write a check but you have to wait until the check clears before you can claim your object.

When you pay for an object, it's yours. The responsibility for packing, insuring, and shipping it is also yours. If the object is small, you can carry it home. Although the auction house will be happy to give you the name of a professional shipping agent, it won't do the shipping for you. If you leave the work at the auction house for more than a few days (three to five days at most leading establishments), you must pay a storage fee. At most country auctions you must take possession of the work at the end of the sale.

What can you do if your new acquisition has been damaged between the presale exhibition and the sale? Very little. You buy a work "as is," and that generally means "as is" at the time of the sale, not at the time of the presale exhibition.

How to Find a Good Auction House

Just as some dealers are better than others, some auction houses are better than others. You want an auction house that features items of high quality, that provides the broadest guarantees, and that is honest (some houses hire "plants" or "shills" to push the bids higher). Finally, you want an auction house where the officials are both knowledgeable and helpful.

You may evaluate an auction house the same way you evaluate a private gallery. However, while there are hundreds of reputable dealers, there are only a few reputable auction houses. For a full listing of all auction houses and their addresses, buy a copy of *Art & Antiques* magazine (250 West 57th Street, New York, N.Y. 10011). Listed below is a selection of the best of these houses.

California

Christie Manson & Woods
   International, Inc.
9350 Wilshire Boulevard
Los Angeles, California 90212

Sotheby Parke Bernet, Inc.
7660 Beverly Boulevard
Los Angeles, California 90036

District of Columbia

C. G. Sloan & Co., Inc.
715 13th Street N.W.
Washington, D.C. 20005

Adam A. Wechsler & Son, Inc.
905-9 E Street N.W.
Washington, D.C. 20004

Florida

Trosby Auction Galleries
905 North Railroad Avenue
West Palm Beach, Florida
   33401

Louisiana

Mortons Auction Exchange
P. O. Box 30380
643 Magazine Street
New Orleans, Louisiana 70190

Maine

Barridorff Galleries
242 Middle Street
Portland, Maine 04101

Massachusetts

Robert W. Skinner, Inc.
Main Street
Bolton, Massachusetts 01740

Richard A. Bourne Co., Inc.
P. O. Box 141 A
Hyannis Port, Massachusetts
   02647

Robert C. Eldred Co., Inc.
P. O. Box 796AQ
East Dennis, Massachusetts
   02641

Michigan

Du Mouchelle Art Galleries
409 East Jefferson
Detroit, Michigan 48226

New York

Christie Manson & Woods
 International, Inc.
502 Park Avenue
New York, New York 10022

Christie's East
219 East 67th Street
New York, New York 10021

William Doyle Galleries, Inc.
175 East 87th Street
New York, New York 10028

John C. Edelmann Galleries,
 Inc.
123 East 77th Street
New York, New York 10021

Phillips Fine Art Auctioneers
867 Madison Avenue
New York, New York 10021

Sotheby Parke Bernet, Inc.
980 Madison Avenue
New York, New York 10021

Sotheby's York Avenue
 Galleries
1344 York Avenue
New York, New York 10021

Ohio

Garth's Auction House
2690 Statford Road
P. O. Box 369
Delaware, Ohio 43015

Pennsylvania

Samuel T. Freeman Company
1808 Chestnut Street
Philadelphia, Pennsylvania
 19103

In addition to their main operations listed above, several of the leading auction houses have representatives and hold occasional auctions in other cities. For example, Sotheby's has branch offices in Boston, Chicago, Honolulu, Houston, Palm Beach, Philadelphia, San Francisco, and Washington, D.C.

Although the above list of reputable auction houses may seem short, many art experts don't recommend even this many to collectors. These experts would abbreviate the list of recommended auction houses to Barridorff in Portland, Maine; Butterfield & Butterfield in San Francisco; Du Mouchelle in Detroit; Freeman in Philadelphia; Mortons in New Orleans; and Christie's, Edelmann, Phillips, and Sotheby's in New York and elsewhere.

OTHER OUTLETS: FLEA MARKETS AND GARAGE SALES

Many collectors think that real art bargains are not found in established galleries or auction houses but in flea markets and garage sales. They consider such events the "bargain basements" of the art market. The reputation is partially deserved. Occasionally, a great bargain can be found amidst the heaps of relatively worthless junk. If there is a good item, you're more likely to be the only person in the crowd capable of recognizing it.

Before you decide to buy at flea markets and garage sales, however, you should know how much effort is required—and how futile that effort can be. Superb works of art are not, as a rule, the stock in trade of such events. For every good piece of Mission furniture or art pottery that you find at a flea market, you will have to wade through mountains of "antique" plastic dinnerware and cheap used furniture. Although many of your fellow bargain hunters probably can't tell the difference between Rookwood and Melmac, you can't count on being the only expert there. At any good flea market, you're likely to encounter one or two other knowledgeable buyers who will be looking for the same bargains you are.

Finally, although many objects are vastly underpriced at flea markets and garage sales, many are vastly *overpriced*. It's only when you're buying from a seller who doesn't know his merchandise that your expertise becomes an advantage. Unfortunately, an ignorant seller is often the one who thinks every work of art is a museum masterpiece. He may think his lone oil painting is worth millions, and no amount of expertise will convince him to the contrary.

While an ignorant seller may overestimate the value of a flashy object, subtler virtues may escape his notice. He may think that his Rococo Revival sofa once occupied an important spot at Versailles, but he won't know that his plain-looking green ashtray is really a rare Ming celadon porcelain dish. In either case, you should know what he doesn't know. You'll need some expertise to distinguish both the excellent work that is priced too low *and* the mediocre work that is priced too high. The principle of the auction house applies at flea markets and garage sales as well: Knowledge is more important than money.

Some Ground Rules

Come Prepared to Take the Object Home with You. There are no delivery or storage facilities at flea markets or garage sales. So bring adequate packing materials and a car or truck big enough to hold your purchase.

Bring Cash. Sellers will not accept credit cards and may not accept personal checks—even for the more expensive items. So have enough cash on hand. (Traveler's checks, however, are generally accepted.) If you plan to make small purchases, carry small bills and plenty of change since the seller himself may run out during the day.

Don't Dress Up. There's no reason to dress up for a flea market, and every reason to dress down. You want to be able to carry that fine but filthy Mission desk home with you.

Arrive Early. The best purchases are often made at the beginning of the day, so arrive early. In fact, since the sellers often arrive long before sales officially open, you should too. You can get to the flea market, purchase the best items, and be back on the road before most buyers have even arrived.

How to Find a Flea Market

For lists of flea markets, see:

Barbara Beddoe and Marie Baxter Pace, *Where 2,000 Antique Shows and Flea Markets Are* (Old Chelsea Station, N.Y.: P.O. Box 33, 1976).
Irene Copeland, *The Flea Market and Garage Sale Handbook* (New York: Popular Library, 1977).

SELLING WORKS FROM YOUR COLLECTION

Why would you ever *sell* a work, especially if you've gone to a lot of trouble to acquire it?

There are several good reasons for selling a work; even museums do it, although they call it "deacquisition." The first reason, of course, is money. Sometimes it's a choice between the Tiepolo drawing and the kid's tuition. The second reason is changing tastes. When you first began to collect, you liked Chinese export ware; now you prefer Chinese domestic ware. The final reason is upgrading your collection. You want to sell a mediocre impression of a Dürer print so you can afford a better one.

Whatever your reasons, selling an art object is always difficult. A collector tends to develop special emotional ties to each work in his collection. Selling a work is also a practical difficulty. First, you have to know how to place the work in a gallery or auction house. Once you've placed it, months or even years can pass before it sells. And when it does, it probably won't bring as much as you hoped for.

Here are some tips that will help you sell a work more easily. First, secure an expert appraisal. Next, investigate the relative advantages of selling through a dealer or an auction house by checking with several of each. Finally, before you actually sell the work, weigh the pleasure—and profit—of giving it away.

Appraisals: Taking Stock

The first step in selling a work is to have it appraised. You should know how much an object is worth before you decide how much to ask for it.

Unofficial Appraisals. There are two kinds of appraisals: official and unofficial. Whenever you calculate the value of a work by comparing it to similar items, you are making an unofficial "appraisal." It's also possible to get an unofficial appraisal from someone more knowledgeable than yourself. Simply send a description and a photograph to a relevant dealer, auction official, or museum curator. Better yet, visit the expert in person and take the object along. Many of them will be happy to tell you unofficially what your object might be worth. The expert opinion is a free service to the community.

Heirloom Discovery Days. Since 1975, Sotheby's has set aside special "Heirloom Discovery Days." Officials from the auction house travel to small cities where, for a $5 fee, owners can bring their objects for a quick appraisal. Many of the items that turn up on Discovery Days are practically worthless. On occasion, however, a remarkable object surfaces. One man in upstate New York brought in a plate he'd bought for $6 only to learn that he was the owner of a rare piece of Ming porcelain. The man later sold the plate for $70,000. A version of Edward Hicks's *Peaceable Kingdom* appeared at a Discovery Day in Montclair, New Jersey; the startled owner soon sold it for $125,000.

Official Appraisals. But sometimes a quick, unofficial appraisal isn't enough. For example, if an unofficial appraisal indicates that you should sell an object, you'll want to have it *officially* appraised before making a final decision to sell. Official appraisals are also essential, or at least helpful, in *buying* an object, obtaining insurance, writing a will, settling an estate, and recovering stolen items. In each case, you will need the services of a professional appraiser: one with experience in the relevant area, recognized skill in assessing objects, and—not least—unquestioned integrity.

1. *Relevant expertise.*   Appraisers appraise everything from business machinery to real estate. You want an appraiser who is not only a specialist in art, but also a specialist in the particular kind of art you are having appraised. "Gone is the day of the 'general appraiser,' who is prepared to tackle the Remington bronze and the Remington razor," says Hugh Hildesley, head of appraisals for Sotheby's.

2. *Proven ability.*   The potential for error in an appraisal is very high, especially if the appraiser doesn't know his business. One collector inherited a work attributed to Jean-Baptiste-Camille Corot and appraised at $125,000. Based on this appraisal, he paid $35,000 in estate taxes. Some time later, the work was determined to be a copy of a Corot and reappraised at only $1,000. The inaccurate first appraisal cost the heir far more in estate taxes than the painting was actually worth.

3. *Integrity.*   In appraisals, there is as much scope for corruption as for error. If the appraiser charges a percentage of the appraised value, he may up the value in order to up his fee. On the other hand, if the person appraising the work is a dealer who wants to buy the work from you, it's obviously in his interests to underestimate the value.

How to Find an Appraiser

How can you locate a competent appraiser? Ask a banker or lawyer; he can refer you to an appraiser he has confidence in. Museum curators are another good source. Finally, consult a dealer or auction official. If he can't give you the appraisal himself, he'll be able to recommend someone who can.

You may also wish to consult the membership lists of The Art Dealers Association of America (575 Madison Avenue, New York, N.Y. 10022) or of the two main appraisers' associations: The American Society of Appraisers (60 East 42nd Street, New York, N.Y. 10016) and the Appraisers' Association of America (541 Lexington Avenue, New York, N.Y. 10017). Of the two, the ASA is the more highly respected. It has both an elaborate entrance examination and a required program of continuing professional education.

Once you have a list of candidates, you should interview each of them. Even the American Society of Appraisers emphasizes the importance of checking an appraiser's credentials: his special expertise, membership in professional associations, and prior experience.

What Should an Appraisal Contain?

An appraisal should be recorded in writing and should include the following items:

1. Date of the appraisal.
2. Client's name and address.
3. Purpose of the appraisal.
4. Statement of disinterest.
5. Artist's name.
6. Title of the work.
7. Exact size.
8. Medium.
9. Support.
10. Signature and/or date.
11. Condition.
12. Complete description.
13. Provenance.
14. Exhibition history.
15. Bibliography.
16. Special conditions affecting the valuation.
17. Statement of corollary opinions.
18. Sales record.
19. Value.
20. Photograph, preferably in color.
21. Appraiser's qualifications.
22. Appraiser's signature.

Prepare in Advance.   The best way to lower the cost of an appraisal is to prepare for it in advance. Before the appraiser arrives, assemble as much of the information listed above as possible, including a photograph of the object.

Update Appraisals Periodically.   Sometimes an appraiser will exaggerate the value of an object to account for inflation. A better way to keep an appraisal current is to update it periodically: every three or four years, depending on the inflation rate.

Second Opinions.   If you have any reason to doubt an appraisal, get a second opinion. Unless the object is worth more than $10,000, a second appraisal need not be a written one; a quick verbal appraisal will suffice. Just ask a dealer or auction official how much he thinks the object is worth. If there's a significant discrepancy between this second estimate and the one from the appraiser, seek another written appraisal.

Selling Through a Dealer

Generally speaking, there are three reasons to sell through a dealer. The first two (the sale of a specialized collection or a single spectacular work) are relevant only to experienced collectors. The third reason, however, is relevant to any collector who wants to sell an object. The dealer alone is prepared to give you immediate cash for a work.

Outright Sale. There are two ways to sell through a dealer: by outright sale and by consignment. Only the outright sale is absolutely certain and produces immediate payment. When selling outright to a dealer, you should expect to receive 50 to 75 percent of the object's current market value. If you bought the work a decade ago for $10,000 and its current appraised value is $25,000, the dealer should give you between $12,500 and $18,750 for it. If the object can be sold easily, you might get as much as $20,000 or $21,000.

Consignment. In an outright sale, you sell *to* the dealer. In a consignment sale, you sell *through* the dealer. *You* maintain possession of the work; the dealer merely sells it for you. The advantage of such an arrangement is that the dealer takes a smaller piece of the profits. Instead of taking 25 to 50 percent off the value of the work, a dealer will accept a commission of 10 to 30 percent on the sale price. In other words, for an object valued at $25,000, you would get $17,500 instead of $12,500. The major disadvantage of selling on consignment is that you don't get paid until the work is sold—*if* the work is sold.

If you decide to sell on consignment, don't be afraid to bargain. If a dealer asks for a 30 percent commission, offer 10. Also, be sure to agree in advance how long the consignment will last: Three to six months is typical. If the work has not sold by the end of the agreed-upon period, you can take it elsewhere. Of course, all of these terms should be put in writing.

If you decide to sell a work through a dealer, go first to the gallery where you bought it. The dealer who sold the work to you will probably want to buy it back. You should shop around before you commit yourself, however. Another dealer may offer you a better price. At the very least, other bids will strengthen your bargaining position with the original dealer.

Selling at Auction

Increasingly, collectors are turning to auction houses to sell their unwanted works. The primary reason, of course, is that auction houses charge a lower commission than dealers: generally no more than 10 percent at the major houses—and even less on expensive items. Just try to make sure your object will bring a competitive price at auction, or you might be better off paying a higher commission to a dealer.

Also, because more collectors are buying at auction, more works are being sold at auction. Auction houses have become the hub of activity in the art market, especially for moderately priced and highly specialized objects. Richard H. Rush, the investment expert, has said, for example: "I don't see how you could move a good Persian rug these days outside a rug auction."

But the disadvantages of selling at auction are often as compelling as the advantages. First, once you decide to sell an object, it may take three or four months (even longer, perhaps) for it to reach the auction block. When it finally does, it may not reach the reserve price—in which case it doesn't sell at all. As an added injury, you even have to pay a penalty fee (generally around 5 percent).

Sotheby's York Avenue Galleries. Sotheby's has recently devised a system to help ease the problem of long delays. Traditionally, all objects sold at Sotheby's were submitted to extensive research and restoration and featured in elaborate catalogues. Now, most objects worth less than $300 bypass the time-consuming aspects of research and restoration and reach the block within two to three weeks of their arrival. Instead of glossy catalogues, the objects are listed in daily computer printouts.

The Best Auction Houses Are Best. If you decide to sell a work at auction, you should entrust it to the best possible auction house. Because of their broad-ranging expertise and loyal following, the major auction houses are generally the best places to auction art works regardless of quality. Because they have outlets throughout the world, the major houses can also ensure that your object is sold where it is likely to bring the highest price. Finally, major houses now charge the seller less commission. Instead of charging the 20 to 25 percent still common at smaller houses, they split the fee equally between the seller and buyer, charging each 10 percent. And even that 10 percent is negotiable if the item is particularly valuable.

Sending a Work to Auction. The first step in selling a work at auction is to send a good photograph of the work and a complete description to several houses for a preliminary appraisal. "We can determine salability by mail," says Annette S. Benda, head of consignment services for Sotheby's. This informal appraisal is usually free. If you want to sell an entire collection, the houses will send a representative to appraise your works in person. A personal visit by an auction house appraiser is *not* free. At Sotheby's, for example, it will cost you $25 for a visit in Manhattan, $50 elsewhere in New York City, $100 in the New York City area, and $250 elsewhere in North America—plus full travel expenses, of course. However, if you consign your objects to Sotheby's within a year of the visit, the charges will be refunded.

Once you've decided on a house, a number of issues will need to be resolved: shipment, cleaning, restoration, and research of the work; catalogue illustrations; reserve price; insurance coverage; and the date of sale—to mention just a few. All of these details must be negotiated, then specified in a written contract. If the work sells, you will receive a check about a month after the auction for the final sale price minus your 10 percent seller's fee and a charge for most of the services listed above.

Tax Consequences of Selling a Work

Selling a work of art is a financial transaction. You'll probably earn a profit; you may incur a loss. Either way, you'll incur some expenses. All of these contingencies have tax consequences.

The nature of those consequences depends largely on your status as a collector. Many collectors have found significant tax advantages in assuming the status of "art investors" rather than simple collectors. On the other hand, the IRS sometimes looks upon active collectors as "dealers," whether or not they own established galleries. The "dealer" status entails some serious disadvantages.

Art-Investor Status. In order to convince the IRS that you're an art investor, you have to demonstrate that you buy art primarily as an investment; that you buy art for profit, not for pleasure. There are several ways to do this: You can employ professional investment counselors, keep your works of art in storage instead of displaying them, maintain careful records of the rates at which your objects appreciate, and sell works frequently, instead of holding them for many years. In addition, it's helpful if your collection represents a major portion of your assets.

There are several important advantages to the art-investor status which may make these efforts worthwhile. First, as an art investor, you can deduct the costs of collecting: investment advice, appraisals, buying trips, conservation, storage, and insurance. Even more important, you can deduct any losses you may incur in selling a work. Before you pursue art-investor status, however, you should be aware that the IRS is suspicious of the classification. In 1970, a court ruled that Mr. and Mrs. Charles B. Wrightsman, a couple who spent a great deal of money on art works, kept detailed records, and displayed their collection in an apartment they rarely lived in, were *not* "art investors." They were "collectors," the court said, because they didn't buy and sell works often enough and they enjoyed them too much.

Dealer Status. Another risk of trying to achieve art-investor status is that all of your buying and selling and all of your professionalism will only turn you into a dealer in the eyes of the IRS. If you're considered a dealer for tax purposes, you can also deduct all expenses and losses, but you may not be able to declare profits derived from the sale of works as a capital gain.

Capital-Gains Treatment. If you are a collector or an art investor but not a dealer, you can declare all of your profits on the works you sell as capital gains. Works held for less than one year will receive short-term capital gains treatment; works held for more than a year will receive superior long-term capital gains treatment.

Gifts to Museums

Instead of selling your works, consider donating them to a museum. Giving works away is generous, of course, and good for the soul, but it also has considerable tax benefits. Especially if you're in a high tax bracket, you can actually make *more* money by giving an object away than by selling it. In the art world, charity definitely begins at home. "It's gotten very expensive to die with a collection," says J. Carter Brown, director of the Washington National Gallery. "People really can't afford to do that."

Consider the Figures. Suppose a collector bought for $10,000 a work that is now worth $100,000. If he sells the work through a gallery and pays a 25 percent dealer's commission, his profit is $65,000 ($75,000 minus the initial investment of $10,000). If the collector is in the highest tax bracket, the tax on the sale could be 40 percent, or $26,000. His after-tax profit, then, is $39,000.

If, on the other hand, the collector gives the work away, he can deduct the full market value of the work, $100,000. For someone in the highest tax bracket, that translates into a tax savings of $70,000, and a profit of $60,000—as compared with $39,000 on a sale.

There are, however, several restrictions on deductions for charitable donations:

1. *Must be a long-term capital asset.* The work must be a long-term capital asset, meaning that it must have been in your possession for at least twelve months. You should also have assembled a collection and displayed it for several years before you begin to donate individual works. Otherwise, the IRS may determine that you are not a collector but a dealer, severely limiting the amount you can deduct.

2. *Not applicable to gifts.*   Profits from the sale of a work given to you by the artist are treated as ordinary income, not capital gain. Therefore, if an artist wants to give you something, try to pay him something for it —the amount is irrelevant.

3. *No more than 30 percent of your income.*   You can deduct the market value of a work against no more than 30 percent of your adjusted gross income. If the value exceeds the 30 percent limit, the excess can be carried over for as many as five years. The way the law sees it, you're making your donation in installments. To satisfy the IRS, however, you should probably surrender physical possession of the work as soon as you deduct the first "installment." Unfortunately, the days have passed when a collector could donate a work to a museum but keep it on his walls until his death.

4. *Only to "related" institutions.*   The work must be donated to an institution that will use it for a "related" tax-exempt purpose. As a general rule, the work must go to an institution—a school or, more probably, a museum—that will put it on exhibition. You can't give a painting to a hospital that will turn around and sell it to raise money and still reap the full tax benefits.

5. *Only to publicly funded institutions.*   The work must also be donated to an institution that is publicly funded. Donations to *private* institutions can only be deducted up to 20 percent of adjusted gross income and excess amounts can't be carried over into following years.

6. *Adequate appraisals required.*   The IRS examines deductions for art donations, especially large ones, with great care. Before you give a work away, therefore, you should have it appraised by the most reputable appraiser you can find.

Bargain Sales.   Instead of donating a work to a museum, you can sell it on the open market and then donate the proceeds. There are tax advantages in this arrangement, but they don't match the advantages of donating the work itself, since your deduction will be set off against your profit from the sale. If you want both a deduction and immediate cash, however, there's a way to combine a sale with a donation without sacrificing tax benefits. You can sell the work to an institution for the amount you paid for it, then donate the appreciation. This procedure is called a "bargain sale."

The tax consequences of an art gift are very complicated. Therefore, before you decide to give a work away, you should consult a tax lawyer or accountant. A museum official will also be happy to discuss the details of donating art.

Lifetime Family Gifts. The typical collector wants to keep at least a part of his collection in the family even if he donates the bulk of it to a public institution. There are, however, significant tax problems to be considered. Whether you give works to family members during your lifetime or will them at your death, the tax on such transfers can be breathtaking. The only way to avoid these taxes is to use the *annual lifetime gift-tax exclusion.*

The law permits both you and your spouse to give each member of your family up to $3,000 per year, or $6,000 jointly. These payments can take any form, including art. Thus, over a period of a decade, you and your spouse can give two children $120,000 worth of art without subjecting them to any additional tax liability.

There are two principal problems with tax-exempt lifetime gifts. First, if you use your gift-tax exclusion to transfer works of art, you can't use it to avoid tax on the transfer of other assets, such as cash, real estate, or stocks. Second, if you die within three years of making a lifetime gift, the IRS reclassifies it as a gift made "in contemplation of death." The government voids the tax exclusion and the gift is "added back" into the estate.

This is only a rough outline. For example, it doesn't account for gift, inheritance, and estate taxes imposed by the state. In the likely event that your collection turns out to be worth more than $100,000, your lifetime gifts should be incorporated into a larger program of estate planning prepared with the assistance of a competent attorney.

What to Collect

Art comes from many periods, from many countries, from the hands of many artists. It also comes in every price range, from under $5 to over $5,000,000. Within this vast diversity, what you decide to buy will depend on the breadth of your tastes and the size of your budget. Chances are, you'll want to buy more than one kind of art. No book can tell you what you should or shouldn't buy, but it can give you a sense of the numberless possibilities.

Here, then, begins a quick tour of the art market, divided into three unequal excursions. First, the current art market's most competitive areas: paintings by the old masters and Impressionists. While the finest works in this category are entirely beyond the reach of the new collector, an occasional work is still available to the educated collector—new or old. In short, bargains can be found even here.

Second, a slower and more detailed look at three areas where the new collector is likely to spend most of his time: prints, photographs, and posters. Prints have long been favorites among true collectors; only in the past few years, however, have large numbers turned seriously to photographs and posters. All of these fields share one important characteristic: reasonable prices. First-rate works are regularly available for several hundred to several thousand dollars.

Third, a rapid tour through the less-traveled regions of the art market. This more esoteric area of the market includes both the oldest works of art and the newest, art from the South Pacific islands and art from around a hometown corner.

THE BIG TIME: IMPRESSIONISTS AND OLD MASTERS

The Big Time is a game in which the very rich compete for the few remaining masterpieces of Western art: the paintings and sculptures of the leading old masters and Impressionist artists. The National Gallery in London and the Norton Simon Museum in Pasadena recently played a round of the game over *The Resurrection* by Northern Renaissance master Dieric Bouts. The Norton Simon Museum won that one for a mere $3,740,000. The National Gallery soon came back, however, and won the next round: *Samson and Delilah* by Peter Paul Rubens for $5,400,000.

Any collector, old or new, would love to play the Big Time. Rembrandts and Monets are the stuff of every collector's fantasies. The sad truth, however, is that only a handful of private collectors can still play the Big Time. And only a handful of masterpieces are left to play it with. A few still hang on the walls of private homes, and when one of them does come on the market (a rare event), only the richest museums and richest men can afford to play for it.

If you're willing to lower your sights, however, you can find similar and equally spectacular works, even by Impressionists and old masters, for less than $10,000. Just remember the various factors governing the prices of works of art, and use them to your advantage.

Subject. For example, some subjects are more popular than others, and therefore more expensive. Collectors compete heatedly for flower paintings but shun portraits. Bouquets of lilies, roses, irises, and tulips by little-known seventeenth- and eighteenth-century Dutch painters such as Osias Beert and Baltasar van der Ast can cost $100,000 or $150,000. By contrast, you can find works by many of the brilliant eighteenth-century English portraitists, including Sir Thomas Lawrence, George Romney, and Sir Henry Raeburn, for $10,000 or less. Although one Raeburn portrait sold recently for $60,000, two others in the same sale went for less than $3,000 each. "We've become rather bored with the Romneys, the Raeburns, and so forth," says Harry Brooks, president of Wildenstein & Co. in New York. "But I wouldn't be surprised to see judicious buying in this area of English painting. It may be a reawakening of the whole school."

Top left, Baltasar van der Ast. *Upright Flowers in Vase.* Oil on panel. 21½″ x 14″. Courtesy Christie's, New York.

Top right, Jacopo Negretti, Il Palma Giovane. *St. Jerome.* Black chalk and oil on brown paper. 11⅝″ x 8¾″. Courtesy, Christie's, New York.

Left, Sir Peter Lely. *Portrait of Lady Killigrew-Hesse.* Oil on canvas. 49″ x 39″. Courtesy Christie's, New York.

Media. Also, some media are more popular and expensive than others. Even if you can't buy a painting by your favorite artist, you probably can buy one of his drawings or prints. The record price for a painting by Picasso is $5,300,000 (for an early self-portrait). Even Picasso's mediocre paintings routinely bring six-figure prices. But a fine Picasso drawing can still be purchased for about $10,000. That's not cab money, but it's still relatively cheap for a signed work by one of the greatest artists of all time.

Style. Finally, some styles are more popular than others. Peregrine Pollen of Sotheby's, for example, suggests that collectors take advantage of the relative unpopularity of early Italian Renaissance art: "If you compare Italian paintings of the 14th and 15th centuries with third-rate Impressionist and post-Impressionist works that are fetching a lot more, it doesn't make sense. So the Italian paintings must be undervalued—particularly minor Florentine and Sienese artists of that period." David Bathurst of Christie's recommends other areas of art that have fallen in popularity, such as Spanish art and medieval art: "Surely such areas will come back into style sometime."

If you decide to venture into the most established and competitive areas of the art market, you'll have to develop a special kind of flexibility and ingenuity. Look only for those objects ignored by less adventurous collectors, and *you* can be the real winner, even in the Big Time.

PRINTS

Given a choice, most collectors would undoubtedly prefer to collect major works by the old masters or the Impressionists. Everyone has visions of a Rembrandt over the mantel. The problem is that most collectors can't afford the million-dollar-plus price tags. Often, they can't even afford $50,000 for the work of a living master like Robert Rauschenberg.

Does that mean you'll never be able to collect the works of great artists? Not at all. You may have to pass up Rauschenberg's paintings, but you may be able to afford a Rauschenberg silk screen for $5,000, or one of his lithographs for $500. In fact, if you're willing to take an impression of moderate quality in moderate condition, you can find prints by the old masters, even Rembrandt, in the same price range. Prints make it possible for you to collect the works of the artists you like most.

The Print Market

The last two decades have witnessed an unparalleled explosion in the print market. A survey made for *Barron's* in 1973 showed that etchings had shot up in value by 400 percent in one year, outperforming everything in the art market as well as the investment market, including stocks, bonds, and gold.

Humble Beginnings.   Despite their current high prices and investment appeal, prints have humble origins. Ironically, the print medium was developed as a way of disseminating images cheaply to a large audience. Albrecht Dürer, for example, sold a set of sixteen small Passion woodcuts in 1515 for four florins. Even allowing for a half-millenium of inflation,

Left, Thomas Moran. *Children of the Mountain.* 1866. Oil on canvas. 62⅛″ x 52⅛″. Courtesy Christie's, New York.

Below, Thomas Moran. *The Much Resounding Sea.* 1886. Etching. 14⅞″ x 32⅝″. Courtesy Hirschl & Adler Galleries, Inc., New York.

that's about $20 for the set, or $1.25 per print. As recently as the 1950s, $20 would have bought any of the prints that Ellsworth Kelly, the abstract artist, made for the prestigious Galerie Maeght in Paris.

Unfortunately, those days are gone forever. Today, print prices can rival those of paintings, although they vary widely. The paintings of the great American nineteenth-century landscape painter, Thomas Moran, for example, now command prices in the hundreds of thousands of dollars. His *Children of the Mountain* brought $650,000 at Christie's in 1981. Yet most of his prints sell for between $150 and $350. By contrast, the prints of Edvard Munch, the Norwegian Expressionist, are almost as expensive as his paintings. One of his prints sold for a record price of $180,000 in 1980. In 1978, an American museum purchased an impression of Rembrandt's *The Three Crosses* from a European dealer for $350,000: a price that few paintings can command.

The market for prints is unusually volatile. *La Clownesse Assise*, a lithograph by Toulouse-Lautrec from 1896, sold for $16,000 in 1972, then for $25,000 in 1973, and finally, a month later, for $48,000.

A Multiple Art Form

A print is a work of art, usually on paper, that is reproduced from another surface—a wood block, a metal plate, a slab of stone, a silk screen. One of the key features of the printmaking process is that the block, plate, stone, or screen can yield more than one print. Nevertheless, some prints are unique: either because the artist made only one impression—these are called *monotypes*—or because only one impression has survived. These are rarities, however; most prints exist in numbers.

Not Reproductions. A print is *not* a reproduction. It is an original work of art that comes to you directly from the hand of the artist. He does not merely make a photographic copy of an image created in another medium (although Jasper Johns, Robert Rauschenberg, Andy Warhol, and others have confused the issue in recent years by incorporating photographs into etchings, lithographs, and silk screens). A print is a direct link between you and the artist, an essential part of any genuine art experience.

More Is More. Some collectors who move from paintings to prints regret losing the sense of uniqueness, the sense that they own a one-of-a-kind object. Other collectors consider the multiplicity of prints an advantage—and not just because it lowers the price.

For one thing, it means that the same image may come up for sale more often. In 1975, Randy Rosen, an art consultant, asked Donald Marron, a prominent print collector, why he collected prints instead of paintings. "Prints," Marron told her, "are the only art form where you can build a collection of original art with some kind of consistent logic. . . . You can decide on an artist you like, you can often check his whole body of work in a *catalogue raisonné*. Then, barring the print being extraordinarily rare or prohibitively priced, and assuming you have the patience to wait, you can wind up owning precisely the art you want." In other words, you won't have to settle for the only Edward Hopper painting you can find—or afford. You can buy the Hopper print you really want, the same one that's the centerpiece of a major museum's collection.

A Pleasure Shared.　Print collecting is also a more communal activity. You can share your appreciation of a print with all the other collectors who have chosen to buy it. John Russell, art critic of *The New York Times*, wrote in 1979 that buying a print "is quite a different matter from buying a work of art that exists once and only once and may never be seen, let alone coveted, by anyone else. To buy even one print is to become enrolled in a secret society whose functioning is largely benign."

The true print collector looks forward not only to selecting an artist and an image, but also to the search that follows. It becomes a kind of courtship in which the pursuit is part of the enjoyment. The collector studies different impressions of the image in various museum collections (often the same museum will have impressions of varying quality), then scouts all the dealers and auction houses to see which impressions are currently available. The search for just the right impression may take months or even years. But by the end of it, the collector will really *know* the print—far better than he would know a painting bought in an afternoon off a dealer's walls.

A Multiple Medium with Multiple Possibilities.　For the collector who wants something to hang on his walls, prints are often less expensive than paintings but more "dramatic" than drawings. Andy Warhol's silk screens of Marilyn Monroe are as large and colorful as the paintings of the same subject—at a fraction of the cost.

On the other hand, for the collector who has too little wall space, a small etching or engraving is smaller than a painting and more finished than a drawing. The more a print looks like a painting, the more it's priced like a painting. Martin Gordon, a New York dealer, said recently that he can "sell a color print five times faster than a black and white" one. As a result, black-and-white prints are generally the best bargains. A collector can assemble a sizable group of small prints, keep them stored away, and occasionally bring them out, Japanese fashion, for intimate contemplation alone or with a small group of friends.

With prints, you can find a bold, colorful lithograph to decorate your walls, or a delicate drypoint etching to enjoy on special occasions. It is a flexible medium that can accommodate the tastes (and budget) of any collector.

Printmaking Processes

Woodcut. Developed in seventh-century China, woodcutting is the oldest printmaking process still in use. A woodcut artist cuts his design into a smooth block of wood, cutting away those portions he does not intend to print, then applying ink to the raised surfaces. When the block is printed, the image is reversed. A woodcut print of more than one color can be made from either a single hand-inked block or several single-color blocks.

The greatest master of the woodcut medium in Western art was probably Albrecht Dürer. The medium changed little until the nineteenth century, when the English artist, Thomas Bewick, recognized that using wood taken from parts of the tree where the branches met permitted much more control over tonality and detail, initiating a great period of Romantic woodcut book illustrations. Early in the twentieth century, a reaction to Bewick's innovation set in and Paul Gauguin, Edvard Munch, and the German Expressionists found a kind of primitive strength in the medium's harshness and intractability.

Pablo Picasso. *Buste de Femme d'Après Cranach le Jeune.* 1958. Linocut. 25⅝″ x 21″. Courtesy Christie's, New York.

Variation: Linocut. A recent variation on the woodcut, the linocut, uses linoleum instead of wood as a "plate." Traditionally the medium of the children's classroom, Picasso elevated it to a major art form, notably in *Bust of a Woman After Cranach the Younger*, 1958, which sold for $85,000 in December 1980.

Intaglio.   An intaglio print is made by cutting a design into a metal plate, then spreading ink into the incised lines—not across the raised surfaces as in a woodcut. The plate is covered with a dampened piece of paper and run through a press. The principal advantage over the woodcut is that the artist cuts the lines that will be printed, he doesn't cut away from them. The cutting itself is also somewhat easier, which gives the artist more control over the image.

Of course, cutting designs into hard surfaces goes back a long way. Cavemen regularly cut designs into animal bones and tusks. It took a long time, however, before artists had the clever idea of printing these designs on paper. The first dated intaglio print in Europe was made in Italy in 1446, probably by an artisan in a goldsmith's shop practiced in the art of decorating metal surfaces with designs of incised lines.

Variation: Engraving. The design of the print is cut directly into a metal plate, usually made from copper, with a steel tool called a *burin*. A *drypoint* engraving is made with a fine steel needle instead of the blunter burin. Dürer was the great master of engravings as well as of woodcuts.

Variation: Etching. In etchings, the image is cut into the metal plate by acid rather than by the artist. After the plate is covered with an acid-resistant resin, a design is created by scraping away the resin with a sharp tool called a *stylus*. This exposes the copper surface of the plate. The plate is then dipped in acid, which eats into the exposed copper. After the resin is removed by heating, the plate is inked and printed, just like an engraving.

The etching process gives the printmaker even more control over his medium than the engraving, permitting him a wider range of nuance in the thickness and character of the lines. Rembrandt did for the etching what Dürer did for the woodcut and the engraving: The Dutch master took full advantage of the new medium's potential for subtlety and detail.

Variation: Aquatint.   There are many kinds of etchings, the most important being the aquatint. Invented in 1650, it was largely forgotten until 1780, when Francisco Goya used it for his *Los Caprichos*. An aquatint is like a traditional etching except that parts of the metal plate are dusted with a rosin powder which, when heated, fuses to the plate. When the plate is dipped in acid, the acid goes through the pores in the ground and eats little cavities into the metal surface. On the final print, the result is a fuzzy gray which approximates the softer, more painterly look of a watercolor.

Albrecht Dürer. *The Virgin with the Dragonfly*. c. 1495. Engraving. $9\frac{5}{16}$ x $7\frac{1}{4}''$.
Courtesy Christie's, New York.

Above, Rembrandt van Rijn. *Christ Preaching.* c. 1652. Etching with engraving and drypoint. 6″ x 8⅛″. Courtesy Christie's, New York.

Left, Francisco Goya. *Los Caprichos.* 1799. Aquatint with etching. 11¹³⁄₁₆″ x 8¹³⁄₁₆″. Courtesy Christie's, New York.

Lithography. For a lithograph, a design is made with an oily crayon or other greasy material on a stone slab or (more recently) a metal plate. When the slab or plate is moistened, the water runs off where the greasy design has been applied. When ink is then applied, it avoids the water and sticks only to the design. The plate is then printed.

Lithography was invented almost by accident by Aloys Senefelder, a penniless playwright, in 1796 when he wrote a laundry list on a stone slab. The medium was seen first as a cheap printing process for textual materials and musical scores and only somewhat later as a new medium for artists.

Silk Screen. Silk-screening is essentially a stencil process like that used to print designs on T-shirts, addresses on steamer trunks, and everything in the army. On a fine screen—made of nylon, not silk—an image is made by blocking out the negative areas either with a stencil cut from paper or acetate film, or with a gluelike substance applied with a brush. The screen is then pressed against a piece of paper and ink is squeezed through the back of the screen to form the image. The process is repeated for each additional color.

To distinguish them from commercial silk screens, fine-art silk screens are now sometimes called *serigraphs*. The terms, however, are used interchangeably.

Impressions. Although most prints exist in numbers, not all impressions of the same print look or cost the same. The general rule that the condition of a work of art affects its price applies to prints as well as to paintings. In fact, condition is often more important in print collecting than elsewhere in the art world. "Print collectors are more exacting than drawing collectors," says David Tunick, a New York print dealer. "With prints, people figure they may have another chance."

Condition. An impression in pristine condition will cost a great deal more than one that has been cropped, torn, stained, foxed, faded, or repaired in any way. You can get a late impression of a damaged Dürer woodcut for $200, whereas you would probably have to pay $100,000 or more for the finest impression of the same print in perfect condition.

Quality. Sometimes two different impressions, even if pulled on the same day, can vary in quality. This is especially true of etchings. By wiping the plate carefully with the ink prior to printing it, the artist can control the tonal qualities of each impression. He can make it linear and stark or soft and atmospheric; he can make the whites bright and clear, the blacks rich and dark, depending on the effect he wants to achieve.

Left, Grant Wood. *Honorary Degree*. 1937. Lithograph. 11¾" x 7". Courtesy Hirschl & Adler Galleries, Inc., New York.

Below, Andy Warhol. *Campbell's I*. 1968. Silkscreen. 35" x 23". Photograph by Eric Pollitzer. Courtesy Leo Castelli Gallery, New York.

Rembrandt took particular care in wiping the ink on his plates. One impression of a Rembrandt etching may be nuanced and evocative (if printed by Rembrandt himself), another dull and lifeless (if printed years later by some anonymous lackey). In May 1973, an undistinguished impression of Rembrandt's *Agony in the Garden* (c. 1657), one of his major prints, sold at Sotheby's for $3,600. At the same auction, another impression of the same print came up for sale. This one, by contrast, was one of the finest to appear on the market in years. The price: $70,000. The point: Anyone who seriously wishes to collect prints should learn to distinguish a mediocre impression from a great one.

What Is an Original Print?

What makes a print an original work of art and not just a reproduction? When is a print "original"? The question is an important one for those who plan to collect prints, and the answers are elusive. The meaning of originality has always been ill-defined and it varies considerably from one period to the next. For example, there is a higher standard of originality for recent prints—prints made since about 1930—than for prints made before that time.

Early Concepts of Originality. The whole concept of originality is essentially a modern one. Before the mid-nineteenth century, many prints were not independent works of art but engraved "reproductions" of an artist's paintings. Many artists didn't make their own plates; they called instead on the services of a special engraver, often an able and respected artist in his own right. These prints are called "reproductive engravings," and, in most cases, are captioned with the names of both the artist who created the image and the one who engraved it.

Reproductive engravings of a great artist's works are always cheaper than the artist's own prints, yet some are considered very fine works. These are among the true bargains of the print market. Especially notable are Marcantonio Raimondi's sixteenth-century engravings of roughly contemporaneous works by Raphael. One of Raimondi's engravings of Raphael's *Parnassus* sold at Christie's in 1975 for $1,520.

Albrecht Dürer. Even in Raimondi's lifetime, however, the controversy over originality was already beginning to boil. Albrecht Dürer, another of Raimondi's contemporaries, was so outraged by the Italian's unauthorized copies of his own prints that he travelled to Venice in 1505 to try to put a stop to them. Despite Dürer's protest, the Italian authorities agreed only to prohibit Raimondi from replicating Dürer's well-known monogram, consisting of an A superimposed on a D.

Marcantonio Raimondi. *The Climbers*. Engraving. 11⅛″ x 5¹⁵/₁₆″. Courtesy Christie's, New York.

Although Dürer generally cut his own plates, he rarely printed them himself. He left that to students and assistants in his workshop. He neither limited the size of his editions—often printing as many impressions as he thought the market would bear—nor signed his prints, carving his monogram directly into the plate. Despite all this, despite the fact that Dürer did not print, number, or sign his works, they are still "original": No one else at the time did either.

The Concept of Originality Today. If an artist today followed Dürer's procedure, the results would be called "reproductions," not "original prints." Why the double standard?

The distinction arose with the invention of photography and photomechanical reproduction in the nineteenth century. Before that, printmaking was the only one way to reproduce images quickly and cheaply so they could be made available to the general public. Prints were less an art form than a means of popular communication. With the arrival of the cheaper and more efficient photographic process, however, printmaking soon lost its mass market. Only artists continued to have a use for the older medium's expressive potential.

Current Standards. Because we now tend to think of printmaking as an art form rather than a form of reproduction, we expect the artist to be involved in every step of the process. He should make the plate, certainly, and he should at least supervise the printing. He should make only as many prints in an edition as he can adequately supervise. Finally, his signature is a guarantee that the print is authentic and that it meets his personal standards in every respect.

Making an Edition

An artist indicates that he has limited the size of an edition by numbering each print. After he decides how many prints he wants to make— almost never more than 250, usually far less—he then *numbers* each print. (Editions today generally run from 10 to 100, with the majority falling between 35 and 50.) There are, in fact, two numbers: the number of the print, and the number of prints in the edition. They appear separated by a slash, like this: 1/250, which means the first print in an edition of 250.

Artist's Proofs. Actually, the numbers can be misleading. There are almost always more prints than the numbers indicate. Custom permits the artist to pull a few extra prints for himself and for the printer. Logically enough, these are called *artist's proofs* (or *épreuves d'artiste*). Such proofs are sometimes distinguished from the regular edition by "A.P." or

"E.P." instead of an edition number. They might also be labeled "H.C." for *hors de commerce* (not for sale).

Labels notwithstanding, many of these "not for sale" items do, in fact, come up for sale. If you see a print marked A.P., E.P., or H.C. from time to time, don't be afraid to buy it. It's exactly the same as the numbered prints in the same edition.

Counterproofs. There are further complications. In the process of making a plate, an artist may want to experiment with changes without altering the plate itself. To do so, he makes a print from the plate, then, while the impression is still damp, presses another piece of paper against it. The result is a *counterproof*. After making changes on the counter-proof, he can transfer them to the plate.

Bon à Tirer Impressions. When the artist considers an image complete, he often pulls a *bon à tirer* (good to pull) impression. This ideal impression serves as a standard of quality for the rest of the edition. As each new print is pulled, it is measured against the *bon à tirer* impression. If the print measures up, it becomes part of the numbered edition; if not, it's thrown out.

States. Sometimes an artist isn't sure when he's finished work on a plate. As a result, he wants to print from the plate at various stages in its evolution. These "in-progress" printings are referred to as different *states* of the same print. If a print exists in many states, it doesn't mean that the artist was indecisive or that the print is less accomplished. Even Rembrandt frequently developed his images incrementally. Seeing all the states of a print assembled at one time provides a rare insight into the creative process. Many collectors and museums try to acquire one of each.

Canceling the Plate. When an artist has finished printing the entire edition, he usually destroys—or *cancels*—the plate: He cuts the wood block in two, scratches an X across the metal plate, erases the stone slab, or tears up the silk screen. Each procedure ensures that no more prints can be produced.

Editions and Restrikes. Sometimes, instead of being canceled, a plate is merely set aside or *retired* after the first edition. When this happens, additional prints are often made. If they are made by the artist or during the artist's lifetime, they are generally called subsequent *editions*. If, however, they are made by a third party or after the artist's death, they are called *restrikes*. Several European museums that maintain collections of old-master plates will occasionally use their plates to issue new editions. Here in the United States, in 1971, the Whitney Museum of American Art issued limited editions of one hundred etchings from four plates it owns by the 1930s artist, Reginald Marsh.

As long as no attempt has been made to cancel the plates, restrikes and subsequent editions can be of very good quality. As long as you pay less than for impressions from an early edition, restrikes can even be good bargains. The Reginald Marsh restrikes, for example, were published at prices ranging from $40 to $90.

Sometimes, however, what looks like a bargain is definitely not. Sometimes, the plate is so badly damaged or worn that the original image is almost unrecognizable. This is often true of Rembrandt restrikes, for example. Many of Rembrandt's plates were printed time and again before they were deposited in the Bibliothèque Nationale in Paris. If you find a Rembrandt print in good condition for less than $500, it may be a late, badly worn restrike. If you want a work by Rembrandt, but can't afford to pay too much, this may be the solution. Just remember that what you're getting is only a shadow of the real thing.

Edition Size. How important is the size of an edition? It depends on the nature of the print. The first engravings and etchings pulled from a plate are generally the best. After a while, the lines in the plate begin to weaken and blur. A copper engraving is said to yield about 500 good impressions; a drypoint etching only about 150—and not all of the same quality. A lithographic stone yields between 800 and 1,000 impressions of varying quality. The first few are *not* the best, however. It takes some time for the stone to "warm up." The silk screen, the most democratic of all the printmaking media, yields thousands of impressions of equal quality.

Extending the Life of a Plate. It is possible to extend the life of a plate, and with it the size of the edition—but not without some loss of quality. A lithographer can transfer an image from one stone to another, then print from the second stone. Naturally enough, these secondhand impressions are called *transfer* prints. It's also possible to "face" the metal plate of an etching or engraving with steel. The procedure significantly reduces the nuance in the original plate, however.

Effect on Prices. The number of prints in an edition usually affects the value of each individual print. Cecile Shapiro and Lauris Mason, authors of *Fine Prints: Collecting, Buying, and Selling,* point out a rough correlation between the price of an Edward Hopper print and the size of its edition. For example, *Night Shadows,* which comes in an edition of more than five hundred, is Hopper's cheapest print. The correlation is not perfect, however. Grant Wood's most popular print, *Honorary Degree,* which was also issued in a large edition, is Wood's most expensive print. Why the discrepancy? Although collectors generally prefer prints from small editions, the popularity of a particular image can sometimes overide considerations of scarcity.

The Numbers Game. Does it matter which number in a small edition you buy? Almost never. If you have several impressions to choose from, look to the quality of the individual print, not the number. Most artists number their prints long after they've been pulled. By the time the prints have been dried and stacked to await the artist's signature, no one can recall which print was pulled first. So much for collectors who pride themselves on having the "first" print in an edition.

The Signature. Most prints today are signed as well as numbered. Yet you should be aware that signing, like numbering, is a recent invention. James Abbott McNeill Whistler (the painter of "Whistler's Mother") was one of the first artists to employ the practice. Whistler was not unaware that signing his prints made them more marketable: In 1887, he issued a series of prints in both signed and unsigned editions, charging twice as much for the signed versions. If you find an old-master print that's signed in pencil, be on guard. The signature is a fake, and the print may be, too.

Most artists today sign their prints in pencil. This isn't just a matter of convention. If they used ink, it would be difficult to see whether the signature was signed or reproduced. It would be especially difficult to see if the print were covered with glass.

The usual place for the artist's signature is at the bottom right-hand corner; the usual place for the number and edition is at the bottom left-hand corner. Some artists, however, prefer to sign and number their prints on the back. It doesn't matter where the artist signs his name as long as he signs it.

Consider the Individual Artist's Practice. Before you turn down a modern print just because it isn't signed, however, you should be aware that the practice, although common, is not universal. Several artists, including the Americans George Bellows, Arthur B. Davies, and John Sloan, signed only some of their prints. The others were generally stamped by the artists' estates. Signed prints, obviously, are more expensive and better investment values. But if you're more interested in the beauty of the image than in its investment potential, or if you don't want to spend as much, look for the unsigned bargains.

Fake Signatures. A *fake* signature may actually lower the value of the print. Yet never try to remedy the situation by erasing a fake signature. This will only damage the print and lower its value still further.

There are even cases in which the signature and number are original but the print is not. Unscrupulous dealers often take books with high-quality reproductions of prints by artists such as Georges Braque, Marc Chagall, and Fernand Léger, cut out the reproductions, frame them, and sell them as original works of art. In some cases—Braque, Chagall, and Léger, for example—the artists have contributed to the confusion by signing and numbering the *reproductions*. Ben Shahn, the modern American artist, indulged his fans by signing reproductions on request.

Standards in the Industry. The concept of originality is so confusing that the Print Council of America felt it necessary to provide a definition:

"An original print is a work of art, the general requirements of which are:

1. The artist alone has created the master image in or upon the plate, stone, wood block, or other material, for the purpose of creating the print.

2. The print is made from said material, by the artist or pursuant to his direction.

3. The finished print is approved by the artist."

Even this definition is loose. It doesn't mention the signing and numbering of a print, and it doesn't cover prints made before 1930. In 1976, the College Art Association tried to formulate a more workable definition, but gave up. Instead, they recommended that a buyer request from the seller a written description of the print being purchased.

Here is the information that should be included in such a description:

1. The artist's name and the year he made the print;

2. The printmaking process;

3. The limits of the edition, if any;

4. Whether the plate has been canceled or altered in any way after the edition was printed;

5. Information concerning any prior editions;

6. Whether the print is a restrike, and, if so, whether the plate has been reworked;

7. The name of the workshop that produced the print.

Of course, as always, the best guarantee of a work's originality is to do business only with a reputable dealer. A good dealer will provide this documentation as a matter of course.

Four states—California, Hawaii, Illinois, and Maryland—have enacted laws requiring print dealers to disclose all pertinent information about the prints they sell. In response, some dealers have claimed that the necessary information is either unavailable or unreliable. Others have simply refused to cooperate. Unfortunately, few collectors are aware of their remedies under the new print laws. In Illinois, for example, no one has taken advantage of the print-disclosure law in the ten years since it was passed.

Contemporary Master Prints

During the past twenty-five years, the finest artists in this country have led a revolution in printmaking. Earlier in this century, great American painters occasionally made prints, but adequate printmaking facilities were hard to find. Printmaking remained, for the most part, a second-class affair. Then, in 1957, Tatyana Grossman founded Universal Limited Art Editions in the garage of her home outside New York City. Grossman did all the work herself: She commissioned the artists, provided them with first-quality facilities supervised by skilled printers, and, finally, went among unconverted curators and dealers promoting the rediscovered medium.

In 1960, with a grant from the Ford Foundation, June Wayne founded the second important printmaking mission in America, the Tamarind Lithography Workshop in Los Angeles (now in Albuquerque, New Mexico). A few years later, Ken Tyler founded Gemini G.E.L. These three new facilities soon converted many of the country's finest painters to printmaking.

Freeing the Imagination. The print workshops urged their artists to be inventive and worked with them in overcoming the medium's traditional limitations. If an artist felt constrained by the small size of the conventional lithographic stone, the workshops constructed a larger one. Gemini G.E.L. made one a mammoth seven feet long. If an artist wanted to make richly colored silk screens, the workshops developed multiple-screen capabilities, sometimes using fifty or more screens in the creation of a single image. If an artist was bored with the traditional paper surface, the workshops invented processes for printing on almost any surface. During the mid-1970s, Robert Rauschenberg printed on large sheets of silk chiffon, silk taffeta, and grocery bags.

John Russell of *The New York Times* wrote in 1979, "The master printer—the man in charge of the workshop—began to serve the artist the way a recording engineer serves the recitalist. He showed the artist how to do things that the artist never dreamed were possible. Given, in some cases, the merest outline of an idea, the master printer came up with an end product that was astonishing in its vigor, its assurance and its breadth

Jasper Johns. *Coat Hanger II*. 1960. Lithograph. 35½" x 24¾". Courtesy Castelli Graphics, New York.

of resource. What the master printer had to offer was not printmaking, in the old sense: it was printmaking as metamorphosis, and it was irresistable.''

Prints–or Paintings?   These technical advances helped bridge the gap between printmaking and painting: Many of the new prints were as large and colorful as any canvas. Collectors were as captivated by the new possibilities in printmaking as the artists themselves. Suddenly, they could buy large, colorful, richly textured—and original—images by leading contemporary artists for a fraction of the cost of similar images in paint on canvas. Contemporary master prints were soon among the most sought-after items in the art market.

Soaring Prices.   Unfortunately, the market's infatuation with the new medium soon sent prices soaring. Two or three years ago, you could buy a first-quality print by almost any of the contemporary masters for $2,000 or less. No longer. The upper limit has risen to about $4,000, and at that price the prints are not the bargains they once were. Despite the sudden rise, however, contemporary master prints are still safe investments and first-quality works of art.

A Who's Who of Contemporary Master Printmakers.   Who are the leading contemporary printmakers? I've compiled below a list of the leading American artists who regularly make prints today. The prices for their works range between about $500 and $10,000. You should be able to buy a great print by any of them for $4,000 or less.

Willem de Kooning	Roy Lichtenstein
Richard Diebenkorn	Brice Marden
Jime Dine	Robert Motherwell
Richard Estes	Claes Oldenburg
Helen Frankenthaler	Robert Rauschenberg
Jasper Johns	Robert Ryman
Alex Katz	Frank Stella
Ellsworth Kelly	Andy Warhol
Sol Lewitt	

Where to Buy Contemporary Master Prints

Most of the leading printmakers sell their works through one of three or four prominent New York dealers. But in several large cities throughout the country, there are private galleries that maintain an excellent selection of their prints along with a few of their paintings. I recommend you start your search at these galleries. If the gallery you go to doesn't have a particular print, simply ask the dealer to request it from another gallery. You'll find that all the major galleries will cooperate with you and with each other to find the print you want.

Here are the major galleries that sell contemporary prints in New York and elsewhere:

California

Margo Leavin Gallery
812 North Robertson Boulevard
Los Angeles, California 90069

John Berggruen Gallery
228 Grant Avenue
San Francisco, California 94108

District of Columbia

Fendrick Gallery
3059 M Street N.W.
Washington, D.C. 20007

Middendorf/Lane Gallery
2009 Columbia Road N.W.
Washington, D.C. 20009

Illinois

Richard Gray Gallery
620 North Michigan
Chicago, Illinois 60611

Massachusetts

Alpha Gallery
121 Newbury Street
Boston, Massachusetts 02116

Harcus Krakow Gallery
7 Newbury Street
Boston, Massachusetts 02116

Minnesota

John C. Stoller & Company
12th Floor, Dayton's
700 on the Mall
Minneapolis, Minnesota 55402

New York

Brooke Alexander, Inc.
20 West 57th Street
New York, New York 10021

Castelli Graphics, Inc.
4 East 77th Street
New York, New York 10021

Getler/Pall Gallery
50 West 57th Street
New York, New York 10019

Pace Editions Inc.
32 East 57th Street
New York, New York 10022

Pennsylvania

Makler Gallery
1716 Locust Street
Philadelphia, Pennsylvania
19103

Texas

Janie C. Lee Gallery
2304 Bissonet
Houston, Texas 77005

Publication and Prepublication Prices. Prints are cheapest when they are first issued. Thus you can save money by buying a print the minute it arrives in a gallery. In 1980, for example, David Hockney, the English artist, published a print in his swimming-pool series at a price of $2,250. Within less than a year, the same print was selling for $8,800.

Of course, most dealers offer prints at publication prices only to their best customers. As always, the best clients get the best deals.

Other American Prints

I've said that the great contemporary masters of American art have led a renaissance of the print medium during the past twenty-five years. Yet the medium was far from dead at the time: Excellent prints have been made in this country during almost all periods. If the prices of contemporary-master prints are too expensive, you should look carefully at the work of earlier artists—or somewhat less fashionable recent ones. You'll find that, like most prints—including most old-master prints—they're surprisingly affordable.

Underrated and Undervalued. William P. Carl of Childs Gallery in Boston has assembled the following list of underrated and undervalued American printmakers. You'll be able to find a good impression of one of their prints in good condition for the stated amount:

Less than $500

George Elbert Burr (1859–1939)
Samuel Chamberlain (1895–1975)
Kerr Eby (1890–1946)
Clare Leighton (b. 1901)
Mary Nimmo Moran (1842–1899)

Thomas Nason (1889–1971)
Joseph Pennell (1857–1926)
Walter Tittle (b. 1883)
Stow Wengenroth (1906–1977)
Levon West (1900–1968)

$500–$2,500

George Bellows (1882–1925)
Frank Duveneck (1848–1919)
Martin Lewis (1881–1962)
Louis Lozowick (1893–1973)

Reginald Marsh (1898–1954)
Thomas Moran (1837–1925)
Grant Wood (1894–1942)

$2,500–$5,000

Fitz Hugh Lane (1804–1865)

James A. McNeill Whistler
(1834–1903)

Where to Buy Prints

California

Marilyn Pink Master Prints and
  Drawings
817 North La Cienega Boulevard
Los Angeles, California 90069

O. P. Reed, Jr.
521 North La Cienega Boulevard
Los Angeles, California 90048

Zeitlin & Ver Brugge
815 N. La Cienega Boulevard
Los Angeles, California 90069

Walton-Gilbert Galleries
590 Sutter Street
San Francisco, California 94102

R. E. Lewis, Inc.
P. O. Box 1108
San Rafael, California 94902

Robert M. Light & Co., Inc.
P. O. Box 5597
Santa Barbara, California 93108

Connecticut

The Print Cabinet
Cannon Crossing
Wilton, Connecticut 06897

District of Columbia

Hom Gallery
2103 O Street N.W.
Washington, D.C. 20037

Illinois

Merrill Chase Galleries
800 North Michigan Avenue
Chicago, Illinois 60611

Allan Frumkin Gallery, Inc.
620 North Michigan Avenue
Chicago, Illinois 60611

R. S. Johnson-International
  Gallery, Inc.
645 North Michigan Avenue
Chicago, Illinois 60611

Mainstreet Gallery
620 North Michigan Avenue
Chicago, Illinois 60611

Massachusetts

Childs Gallery
169 Newbury Street
Boston, Massachusetts 02116

New York

Harbor Gallery
43 Main Street
Cold Spring Harbor, New York
  11724

Associated American Artists
663 Fifth Avenue
New York, New York 10022

Carus Gallery
1044 Madison Avenue
New York, New York 10021

Fitch-Febvrel Gallery
5 East 57th Street
New York, New York 10022

Lucien Goldschmidt, Inc.
1117 Madison Avenue
New York, New York 10028

Martin Gordon Inc.
25 East 83rd Street
New York, New York 10028

Isselbacher Gallery
41 East 78th Street
New York, New York 10021

Kennedy Galleries, Inc.
40 West 57th Street
New York, New York 10019

William H. Schab Gallery, Inc.
37 West 57th Street
New York, New York 10019

David Tunick, Inc.
12 East 91st Street
New York, New York 10028

For More Information

Riva Castleman, *Prints of the Twentieth Century: A History* (New York: Oxford University Press, 1976).

Riva Castleman, *Printed Art: A View of Two Decades* (New York: Museum of Modern Art, 1979).

Theodore B. Donson, *Prints and the Print Market: A Handbook for*

Buyers, Collectors, and Connoisseurs (New York: Thomas Y. Crowell, 1977).

A. Hyatt Mayor, *Prints and People: A Social History* (New York: The Metropolitan Museum of Art, 1971).

Randy Rosen, *Prints: The Facts and Fun of Collecting,* a Dutton Paperback (New York: E.P. Dutton, 1978).

Cecile Shapiro and Lauris Mason, *Fine Prints: Collecting, Buying, and Selling* (New York: Harper & Row, 1976).

Carl Zigrosser, *Prints and Their Creators: A World History*, second revised edition (New York: Crown Publishers, 1974).

Carl Zigrosser and Christa M. Gaehde, *A Guide to the Collecting and Care of Original Prints* (New York: Crown Publishers, 1965).

PHOTOGRAPHS

Of all the markets open to the beginning collector, photography may offer the most opportunity and excitement. Although prices have risen dramatically in recent years, you can still buy the work of almost any photographer, no matter how famous, for less than $1,000. Photographs by the best new photographers sell for as little as $300. No other field of collecting offers you so much quality for so little money.

Although people began collecting photographs almost as soon as they began taking them, serious collectors discovered photography relatively recently. Only about ten years ago did they begin to pay high prices and compete heatedly for the best photographs. According to most experts, the photography boom dates from 1969, the year Lee D. Witkin opened his specialist gallery in New York.

Witkin was not the first person to consider dealing exclusively in photographs, just the first to succeed. Alfred Stieglitz opened the famous Little Galleries of the Photo-Secession, also in New York, at turn of the century. But Stieglitz failed to convert collectors to the new medium, as did all others who took up the cause in the intervening years. Witkin himself had to overcome considerable skepticism: "I was warned that six months, one year at most, was as long as I could expect to last—because no one collected photographs." Fortunately, the skeptics were wrong. Witkin did last, soon to be joined by almost 120 other photography dealers across the country.

But Is It Art?

Photography took so long to gain acceptance as an art form for two basic reasons. First, people harbored doubts about the expressive potential of the "little brown box." After all, they said, *anyone* can take a photograph—it doesn't require the skill of an artist. "Because the photograph involves in some part the use of a machine," Witkin says, "some people believe it should not be considered art."

Second, there is no way to ensure the scarcity of photographs—a major obstacle to the investment-minded collector. Alan Shestack, director of the Yale University Art Gallery, notes that "one question often asked about photographs (but almost never about Rembrandt etchings or Daumier lithographs) is how they can be valuable, since the negative can, theoretically at least, yield an infinite number of prints."

Acceptance. During the past decade, many collectors have obviously overcome these two concerns—or put them out of mind. It should come as no surprise that many of them are finally willing to acknowledge photographs as a legitimate art form on a par with paintings or prints. After all, photography is the form of art most of us know best. "I think it's because we have a greater sensitivity to photography now—we've been exposed to movies, advertisements, and college photography courses," says Ben Breard, owner of the Afterimages Gallery in Dallas. Robert Mann, of the Harry Lunn Gallery in Washington, D.C., notes that about 90 percent of the new collectors who come into the gallery have a camera dangling from their necks.

Not everyone, of course, agrees that photography is art—not yet, at least. Susan Sontag, the influential critic, wrote an eloquent book called *On Photography*, in which she denies that photography has the expressive potential of the other plastic arts. On the other hand, Janet Lehr, a New York dealer, argues passionately that photography *is* art. In fact, she believes that it's precisely because photography is less plastic than the other media that it is more demanding: The photographer "must capture what he sees in the instant he sees it—dealing with all the problems of light and shadow, form and composition, as they are at the moment. His only tools are his camera and light."

A Fast-Moving Market

Art or not, photography *is* a good investment. A few prices should be enough to convince even the most skeptical collectors. In 1952, long before the boom began, when the Swann galleries in New York auctioned the Albert E. Marshall collection of photographs, 1,100 prints from *Animal Locomotion* by Eadweard Muybridge sold for $250. Three issues of *Camera Work,* the illustrated journal published by Stieglitz to publicize the Photo-Secession movement, sold for $11. And *Pencil of Nature* by

Fox Talbot, the first book illustrated with photographs, and published during the 1840s, sold for $200.

Things have certainly changed. A single print from Muybridge's famous series, *Animal Locomotion,* is now worth more than all 1,100 at the Marshall sale. A single issue of *Camera Work* sold in 1975 at Sotheby's in New York for $5,500. No complete copy of Talbot's *Pencil of Nature* has reached the auction block in recent years, so it's impossible to set a precise value on the illustrated book. However, dealers estimate that it would bring at least $50,000 today—250 times the price it brought in 1952.

The record auction price for a photograph was paid by a German collector in 1980. The photograph: a daguerreotype of the Acropolis taken by a French diplomat, Baron Jean-Baptiste Gros. The price: $50,000. Six months later, the auction record fell to a large print of *Moonrise, Hernandez, New Mexico* (1948), the most famous work of the living American photographer, Ansel Adams. The price: $71,500.

The Adams Chronicle. All along, however, I've said you can't measure a market by record auction prices alone. Despite the surging prices in the

Ansel Adams. *Moonrise, Hernandez, New Mexico.* 1941. Gelatin silver print. 16″ x 20″. Courtesy Christie's East, New York.

photography market—or because of them—there have been several major setbacks since the boom began. The most notable setback hit the work of Ansel Adams. Because so many valuable lessons can be learned from the incident, it's worth relating in some detail.

Adams has long been admired for his dramatic views of aspen forests; Yosemite National Park, where he makes his home; and, above all, Hernandez, New Mexico, site of the now-famous moonrise. Despite the popularity of his work, however, Adams's prices stayed at the same low level through the early 1970s. As late as 1972, you could buy any of his prints for only $150. Adams himself was responsible for the depressed market. Instead of restricting the supply of his work, he persisted in obliging anyone who ordered a print of one of his images.

Prices Soar.   In 1972, a friend convinced Adams that the way to make more money was not to lower prices, but to raise them. Despite the risks, the proposition soon paid off. Prices rose from $350 a print in 1973 to $500 a print in 1974 and $800 a print in 1975. In that year, Adams let it be known that, beginning in 1976, he would accept no further orders for individual prints. A few dealers and collectors accepted the challenge and bought quantities of Adams photographs at the current price of $800. Harry Lunn, the Washington dealer, ordered 1,000.

After 1976, it was up to Lunn and other dealers to set the prices for Adams's work. Adams, who frequently printed the same image in different sizes, had always charged by the size; Lunn charged instead by the image, with prices ranging from $800 to $1,200 (the price of *Moonrise*).

By 1978, *Moonrise* had risen to $2,500. In May 1979, a print sold at auction for $6,000. The price doubled to $12,000 in only four months, and jumped to $15,000 one month later. At Christie's, a print of *Moonrise* soon set the record of $16,500 for a twentieth-century photograph.

What Goes Up Comes Down.   But things couldn't continue in the same direction, at the same pace, forever. First, these prices were being paid for works that were relatively common. According to some estimates, Adams had printed the negative about eight hundred times. That's a great many photographs to be selling at $16,500 each. Moreover, the prints were not all of the same size or quality. Although most of them were sixteen by twenty inches, a few were somewhat larger. Also, since Adams printed them over a period of more than thirty years, the tonal quality differed significantly from one print to another. Some of the prints were light and airy, with great clarity in the details. Others, especially the latest ones, were dark and moody. Finally, there were inevitable differences in condition.

Watching prices rise rapidly out of sight, more and more collectors who

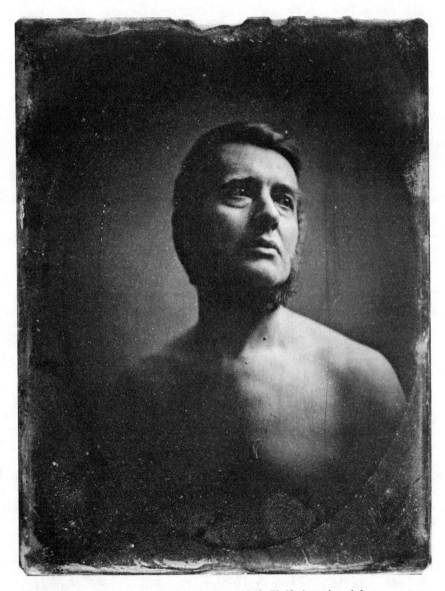

Albert Sands Southworth. *Self Portrait*. c. 1848. Half plate tinted daguerreotype. 4½″ x 3½″. Courtesy Christie's East, New York.

had purchased their prints of *Moonrise* for $150 or less rushed them off to auction, fully expecting to obtain the current record or price or better. As the flood mounted, the market for *Moonrise* collapsed. Within a few months, the price dropped from $16,500 to $8,000.

The Market Recovers. The Adams market soon recovered from this setback, however. Not long after a print of *Moonrise* sold for $8,000, another sold for $13,500. By the end of 1979, a mammoth print sold at Sotheby's for $22,000. In June 1980, the Weston Gallery of Carmel, California, sold a thirty- by forty-inch print for $46,000. In November 1980, however, a large, pristine example was bought in at Christie's at $11,000. Then, in January 1981, a trimmed version of a forty- by sixty-inch print was sold by the G. Ray Hawkins Gallery for the record price of $71,500.

The market for *Moonrise* may seem chaotic, but the lesson for all collectors is clear: You can't get rich quick investing in photographs. But despite the potential of limitless prints of the same image, there is clear investment potential in the medium of photography.

Options

There are four basic kinds of photographs you can collect regardless of your budget limitations:

> Early one-of-a-kind photographs.
> Nineteenth-century paper prints.
> Twentieth-century-master prints.
> Contemporary photographs.

Early One-of-a-Kind Photographs

The first photographs—including daguerreotypes, ambrotypes, and tintypes—were printed without a negative. They were printed directly on the surface of a sheet of copper, glass, or tin respectively. As a result, each photograph is unique. The plates were typically set in leather-bound glass cases, often so attractive they are collected in their own right.

Photography was a popular art form from the start. Between 1840 and 1860, more than thirty million daguerreotypes and other one-of-a-kind photographs were made in the United States alone. That's a lot of photographs. Because the supply of these objects is vast, and the demand relatively small, early one-of-a-kind photographs are generally inexpensive, often costing as little as $5.

Robert Howlett. *Isambard Kingdom Brunel Standing Before the Launching Chains of "The Great Eastern."* 1857 or 1858. Albumen print. 11½″ x 9″. Courtesy Christie's South Kensington, London.

Subject and Artist's Standing. Why do some early photographs cost more—sometimes much more—than others? Occasionally, it's the esthetic merit that commands the higher price. But, as a rule, people buy daguerreotypes and other early one-of-a-kind photographs less for the esthetic merit of the image than for the interest of the subject or the standing of the artist. A record auction price was paid for the photograph of the Acropolis, for example, because it is an unusually compelling image of a compelling subject by a famous person.

A high price is paid if the subject is historically significant. But since relatively few photographs were taken of landscapes, interior views, and still lifes, these also generally bring high prices. Gerard Lévy, a Paris dealer, owns a particularly rare and valuable item: a daguerreotype of a horse and two dogs in front of a stone country house. Exposing a daguerreotype took such a long time that it was unusual to have even a single animal—much less several animals—stand still long enough to provide a clear image.

It also increases the value of an early one-of-a-kind photograph if you can identify the photographer. For example, collectors are willing to pay high prices for daguerreotypes that can be attributed to Mathew Brady, of Civil War fame.

The vast majority of early one-of-a-kind photographs were portraits—portraits, by and large, of unknown people. If you want to assemble a good but inexpensive collection of early photographs, look for unusually appealing anonymous portraits.

Nineteenth-Century Paper Prints

During the decade since the boom in photography began, the main competition has taken place in the market for paper prints by leading nineteenth-century photographers. Most nineteenth-century paper prints are nevertheless relatively inexpensive. There are only a few exceptions: Lewis Carroll, Thomas Eakins, and a few others left so few prints behind that the prices are high.

Whiz-bang Collectors. Works by most other master photographers are expensive only when they have been reproduced in one of the two authoritative histories of photography by Gernsheim and Newhall. A notable example is the portrait taken by Robert Howlett in 1857 of I. Brunel, the designer of a steamship called the *Great Eastern*. In this well-known photograph, Brunel is shown standing against an impressive pile of huge chains. Published in both Gernsheim *and* Newhall, the Brunel portrait has brought as much as $16,000 at auction. One dealer refers to collectors who buy nothing but such frequently reproduced images as "whiz-bang" collectors.

Mathew Brady & Co. *General R.E. Lee and Staff*. 1865. Albumen print. 8½″ x 7″. Courtesy Christie's East, New York.

André Kertész. *Magda—The Satyric Dancer*. 1926 [1970s]. Gelatin silver print. 13½″ x 11¾″. Courtesy Christie's East, New York.

Independent Collectors. If you're independent enough to select your images without cues from Gernsheim and Newhall, you can buy great works by Howlett or almost any other nineteenth-century master photographer for about $1,000 or less. A portrait of General Robert E. Lee and his staff by Mathew Brady sold for the relatively high price of $2,200 in 1980, but other excellent Brady paper prints, with less famous subjects, are available in the $300 to $500 range.

Works by more obscure nineteenth-century photographers cost less than that, often much less. If well-chosen, however, they can form the core of an excellent collection.

You can't begin to understand the beauty of any work of art until you know how it was made. This is as true of photography, with its many technical processes, as of any other medium. Here are some terms you should understand:

1. *Calotypes.* The calotype was the first photograph produced from a negative. Preparing the negative for a calotype required several elaborate chemical procedures, from dipping it in a silver-nitrate solution to fixing it with a hot "hypo" solution. The main chemical used to print the negative was salt, so the prints are often called *salt prints*. You can tell a calotype by its matte brown and often faded colors. (Calotypes are also referred to as *talbotypes,* in honor of Henry Fox Talbot, the man who, in 1840, patented the first calotype process.)

2. *Collodion wet-plate negatives.* Invented in 1851, the collodion wet-plate negative soon replaced both calotypes and one-of-a-kind photographs like the daguerreotypes. The negative was a sheet of glass, coated immediately before exposure with a collodion-based, light-sensitive emulsion. Collodion wet-plate negatives remained standard until the 1870s, when gelatin dry-plate negatives came into general use.

3. *Albumen prints.* Wet-plate negatives were generally used for albumen prints. The main ingredient in the paper of albumen prints was the white of an egg, made photosensitive by the addition of silver salts before the negative was printed. Unlike calotypes, albumen prints have a semigloss finish and look as if they lie on the surface of the paper rather than as if they're embedded in it. They remained popular from the late 1850s through the turn of the century.

4. *Gelatin dry-plate glass negatives.* The gelatin dry-plate process had several distinct advantages over the wet-plate processes it replaced in the 1870s. The photographer did not have to process the negative before exposing it and could store unused negatives for later use.

5. *Platinum prints.* With the new form of negative soon came a new form of positive, the platinum print. Used mainly between 1880 and 1930, the paper in platinum prints was coated with light-sensitive salts, then treated with platinum to form an image that, unlike earlier images, was embedded in the paper.

It pays to know something about the different processes, not just because there are differences in the way the resulting prints *look*—one type of print may appeal to you more than another—but because there are differences in how much they *cost*. Occasionally, a photographer made both albumen prints and platinum prints of the same image, in which case the albumen print is generally worth twice as much.

Twentieth-Century-Master Prints

As a general rule, the highest prices in photography are paid for twentieth-century-master prints, especially for good rare work. Prints by Alfred Stieglitz, Paul Strand, and Edward Weston, for example, have risen beyond the reach of most beginning collectors.

Barbara Morgan. *Martha Graham—Letter to the World.* 1940 [1980]. Gelatin silver print. 14⅝" x 19". Courtesy Christie's East, New York.

Nevertheless, in this category of photographs, as in all others, excellent works remain available even to the budget-conscious. For $1,000 or less, you can buy vintage prints by such major twentieth-century photographers as Brassai, Imogen Cunningham, André Kertész, Barbara Morgan, W. Eugene Smith, and others. You simply have to avoid their most frequently reproduced images. A typical print by Barbara Morgan, for example, costs only $500. That amount won't buy you her elegant and deservedly renowned portrait of dancer Martha Graham, but it will buy you almost any of her other equally beautiful images.

Three Categories. There are three basic categories of twentieth-century-master prints to choose from, although many photographs fall into more than one category:

1. *Fine-art photography.* This is probably the most important category, and the range is correspondingly broad. Fine-art photographs include, on the one hand, the delicately Romantic work of Alfred Steiglitz and, on the other, the starkly understated work of Paul Strand.

2. *Documentary photography.* Walker Evans, who made photographs of the South and of other rural areas for the W.P.A. during the 1930s, is a major example.

3. *Photojournalism.* Fashion photographs by Richard Avedon and Irving Penn prove that a photograph taken to illustrate a magazine article can still be art. W. Eugene Smith's travel photographs for *Life* are also first-quality works of art.

Pictorialist Photography. If you prefer twentieth-century-master prints, but you can't spend as much as $1,000 a print, you might want to consider the works of the lesser *Pictorialist* photographers from the 1920s and 1930s. Those two decades were dominated by the cool, "photographic" style inaugurated by Paul Strand. At the same time, however, soft-focus Pictorialist photography lived on in amateur camera clubs across the land. The best works from these clubs have been gaining in popularity and in price, but good buys are still available. An auction of Pictorialist photographs at Phillips in 1979 produced prices ranging from $150 to $600. The top price went for *On the Elbe,* a beautiful bluish shot by Edward P. McMurty from the mid-1930s.

Contemporary Photographs

Without question, the best buys in photography are works by living photographers who have not yet achieved master status. The going price

Robert Mapplethorp. *Y.* 1978. Gelatin silver print. 7¾" x 7¾". Courtesy Christie's East, New York.

for these prints is about $300, and for that amount you get superior art that has clear investment potential.

The problem, of course, is deciding *which* photographer's work you should collect. After all, the pool of candidates is enormous: Hundreds of thousands of Americans consider themselves to be photographers.

Private Galleries. You can begin your search by looking at the less expensive recent work sold by galleries that handle master prints. Only a few galleries, notably Harry Lunn's, are too elitist to handle anything but master prints.

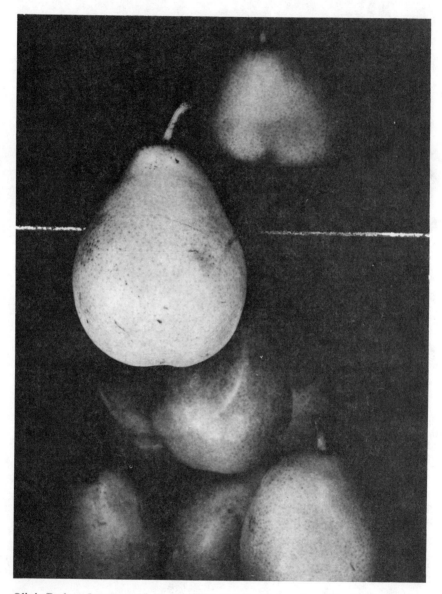

Olivia Parker. *Interior with Pears*. 1979. Gelatin silver print. 10″ x 8¼″. Courtesy Vision Gallery, Boston.

Museums.   Regular presentations in museum exhibitions are another good sign. Unfortunately, this route is not as productive as it might be, since recent photographs are only rarely admitted into the sacred preserve of the art museum. The Museum of Modern Art is something of an exception, but you should be aware that its influential and skilled director of photography, John Szarkowski, has let his own preference for "cool" images shape the character of the exhibitions he mounts.

Recommended Photographers.   The following is a list of talented photographers who have not yet achieved master status, but who are well on their way. It represents several major trends in the medium:

Linda Connor	Jerome Liebling
Robert Cumming	Robert Mapplethorp
Rick Dingus	Joel Meyerowitz
Arthur Gay	Nicholas Nixon
Emmet Gowin	Olivia Parker
Jan Groover	Bill Perronneau
Kenneth Josephson	Howard Read

There should be a photographer on this list whose work will meet every taste and every budget.

Creating Scarcity

Harry Lunn, the Washington dealer, says that photographs still haven't attracted large numbers of collectors. The reason, he says, is the widespread if erroneous perception that photographs are mass-produced. To show that prices depend on scarcity, Lunn likes to tell the apocryphal story of a stamp dealer who owned a pair of stamps, each worth $1,000,000. The dealer reportedly burned one of the stamps so that he could charge $3,000,000 for the other.

Nineteenth-Century Material.   Assuring sufficient scarcity is less of a problem with nineteenth-century material than with twentieth, which may be why the market for nineteenth-century material has generally been the stronger of the two. Of course, you can't prove that all early material is scarce. In most cases, we don't have any idea how many examples of a particular print have survived. But, in fact, many nineteenth-century photographs were unique to begin with. Few were printed in large numbers and fewer still have *survived* in large numbers. Besides, no nineteenth-century photographers are still around to pull an old negative out of the file and print a new batch.

Twentieth-Century Material. The problem of assuring scarcity is more acute with twentieth-century material. Sometimes, as in the case of *Moonrise,* hundreds and hundreds of prints are lying around out there, just begging to be shipped off to auction whenever the price is right. And, if the photographer is still alive, what's to prevent him from printing additional examples whenever the spirit—or the market—moves him?

In fact, many photographers refuse to make an indefinite number of prints from a negative, regardless of the technical possibilities—not just because it would lower the value of each print, but because it would keep them trapped in the darkroom. Photographers don't want to spend all their time printing negatives they took years ago; they want to go out and take new ones.

Artificial Limits. Careful collectors, however, are not satisfied by the fact that most photographers dread the darkroom. They want proof— proof that, when they pay a lot of money for a print, they can be sure the photographer won't turn around and flood the market with hundreds, even thousands, of others. Some photographers have met the demand by setting strict limits on the editions they print. Typically, editions are twenty-five to seventy-five prints, although some young photographers, such as Graeme Outerbridge, make as few as three. Like printmakers, the photographers sign and number the prints. Brent Sikkema, owner of Vision Gallery in Boston, argues that they should also list the date the negative was taken, the date it was printed, and, if they were printed on more than one occasion, the series that the particular print belongs to.

Of course, the only way a photographer can *prove* he'll never print a negative again is to destroy it, just as a lithographer might cancel a stone. Ansel Adams, for example, now destroys all his negatives after they've been printed, using a bank check-canceling device.

Some Photographers Won't Go Along. Not all photographers believe in destroying negatives, or even in limiting editions. Harry Callahan, Aaron Siskind, and other masters believe that one of the great joys of the medium is that it *can* yield an indefinite number of prints, and therefore that many people can own one. According to Evelyn Stassberg of the Light Gallery in New York, "People like Callahan and Siskind believe very much in the democracy of the print." Scarcity may be good for business; they just believe that photography is more than a business.

Vintage Prints

When a negative is at least twenty-five years old, a print of it made by the photographer himself (or perhaps under his direct supervision) soon after he took the negative is called a *vintage* print. Many collectors won't settle for less. Arnold Crane, a major Chicago photography collector, tells prospective buyers, "Run, don't walk, from anything but a vintage print." Crane claims to see in vintage material "an ethereal presence" not found in later prints from the same negative, a view shared by many fellow collectors, though not, by any means, all.

Does it really matter if the photographer himself does the printing? It seems to vary from one photographer to another. Many wouldn't think of letting anyone else near their negatives. They consider printing a negative as important as taking it. W. Eugene Smith, the great photojournalist, has said, "I make my own prints because no language or communication allows me, or anyone else, to tell another person the very subtle balances of print quality only I can register." Still, many other master photographers, such as André Kertész, Henri Cartier-Bresson, and Duane Michals have regularly left the printing to others.

Even if you don't personally object to prints made by someone other than the photographer himself, the difference is by no means academic. The price of a print often depends on who made it, and when.

Vintage prints are only part of the problem. Here are the various types of prints you may run into:

Vintage Print.   A print made by the photographer, or directly under his supervision, about the time when the negative was taken.

Series Print.   A print made by the photographer, or under his supervision, but some time after the negative was taken. Because the negative may have altered with time, or the photographer may have used different printing papers or chemicals, the surface of the image may be significantly different from that in the vintage prints.

Posthumous Print.   A print made after the death of the photographer, perhaps by someone he designated.

Copy Print.   If a negative is destroyed or is unsuitable for printing, it is possible to make a copy negative from a print. Prints made from these copy negatives are called copy prints, and are not considered to be original photographs.

Just how much does the category of the print affect its price? Often, a great deal.

For example, vintage prints by Walker Evans—the great documentary photographer—are notoriously expensive. They sell for between $300 and $4,500 each. Yet all the negatives that Evans made during the highly creative period of the 1930s, when he worked for the Farm Security Administration, are now on deposit at the Library of Congress. (So are tens of thousands of negatives by Dorothea Lange, Ben Shahn, and others.) For only $6, the library's Photoduplication Service will print any of those negatives for you. Six dollars will buy you an Evans photograph made from the same negative used to make a $4,500 vintage print.

For information, write:

The Library of Congress
Photoduplication Service
10 First Street S.E.
Washington, D.C. 20540

Final Points

Here are some points to consider when collecting photographs:

Take a Good Look.   Obviously, it takes time and experience to develop your sensitivity to photographs. You want a print that's in good condition: no scratches or nicks on the surface; no dents in the emulsion. Resist anything that has yellowed or suffers from browning or foxing. Before you buy a work that's in less-than-perfect condition, just remember that the science of conserving photographs is still in its infancy. It's expensive, uncertain, and often ineffective.

Equally important, look to see if the darks and lights are balanced. Is the print gray and fuzzy, or clear and bright? Of course, different photographers want different effects in their prints. You can learn to tell the relative quality of a particular print only if you know something about the photographer's work as a whole.

See If It's Signed.   Signed photographs are desirable, but don't make a signature an absolute requirement. Some photographers simply didn't make it a habit to sign their work. Walker Evans, for example, practically never did. He signed a particular print only if he was loaning it for exhibition or publication.

The Color Controversy.   One thing you should consider in collecting the work of recent photographers is color. Only during the past decade or so have photographers begun to take color seriously, despite the added dimension it obviously brings to a work. One reason for the delay is that many photographers actually prefer the elegance and stark contrasts of black and white.

The other reason is technical. All photographs are ephemeral. But color photographs are so ephemeral you practically have to keep them locked up in an air-conditioned closet if you want them to last as long as thirty years.

Basically, three color processes are currently in use;

1. *Type C.* This is a *subtractive* process, meaning that all the necessary dies are embedded in the printing paper and respond proportionately to the colors in the negative or transparency.

2. *Die transfer.* This is an *additive* process, meaning that three different negatives are required to print the photograph. The process permits good control of balance and contrast and it is much more stable than Type C, especially when kept in dark storage.

3. *Cibachrome.* This, the most stable of the three processes, is appreciated by some—but shunned by others—for the saturated and glaring quality of the color.

Brent Sikkema, the Boston dealer, says that collectors should be aware of the relative instability of color photographs but should not be scared away from them for that reason alone. "Assume a print lasts thirty years," Sikkema tells us. "If you pay less than $1,000 for the photograph, you can consider it a $30 per year rental fee for the life of the print. That's longer than most marriages last."

Buy Limited-Edition Portfolios. It's not uncommon for a living photographer to select a group of his related images and issue them in the form of a limited-edition portfolio. Olivia Parker—whose name is included in the list of recommended photographers above, and who sells more works than any other photographer under the age of forty—introduced such a portfolio of ten prints in 1977. The publication price was $600. It took less than four years for the portfolio to go out of print. Occasionally, one comes up for sale, but when it does the price is now $3,500.

The initial advantage of buying a portfolio of prints is that you spend less per print than you would buying them individually. But there is also often a more rapid rise in the value of a portfolio than of an individual photograph.

Buy the Book. If you can't afford to buy an original print by a photographer you admire, you're not out of luck. Consider instead buying a well-made, well-illustrated book of the photographer's work. The plates rarely convey the full richness of the original prints, but you'll be surprised how beautiful they can be.

You'll also be surprised to find what good investments photography books can be, especially ones that were signed by the photographer.

Irving Penn. *Two Quedras, Morocco.* 1977 [1974]. Multiple coating and printing, platinum and platinum palladium, BF 360 paper on aluminum. 21″ x 17″. Courtesy Christie's East, New York.

Images, an early book by Ansel Adams, is now selling for $500 even *without* a signature. That's five times the publication price of $100.

Buy Into an Edition Early. Some photographers don't just submit to the requirements of the market; they embrace them, manipulating them to their advantage. A good example is Irving Penn, a photographer noted for his elegant pictures of fashions and flowers. Penn's images are often very large and very strong. They have the kind of presence normally possessed only by large, brightly colored oil paintings. Collectors who would otherwise reject a photograph as unsuitable for hanging on their walls—"it wouldn't look good enough"—will sometimes make an exception for Penn.

Also, Penn has cleverly scheduled regular price rises whenever he issues a new edition. The first buyers of a new image are *guaranteed* that it will increase in value. Here's how it works. Penn prints all of his photographs in strictly limited editions. He puts half of the edition away for his estate; he then puts the remaining half up for sale in small increments, each one more expensive than the one before. When he arrives at the final group to be sold, Penn raises the price for each print. Sometimes, it takes only a few weeks to get through the entire edition. Meanwhile, the initial price of, say, $1,800 will have risen to $7,000. Anyone who bought a print from the first group to be sold has made a profit of $5,200 on an $1,800 investment.

Obviously, it pays to know when an edition of Penn's work is being published so that you, too, can be among the first to buy. The same is true of any other photographer who issues his work in editions. The first buys are the best buys.

Where to Buy Photographs

There are approximately 120 photography dealers around the country. Many other dealers, especially those who specialize in modern prints, carry photographs along with their other stock.

I recommend that you buy your photographs from a specialist in photography, just as I would recommend buying prints from a print specialist. A photography dealer knows more about the medium, both its technical side and its esthetic side. Dealers who carry photographs along with other items generally exhibit photographs that look like paintings, or else the best-known images of the best-known photographers. You're always better off with a specialist.

To help you out, here is a list of galleries that specialize in photography:

California

Friends of Photography
San Carlos and Ninth Avenue
Carmel, California 93921

Weston Photographic Gallery
Sixth Avenue and Dolores
Carmel, California 93921

James Corcoran Gallery
8223 Santa Monica Boulevard
Los Angeles, California 90046

G. Ray Hawkins Gallery
9002 Melrose Avenue
Los Angeles, California 90069

Susan Spiritus Gallery
3336 Via Lido
Newport Beach, California
  92663

Grapestake Gallery
2876 California Street
San Francisco, California 94115

Connecticut

Charles B. Wood, III, Inc.
The Green
South Woodstock, Connecticut
  06281

District of Columbia

Lunn Gallery/Graphics
  International
406 Seventh Street N.W.
Washington, D.C. 20004

Sander Gallery
2604 Connecticut Avenue N.W.
Washington, D.C. 20008

Florida

Gallery Gemini
245 Worth Avenue
Palm Beach, Florida 33480

Georgia

Fay Gold Gallery
533 Holldale Court, N.W.
Atlanta, Georgia 30342

Illinois

Graphic Antiquity
P. O. Drawer 1234
Arlington Heights, Illinois
  60006

Allan Frumkin Gallery
620 North Michigan Avenue
Chicago, Illinois 60611

Massachusetts

Harcus Krakow Gallery
7 Newbury Street
Boston, Massachusetts 02116

Michigan

The Halstead 831 Gallery
560 North Woodward
Birmingham, Michigan 48011

New York

Timothy Baum
40 East 78th Street
New York, New York 10021

Castelli Graphics
4 East 77th Street
New York, New York 10021

International Center of
  Photography
1130 Fifth Avenue
New York, New York 10028

Sidney Janis Gallery
6 West 57th Street
New York, New York 10019

Janet Lehr
45 East 85th Street
New York, New York 10028

Light Gallery
724 Fifth Avenue
New York, New York 10019

Robert Miller Gallery
724 Fifth Avenue
New York, New York 10019

Vision Gallery
216 Newbury Street
Boston, Massachusetts 02116

Marcuse Pfeifer Gallery
825 Madison Avenue
New York, New York 10021

Rinhart Galleries, Inc.
818 Madison Avenue
New York, New York 10021

Robert Schoelkopf Gallery
825 Madison Avenue
New York, New York 10021

Sonnabend Gallery
420 West Broadway
New York, New York 10012

The Witkin Gallery, Inc.
41 East 57th Street
New York, New York 10022

Zabriskie Gallery
29 West 57th Street
New York, New York 10019

Texas

Afterimage Gallery
The Quadrangle No. 151
2800 Routh Street
Dallas, Texas 75201

Cronin Gallery
2424 Bissonet
Houston, Texas 77005

For More Information

Richard Blodgett, *Photographs: A Collector's Guide* (New York: Ballantine Books, 1979).

Helmut Gernsheim, *The History of Photography: From the Earliest Use of the Camera Obscura in the Eleventh Century up to 1914,* revised edition (New York: McGraw-Hill, 1969).

Beaumont Newhall, *The History of Photography from 1839 to the Present Day,* revised edition (New York: Museum of Modern Art, 1964).

Susan Sontag, *On Photography* (New York: Farrar, Straus and Giroux, 1978).

John Szarkowski, *Looking at Photographs: 100 Pictures from the Collection of The Museum of Modern Art* (New York: Museum of Modern Art, 1973).

Robert A. Weinstein and Larry Booth, *Collection, Use, and Care of Historical Photographs* (Nashville, Tenn.: American Association for State and Local History, 1977).

Lee D. Witkin and Barbara London, *The Photograph Collector's Guide,* foreword by Alan Shestack (Boston: New York Graphic Society, 1979).

POSTERS

Not long ago, art collectors bought posters only by artists such as Toulouse-Lautrec who had a reputation in a more traditional art form. Posters were considered too commercial to be art. This is no longer the case. Art-Nouveau, Art-Deco, and twentieth-century avant-garde posters are now considered great works of art indeed. Today, connoisseurs prize Toulouse-Lautrec's best posters at least as much as his paintings, and are willing to pay the price. In fact, bargains are already hard to find in the market for posters by less famous artists who established their reputations in other art forms.

Bargains still await the diligent collector, however, in other areas of the poster market: The finest movie posters, political posters, and commercial posters are all beginning to edge their way into the art market. Of course, in these newer areas, the problems of definition have yet to be resolved. Every time you consider a movie poster or a commercial poster, you have to ask, "Is it art, or is it popular culture?"

Jack Banning, owner of Poster America in New York, says, "Few posters are art, and, among the rest, only a few have any popular culture value. Ninety percent of all posters are of purely decorative interest." If you set out to explore the wider frontiers of the poster market, you have to wade through the hundreds of items that have only decorative appeal to find the rare ones that also have both the historical appeal of popular culture and the esthetic appeal of art.

The Poster Market.   The first auction devoted entirely to posters took place at Phillips, Son & Neal in New York in the autumn of 1979. Prices were high: Record after record succumbed to enthusiastic bidders. But, as is often the case in new, little-tested markets, the enthusiasm soon waned. By June of 1980, a second poster auction at Phillips brought only modest prices. Attempts by other auction houses to exploit the new market met with mixed results. A sale at Sotheby's in 1980 did well, but another at Christie's sputtered.

Don't let the faltering market for posters discourage you from buying them. The ups and downs of specific auction sales can be attributed, in part at least, to the quality and condition of the posters offered. Besides, wise collectors can take good advantage of an erratic market. Even though you've missed the "ground floor" in buying posters, you haven't missed it by much. Most poster prices are still within reach.

The Subject Counts Most

By now, you're probably accustomed to evaluating a work of art more by its form than by its content. It will come as a surprise, therefore, to find that you have to reverse the priority in evaluating most posters. For many collectors, visual appeal is a factor; but for most of them, the subject is what really counts.

Transportation Posters.   For example, competition among collectors is particularly keen for transportation posters—posters that advertise airplanes, ships, trains, and automobiles. The highest prices are paid for posters advertising the most unusual or most glamorous vehicles. Count yourself lucky indeed if you find a poster advertising a dirigible, especially the *Hindenberg,* or a superliner, especially the *Normandie*. The famous poster of the *Normandie* by Cassandre, an Art-Deco masterpiece, sold recently for $7,000.

The further you get from the fine arts, the more important the subject becomes in evaluating the work. Movie posters are something of a test case, since they generally stand at the farthest remove. The poster for a popular movie, or one with a popular star, is desirable almost regardless of what it looks like.

Options

The range of collectable posters is very wide. You can buy *Moulin*

Top, Adolphe Mouron Cassandre. *Normandie*. 1935. Lithograph. 38″ x 23″. Courtesy Christie's East, New York.

Bottom, Henri de Toulouse-Lautrec. *Confetti*. 1895. Lithograph. 22½″ x 15⁵/₁₆″. Courtesy Christie's, New York.

Rouge by Toulouse-Lautrec for $52,000. Or you can pick up a political poster free at your favorite candidate's campaign headquarters. The choice depends on your concept of what constitutes art, on your personal tastes, and, of course, on your budget.

Master Posters

Posters, as we know them, are of fairly recent origin, dating back only to the final decades of the nineteenth century. The highest prices are paid for the work of Art-Nouveau masters who pioneered the poster format—such as Jules Chéret, Alphonse Mucha, and Henri de Toulouse-Lautrec—and the Constructivist and other masters who ushered the poster into the twentieth century.

Mucha and Toulouse-Lautrec. Among the Art-Nouveau works, Mucha's poster of Sarah Bernhardt in *Médée* recently sold for $36,000. Fifty-two thousand was recently paid for Toulouse-Lautrec's *Moulin Rouge*, the record price at the time for any poster.

Chéret. Even though Chéret isn't as fashionable now as either Mucha or Toulouse-Lautrec, his high quality, historical importance, and relatively low prices make him the best bargain of the three. As recently as 1981, his posters were selling at Phillips in New York for between $300 and $3,000, most of them below $1,000.

Works by other poster artists from the late nineteenth century should be carefully considered. In particular, you should look at posters by the Scottish Art-Nouveau master, Charles Rennie McIntosh, and the Viennese master, Gustav Klimt. You might also look for works by less famous Art-Nouveau artists from throughout Europe. These are at least as good from an investment standpoint, and they're also much, much less expensive.

Art-Deco Posters. In the poster market today, Art-Deco is almost as popular as Art-Nouveau—and considerably cheaper. Many Art-Deco artists made superb posters: not only Cassandre, creator of the famous *Normandie*, but also E. McKnight Kauffer, Loupot, and Walter Schneckenberg, among others.

Posters by Twentieth-Century Artists. Susan Reinhold, of the Reinhold Brown Gallery in New York, recommends that poster collectors take a close look at posters by the many twentieth-century artists—some famous, some not so famous—who made posters from time to time. Some of the best, Reinhold suggests, were made by Lucien Bernhard and Ludwig

Hohlwein during the first two decades of the century, and can be purchased for between $500 and $3,000.

Other superb posters were made by avant-garde masters from the Russian Constructivist, De Stijl, Bauhaus, German Expressionist, Dada, and Surrealist movements. "Art-Nouveau posters," says Reinhold, "were made in large editions for collectors and they were saved, so many of them have still survived. Posters by these other masters were done in much smaller editions and weren't saved. As a result, they're much rarer." Reinhold cautions collectors to beware of posters that are reproductions of the artists' work in favor of works designed specifically as posters.

Recommended Movements and Artists. Here are some of the movements and artists to look for:

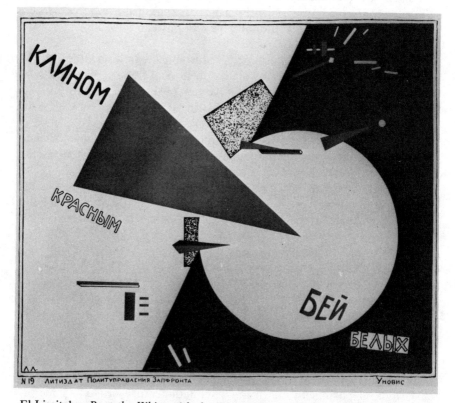

El Lissitzky. *Beat the White with the Red Wedge.* 1920. Letterpress. 58.8 cm. x 47.9 cm. Courtesy Reinhold Brown Gallery, New York.

Russian Constructivism: El Lissitzky, the Stenberg brothers, Alexander Rodchenko

De Stijl: Theo Van Doesburg, H. N. Werkman, Piet Zwart

Bauhaus: Herbert Bayer, Oskar Schlemmer

German Expressionism: Oskar Kokoschka, Karl Schmidt-Rottluff

Dada: Marcel Janco, Kurt Schwitters, Tristan Tzara

Surrealism: René Magritte, Otto Morach

Photomontage and Typographical Posters.   Some posters during the twentieth century have been made by artists who developed styles specifically suited for the poster medium. Their images consist either of superimposed photographs (photomontage) or of pure graphics (typographical). Among the photomontage masters to look for: John Heartfeld, Gustave Klutsis, and Herbert Matter. Among the typographical masters: Walter Dexel, Ernst Keller, and Jan Tschichold. Excellent works by all these masters can be acquired for prices ranging between $200 and $10,000.

American Masters.   The great American poster artists to look for are Will Bradley, Maxfield Parrish, and Edward Penfield. Penfield's works sell for between $200 and $5,000.

Art Posters

These are posters that incorporate a work of art—sometimes an original work, but more often a photographic reproduction. Art posters normally herald exhibitions at art museums and private galleries; occasionally, they announce musical concerts, theatrical engagements, or events entirely unrelated to the arts.

Not *Reproductions*.   Although art reproductions should be avoided, art *posters* should not. This may seem inconsistent. After all, most art posters include art reproductions. But there is an important distinction between the two. While most art posters incorporate photographic reproductions, there are always graphics as well. The graphics keep the posters more *honest* than simple reproductions. Also, since art posters are usually produced by art galleries, and their production often supervised by the artist himself, the level of graphic design in most cases is exceptionally high.

Art Posters Can Be Good Investments. Art posters can be a good investment, especially if you buy them at the "publication" price, the price charged for the poster while the exhibition, musical concert, or other event, is still in progress. In 1966, for example, Vera List—a fine and frequent publisher of art posters—made two large posters for Lincoln Center. List based them on the large paintings by Marc Chagall that hang in the Center's lobby. Because the edition was so large (five thousand examples), the publication price was only $5. In 1979, the two posters brought $600 each at auction—a good investment by any standard.

Buy Early. The moral is clear. Try to buy art posters at the exhibitions or other events they advertise. If you've waited too long, you can find a good selection of recent materials at a New York firm called Poster Originals. Both a catalogue and the posters themselves can be ordered by mail:

Poster Originals, Limited
16 East 78th Street
New York, New York 10021

Limited-Edition Posters

During the past decade, several limited-edition poster workshops have sprung up around the country. The only thing that sets these operations apart from regular commercial workshops is that they strictly limit the size of their editions, generally to about one hundred signed posters and one hundred or two hundred unsigned ones. The small run makes it possible to print the posters by the labor-intensive silk screen process, rather than by the cheaper and faster photo-offset process used by the commercial poster printers. The limited-edition workshops can also afford to employ the best graphic designers and give them a remarkable degree of artistic independence.

Elite Clientele. Because the posters published by such workshops are generally advertisements, limiting the size of the edition also limits the potential clients. Car and soap manufacturers take their business elsewhere. ProCreations Publishing Company, a reputable limited-edition workshop, regularly makes posters for the Albuquerque International Balloon Festival, the New Orleans Mardi Gras, and the Newport Jazz Festival. Also well-recognized is the Graphic Workshop of Boston, which has devoted a splendid continuing series to Endangered Species.

Buy Early. Again, it's wise to buy early. The publication price of a signed, limited-edition poster is often as little as $50. For more information, write:

Agusta Agustsson. *Polar Bear*. 1980. Silkscreen. 39″ x 43″. Photograph by Willa Heider. Courtesy The Graphic Workshop, Boston.

ProCreations Publishing
   Company
4330 Canal Street
New Orleans, Louisiana 70119

Graphic Workshop of Boston
34 Farnsworth Street
Boston, Massachusetts 02210

Political Posters, Commercial Posters, etc.

If you're the adventurous type, you can always try to push back the frontiers of collecting. From time to time, a political poster or commercial poster is successful as a visual image and can be collected as a work of art. The possibilities are limited only by your imagination and your energy— not, as is usually the case, by your budget. One clever collector I know searches the countryside for especially appealing hand-painted billboards (the collector is not just clever, he has a very large house).

These works offer only remote investment potential, but they won't cost you more than a few pennies: Campaign workers and manufacturers work hard to give them away.

Movie Posters

I've saved movie posters for last, because so little good advice on the subject is available elsewhere, because they have so much meaning for many people, and because they remain inexpensive. Of course, certain early Russian Constructivist movie posters, such as the Stenberg brothers' poster for *Potemkin* or Otto Arpke's poster for *The Cabinet of Dr. Caligari*, are worth large sums. Even the most costly Hollywood movie posters, however, are relatively cheap: The record price was paid at a Los Angeles auction not long ago for a "one-sheet" (see later section) of *Alice in the Jungle*, a silent cartoon, eight minutes long, made in 1925 by a youngster named Walt Disney. The price: $5,400. If a movie is either recent or obscure, the poster for it can be acquired for as little as $5.

Only Buy Originals.   Poster collectors can learn a lesson from print collectors: Make sure you get an original. Original posters are the ones

Anton Lavinsky. *Battleship Potemkin, 1905.* 1926. Lithograph. 42″ x 27¾″. Courtesy Reinhold Brown Gallery, New York.

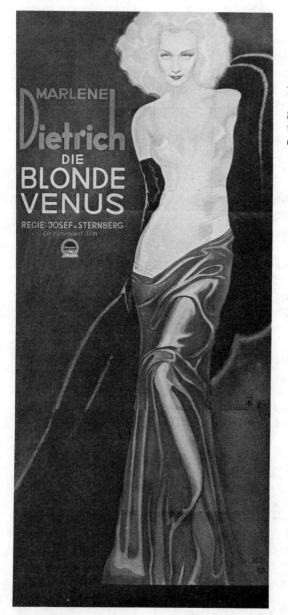

Anonymous. *The Blond Venus*. c. 1932. Lithograph. 37¾" x 81¼". Courtesy Reinhold Brown Gallery, New York.

issued when the film first came out, not when it was re-released. All posters after 1939 are dated and copyrighted. If the date of the poster corresponds to the date of the film, you're in luck.

It's the Movie That Counts, Not the Poster.   More than any other kind of poster, the value of movie posters depends on the subject, not the quality. If you're buying for investment, look for scarce posters manufactured for major movies, with major stars. Only when you're sure of these should you consider the quality of the graphics and the design.

The Reagan Reaction.   If you're still not convinced that most movie-poster collectors care more about the movie than the poster, consider what happened to posters featuring a former movie star named Ronald Reagan.

Not long ago, people bought Ronald Reagan posters only if he happened to be starring opposite a famous leading lady. The election changed that in a hurry.

Before November 20, posters for *Bedtime for Bonzo* cost as little as $10. Only in California did the posters cost more. Within weeks of the election, *Bonzo* had jumped to $1,000. According to Chip Nourse, owner of the Nourse Gallery in Washington, D.C., the posters were "still movie posters, but they were also presidential memorabilia."

The highest prices are now paid for Reagan's best prewar films: *Love Is in the Air, Knute Rockne—All American,* and *King's Row. Bonzo* comes next. Also sought-after are films whose titles became ironic with Reagan's change of career: *Accidents Will Happen, Law and Order,* and *Hellcats of the Navy*—the film he made with leading first lady Nancy Davis. The Nourse Gallery has a five-foot-tall cardboard promotional piece for *The Winning Team* (Reagan and Doris Day) for $5,000.

Shapes and Sizes.   Movie posters come in several shapes and sizes. The jargon is simple, but you have to know it.

The basic size—and the most desirable—is the *one-sheet.* This is the regular 27 by 41-inch poster you find in most theater lobbies.

Less desirable than one-sheets, but still collectable, are *inserts* (14 by 36 inches or 22 by 28 inches), *window cards* (22 by 14 inches), and *lobby cards* (11 by 14 inches). After one-sheets, *lobby cards* are the preferred size. They come in sets of eight. Within the set, the title card and the card showing the main star are the most valuable.

Three-sheets, six-sheets, and *billboards* are too large to appeal to most collectors.

Teasers—generally used before a movie arrives in town—are at the other end of the scale. Collectors shun them, too.

Categories. Here are some categories you might consider:

Early movie posters. Silent-film posters from the teens and twenties and early talkies from the thirties are frequent favorites. A copy of the poster for *Phantom of the Opera* with Lon Chaney recently sold for $6,500.

Science fiction. The big four Sci Fi all come from the fifties: *Forbidden Planet*, *The Day the Earth Stood Still*, *War of the Worlds*, and *When Worlds Collide*.

Anonymous. *City Lights*. 1931. Lithograph. 39½" x 78⅛". Courtesy Phillips, New York.

Horror films. Posters made for horror films are also in heavy demand, especially those for films produced by Universal Studios. Be on the lookout for *I Was a Teenage Werewolf,* an early embarrassment by Michael Landon.

The legendary stars. Major examples include Marlon Brando, James Dean, Marilyn Monroe, and Shirley Temple. Perhaps the all-time favorite of movie-poster fans is Humphrey Bogart. Both *Casablanca* and *The Maltese Falcon* are among the "old masters" of movie posters.

The ground floor. Of course, what the above posters have in common is that they have already begun to rise in value. What posters can you buy and still get in on the ground floor? Several leading poster dealers recommend *Butch Cassidy and the Sundance Kid, Dr. Strangelove, Planet of the Apes, Psycho,* and *Star Wars.*

Preserving and Presenting Posters

In posters—more than in any other form of art—condition is difficult to assess. That's because posters tend to suffer more abuse than other forms of art. Like all works on paper, they are unusually ephemeral. But *unlike* other works on paper, posters are *supposed* to be ephemeral. They're designed to advertise a single event—an art exhibition, a concert, a motion picture, a boat cruise, a political candidacy. After a month or two, when the event has passed, they're supposed to be thrown away. Most posters survive for us to enjoy as art objects only by the rarest chance. As a result, the standards of condition are generally less demanding in posters than in other forms of art.

When you check the condition of a poster, the terms "excellent," "good," "fair," and "bad" take on new meanings:

Excellent condition. A movie poster may legitimately be listed in excellent condition even if it's folded: After all, most movie posters come that way. Collectors prize the rare unfolded one, but no stigma is attached to a poster that has its original creases. Gary Boone, publisher of *Antique Monthly,* notes that an old poster in excellent conditon is one that looks, at first glance, as if it has never been displayed. On closer examination, however, you shouldn't be surprised to find a small tear or blemish.

Good condition. The design should still be clear and bright, but the paper may be yellowed somewhat or noticeably torn.

Fair Condition. The image should still be clear and bright, but the paper may be severely creased. Posters that have undergone extensive restoration are usually described as in fair condition.

Poor condition. If a poster is listed in poor condition, forget it. It's not just poor, it's a total wreck.

The Paper Problem. When you buy a poster, you are faced with a unique problem: the paper it's printed on. In most works of art on paper, the paper is made from the safest nonacidic materials. Not so with posters. Sometimes the paper they're printed on is little better than newsprint.

A conservator will be able to tell you whether a poster is printed on acidic paper, and, if so, whether it's worth the trouble and expense of having it deacidified. This may be difficult to justify if the poster isn't worth much on the market. In that case, you should calculate how much the poster is worth to *you:* How much are you willing to spend to keep it from turning first yellow, and then eventually to powder?

Mounting Posters. If you decide to make the effort to preserve the poster by deacidifying it, you'll need to make sure it stays that way. Most posters are large and fragile. Therefore, you have to mount them to keep them flat. One method is to lay the poster against a piece of acid-free board or foam, wrap it with a piece of clear plastic, then fasten it from behind with heat—much like a package at the supermarket. The advantage of this method is that it can be reversed easily. The disadvantage is that it can't be used permanently: Some conservators worry that the process may do some as yet unrecognized damage to a work.

The second method of mounting posters is more permanent—and more expensive. It consists of lining the poster with a backing of linen or Japan paper. Be sure to use museum-quality nonacidic paste to attach the poster to the backing.

Where to Buy Posters

Almost all American movie posters are distributed by the National Screen Corporation. The NSC retains ownership of these posters, the same way recording companies retain ownership of the "promos" they send out. Of course, the items are available in both cases—but only with some effort and some expense.

You can try the neighborhood theater, of course. But don't count on good results. After all, you're restricted to whatever happens to be playing at the time, hardly the kind of in-depth selection a discriminating collector wants.

Excellent posters of all kinds turn up occasionally at flea markets, and at very cheap prices. Once you know the field, you can also buy or exchange your "paper"—that's how true enthusiasts refer to posters—

with other collectors. Movie-poster collectors form an especially close-knit group, frequently advertising the items they want to sell or exchange at the back of film magazines.

More reliable sources for posters are specialty poster galleries and shops that sell movie memorabilia. Some of the best are one-man operations, operated on a mail-order basis.

California

Hollywood Poster Exchange
965 North La Cienega Boulevard
Los Angeles, California 90009

Icart Vendor
7956 Beverly Boulevard
Los Angeles, California
  90048

District of Columbia

Nourse Gallery
3212 N Street N.W.
Washington, D.C. 20007

New Hampshire

J. H. Beal
38 Cottage Street
Littleton, New Hampshire 03561

New Jersey

The Poster Master
9 North Passaic
Chatham, New Jersey 07928

The Exhumation
10 Bayard Lane
P. O. Box 2057
Princeton, New Jersey 08540

New York

Cinemabilia, Inc.
10 West 13th Street
New York, New York 10011

Reinhold Brown
26 East 78th Street
New York, New York 10021

Poster America/Yesterday
174 Ninth Avenue
New York, New York 10011

Pennsylvania

Miscellaneous Man
P. O. Box 1776
New Freedom, Pennsylvania 17349

For More Information

John Barnicoat, *A Concise History of Posters* (New York: Oxford University Press, 1972).

Mildred Constantine, ed., *Word and Image: Posters from the Collection of the Museum of Modern Art,* text by Alan M. Fern (New York: Museum of Modern Art, 1968).

Mildred Constantine and Alan Fern, *Revolutionary Soviet Film Posters* (Baltimore: Johns Hopkins Press, 1974).

Max Gallo, *The Poster in History,* translated by Alfred and Bruni Mayor, New Concise NAL Edition (New York: New American Library Times Mirror, 1975).

Josef and Shizuko Müller-Brockman, *History of the Poster* (Zurich: ABC Edition, 1971).

Yolande Oostens-Wittamer, *La Belle Époque* (New York: Grossman Publishers, 1970.)

Steven Schapiro and David Chierichetti, *The Movie Poster Book* (New York: E. P. Dutton, 1980).

CONTEMPORARY ART

It takes neither imagination nor great esthetic sensibility to purchase a Rembrandt, all it takes is a lot of loot. And even then the purchase is more in the nature of a gilt-edge investment. To buy a painting that has been critically reviled and that friends, neighbors, and even one's wife will most likely laugh at, however, takes a large measure of both qualities plus a generous dose of independence.—John Rublowsky, 1965

Collectors of contemporary art enjoy a unique advantage: They can get to know the artists themselves. If an artist is relatively unknown (as most contemporary artists are), the relationship can be especially rewarding. The collector becomes a true "patron," an ancient and honorable role. He can give a fledgling artist the support and encouragement he needs to maintain his creative energy. Richard Brown-Baker, one of the country's leading collectors of contemporary art, has said, "I leave the established artist to others. My principal joy in collecting lies in the discovery of new, unrecognized talents. It gives me great satisfaction to watch unknown, young artists grow and develop."

High Risks, High Gains.   Of course, there is also a very practical advantage to collecting the works of living artists. You can buy them for almost nothing and, if you're lucky, watch their value soar. One of the most astonishing examples is Jasper Johns's *Three Flags,* which the Whitney Museum bought in 1980 for $1,000,000. Johns created the encaustic and canvas construction in 1958. Leo Castelli, Johns's dealer, sold it to Mr. and Mrs. Burton Tremaine in 1959 for only $950. Little did they know that, within two decades, the work would appreciate a thousand-fold.

But before you go out and buy your next-door neighbor's art-class exercises, hoping to strike it rich, remember that Jasper Johns is very much the exception. Barbara Krakow, of the Harcus Krakow Gallery in Boston, cautions that "a large proportion of all the paintings that sold for $950 in 1958 are still worth $950—or less."

A Three-Tier Market

In the market for contemporary art, there are three tiers or levels of artists: (1) contemporary master artists, (2) artists of recognized talent, and (3) young, unknown artists. To spend money wisely in the market for contemporary art, you have to know which artists belong to which levels. To *make* money in the market for contemporary art, you must also have the rare foresight to know which artists are destined to move up a level. The bargains in contemporary art are works by third-tier artists who later move into the second tier, and by second-tier artists who later move into the first tier.

The First Tier:
Contemporary Master Artists

Most people are astonished that any work by a contemporary artist, no matter how exceptional, could command a price of a million dollars. It is even more astonishing, however, that several contemporary masters—Helen Frankenthaler, Roy Lichtenstein, Frank Stella—can routinely sell new works at prices of $50,000 or more. There are even some artists who maintain waiting lists. Collectors are willing to pay $75,000 for a Richard Estes and $85,000 for a Richard Diebenkorn—sight unseen. Obviously, prices in this realm are beyond the reach of most collectors.

Expensive and Unreliable. Contemporary master paintings are very expensive, and the resale market is unreliable. Both Sotheby's and Christie's held major auctions of contemporary art in 1980. Although prices were high, a quarter of the objects in the Christie's sale and a third of those at Sotheby's were bought in. Among the works that failed to reach reserve were paintings by such giants as Jackson Pollock and Jasper Johns.

Helen Frankenthaler. *Hope Junction.* 1974. Acrylic on canvas. 77" x 139¼".
Courtesy André Emmerich Gallery, New York.

Don't think, however, that the prices of contemporary art might begin
to fall within reach. Every work that failed to sell at auction in 1980 will
eventually reappear—with even higher reserve prices. If you want great
art at bargain prices, you should look elsewhere than contemporary master paintings.

The Second Tier:
Artists of Recognized Talent

Only about two-dozen contemporary painters and sculptors can obtain
prices of $50,000 or more for their works. Beyond this select group are
other artists whose talents are recognized only in small circles. Their
works are regularly exhibited in museum shows and reviewed in art journals. If their names don't sound familiar, it's only because they haven't
yet been the subjects of museum retrospectives or art-history surveys.
While many of these second-tier artists arrived on the art scene during the
past five to ten years, others arrived decades ago; they simply haven't
achieved the widespread recognition merited by their extraordinary
talents—not yet, that is.

In private galleries, the works of second-tier artists sell for about
$10,000: never less than $5,000 and seldom more than $20,000. Their
drawings and prints are also correspondingly cheaper—the drawings selling for between $250 and $1,500. Second-tier artists are a good choice if
you want contemporary works that may go up in price tomorrow, but you
can afford today.

How to Find Artists of Recognized Talent. There are several ways to find second-tier artists. First, look for artists included in group exhibitions at galleries and museums. Second, look for the second-tier artists represented by the same private galleries that also represent the superstars. Finally, see which artists have their exhibitions regularly reviewed in the leading art journals: *Artforum, Art in America,* and *Arts Magazine.* To help you on your search, I have compiled a list of some of the most promising second-tier artists (many of them are well on their way to the first tier) along with the galleries in New York that represent their work:

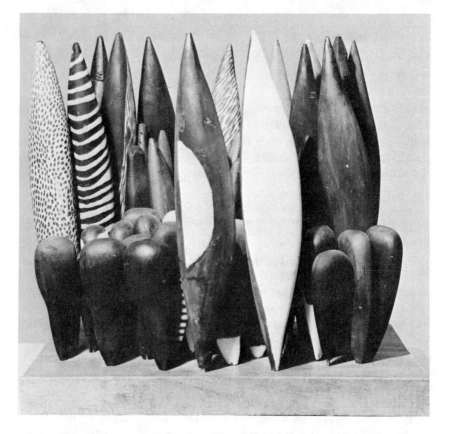

Louise Bourgeois. *One and Others*. 1955. Painted wood. 18¼" x 20" x 16¾". Collection Whitney Museum, New York. Courtesy Robert Miller Gallery, New York.

From the Fifties (Abstract)

Louise Bourgeois
(Robert Miller Gallery, Inc.)

Grace Hartigan
(David Anderson Gallery,
Inc.)

Lee Krasner
(The Pace Gallery of New
York, Inc.)

Joan Mitchell
(Xavier Fourcade, Inc.)

Milton Resnick
(Max Hutchinson Gallery,
Inc. and Robert Miller
Gallery, Inc.)

Richard Stankiewicz
(Zabriskie Gallery)

Myron Stout
(no single gallery)

Esteban Vicente
(Gruenebaum Gallery Ltd.)

Alan Shields. *Sanatee River Cadence*. 1979–1980. Acrylic, thread, canvas. 56″ x 66″. Collection Fried, Frank, Harris, Shriver & Jacobson. Photograph by eeva-inkeri. Courtesy Paula Cooper Gallery, New York.

From the Fifties (Figurative)

William Bailey
(George E. Schoellkopf
Gallery)

Nell Blaine
(Fischbach Gallery)

Alfred Leslie
(Allan Frumkin Gallery)

Alice Neel
(Graham Gallery)

Color-field Painting

Dan Christensen
(Salander-O'Reilly Galleries, Inc.)

Gene Davis
(no single gallery)

Ron Davis
(Blum-Helman Gallery)

Sam Gilliam
(Hamilton Gallery)

Ralph Humphrey
(Robert Miller Gallery, Inc.)

Larry Poons
(André Emmerich Gallery, Inc.)

Alan Shields
(Paula Cooper Gallery)

Phillip Wofford
(Nancy Hoffman Gallery)

Minimal Art

Ronald Bladen
(Max Hutchinson Gallery, Inc.)

Robert Mangold
(John Weber Gallery)

Brice Marden
(The Pace Gallery of New
York, Inc.)

Dorothea Rockburne
(Xavier Fourcade, Inc.)

Richard Serra
(Blum-Helman Gallery and
Leo Castelli Gallery)

Richard Tuttle
(Betty Parsons Gallery)

Photorealism

Robert Bechtle
(O.K. Harris Works of Art)

John Clem Clarke
(O.K. Harris Works of Art)

Richard Cottingham
(no single gallery)

Audrey Flack
(Louis K. Meisel Gallery)

Ralph Goings
(O.K. Harris Works of Art)

Top, Audrey Flack. *Marilyn (Vanitas).* 1977. Oil and acrylic on canvas. 96″ x 96″. Photograph by Bruce C. Jones. Courtesy Louis K. Meisel Gallery, New York.

Bottom, Susan Shatter. *Cambridge Roof Tops.* 1973. Watercolor on paper. 39″ x 62″. Photograph by Greg Heins. Courtesy Harcus Krakow Gallery, Boston.

New Realism

William Beckmann
(Allan Stone Gallery)

Malcolm Morley
(Xavier Fourcade, Inc.)

Susan Rothenberg
(Alexander Willard Gallery, Inc.)

Ben Schonzeit
(Nancy Hoffman Gallery)

Susan Shatter
(Fischbach Gallery)

Neil Welliver
(Marlborough Gallery)

Robert Zakanitch. *Banana Pana*. 1981. Acrylic on canvas. 88″ x 78″. Courtesy Robert Miller Gallery, New York.

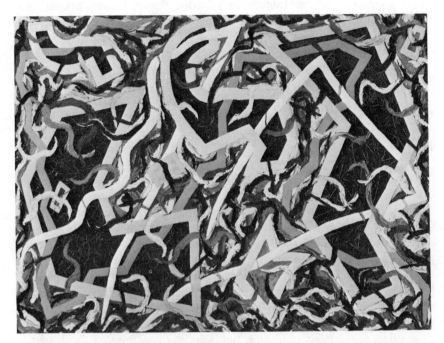

Joan Thorne. *BOVRA*. 1980. Oil on canvas. 75″ x 103″. Collection Roselyne and Richard Swig, San Francisco. Courtesy Willard Gallery, New York.

Pattern Painting

Joyce Kozloff
(Holly Solomon Gallery, Inc.)

Judy Pfaff
(Holly Solomon Gallery, Inc.)

Robert S. Zakanitch
(Robert Miller Gallery, Inc.)

Neo-Expressionism

Jonathan Borofsky
(Paula Cooper Gallery)

Bryan Hunt
(Blum-Helman Gallery)

Neil Jenney
(no single gallery)

Julian Schnabel
(Mary Boone Gallery and
Leo Castelli Gallery)

Joan Thorne
(Alexander Willard Gallery,
Inc.)

Exercise Care. Chris Middendorf, a leading dealer in contemporary art in Washington, D.C., recommends that you exercise great care in selecting works by second-tier artists. The risks involved are sobering: only a very few of their finest works stand any chance of appreciating in value. "If you buy a work by an up-and-coming artist, you stand a much better chance of making a good investment if you buy a major work," says Middendorf. "If you just walk in, get excited, and buy, you won't get the best work possible." How can you be sure you're getting a major work? Visit the artist's studio. Preview the works to be included in the artist's next show. Ask the dealer for his assessment of the artist's work.

Studio Sales. Suppose you visit an artist's studio. You see a painting you think is better than any you've seen before, and you've seen enough of the artist's work for that to mean something. Should you reach for your checkbook and buy the work on the spot, or should you wait and buy the work through a dealer?

The answer depends primarily on the nature of the artist's association with the gallery that represents him. If the artist doesn't have a gallery (unlikely with an artist of this stature) or doesn't have an exclusive contract with the gallery (almost as unlikely), you can save as much as 50 percent of the purchase price by buying the work directly from the artist. The difference—the commission that would go to the artist's dealer—stays in your pocket. Unfortunately, most artists *do* have exclusive dealer contracts, so you won't have this choice.

The Third Tier: Young Unknown Artists

If you want a work by a living artist, but don't want to spend several thousand dollars, you should consider the work of young unknown artists. Actually, young unknown artists aren't always young. Unknown artists can be any age. What they really have in common is obscurity. They're not famous—yet.

Of course, the unknown artists recommended here aren't really "unknown," either. If they were completely unknown, as most living artists are, you'd never see their works. They're "unknown" only in the sense that they're not *well*-known in national and international art circles. The unknowns recommended here have dealers, and have probably shown their works in museums and galleries, perhaps in group shows with other unknowns.

Low, Low Prices.   You can spend as little as $800 on a large painting by one of these third-tier artists; the price is rarely more than $2,000 or $3,000. Drawings will cost substantially less. Even this may sound like a lot of money, especially when you realize that the work will probably not increase in value. But you should also realize that the dealer gets the same 40 to 50 percent commission he'd get on a more expensive work, that the artist has to pay for the materials (very costly for sculptures and large paintings), and, finally, that the artist probably doesn't sell many works. In short, no one is getting rich at your expense.

Other Advantages.   Whatever the financial picture, there are strong reasons for investing in the works of young unknown artists. First, if you choose well, you can get a significant work of art for much less than a similar work by a better-known artist. Second, if you're at all interested in buying art for the purpose of *helping* artists, you couldn't spend your money more effectively. Eight hundred dollars means a good deal more to an artist who sells only a few paintings a year than $8,000 or even $80,000 means to Frankenthaler, Lichtenstein, Stella, or any of the other contemporary masters who sell their works almost as quickly as they make them.

How to Find Third-Tier Artists.   You can locate the works of these third-tier artists the same way you would locate those of more recognized artists: in galleries that sell more-expensive contemporary works and museum-survey exhibitions at museums. If a dealer shows a young artist's works, he's not doing it for profit. He's doing it because he believes in the artist—and most dealers are excellent judges of new talent. The same can be said of museum curators. Much of the best new work in the country surfaces in the annual and biennial survey exhibitions at museums such as the Hirshhorn in Washington and the Whitney in New York. You might also look at work by artists who are recipients of the prestigious fellowships awarded by the National Endowment for the Arts. Although these often go to artists who have already entered the second tier, they go just as often to artists who are about to enter it.

Of course, in assessing the quality of unrecognized art, no one's opinion is foolproof. That is both the challenge and the excitement of collecting the works of unrecognized artists. "When you are in the very contemporary field," says J. Carter Brown, director of the Washington National Gallery of Art, "your guess is as good as anyone's and that can be very liberating."

Where to Buy Contemporary Art

California

James Corcoran Gallery
8223 Santa Monica Boulevard
Los Angeles, California 90046

Margo Leavin Gallery
812 Robertson Boulevard
Los Angeles, California 90069

John Berggruen Gallery
228 Grant Avenue
San Francisco, California 94108

Ace Gallery
185 Windward Avenue
Venice, California 90291

District of Columbia

Diane Brown Gallery
406 Seventh Street N.W.
Washington, D.C. 20004

Fendrick Gallery
3059 M Street N.W.
Washington, D.C. 20007

McIntosh/Drysdale Gallery
406 Seventh Street N.W.
Washington, D.C. 20004

Middendorf/Lane Gallery
2009 Columbia Road N.W.
Washington, D.C. 20009

Florida

Hokin Gallery, Inc.
1086 Kane Concourse
Bay Harbor Island
Miami, Florida 33154

Gallery 99, Inc.
1135 Kane Concourse
Bay Harbor Island
Miami, Florida 33161

Hokin Gallery, Inc.
245 Worth Avenue
Palm Beach, Florida 33480

Illinois

Roy Boyd Gallery
215 West Superior Street
Chicago, Illinois 60610

Jan Cicero Gallery
437 North Clark Street
Chicago, Illinois 60610

Dart Gallery
155 East Ohio Street
Chicago, Illinois 60611

Dobrick Gallery
216 East Ontario Street
Chicago, Illinois 60611

Douglas-Kenyon Gallery
155 East Ohio Street
Chicago, Illinois 60611

Frumkin & Struve
620 North Michigan Avenue
Chicago, Illinois 60611

Richard Gray Gallery
620 North Michigan Avenue
Chicago, Illinois 60611

Hokin Gallery, Inc.
200 East Ontario Street
Chicago, Illinois 60611

Phyllis Kind Gallery
226 East Ontario Street
Chicago, Illinois 60611

Nancy Lurie Gallery
1632 North LaSalle Street
Chicago, Illinois 60614

Betsy Rosenfield Gallery
226 East Ontario Street
Chicago, Illinois 60611

Dorothy Rosenthal Gallery
233 East Ontario Street
Chicago, Illinois 60611

Young Hoffman Gallery
215 West Superior Street
Chicago, Illinois 60610

Zolle-Lieberman Gallery
356 West Huron Street
Chicago, Illinois 60610

Massachusetts

Alpha Gallery
121 Newbury Street
Boston, Massachusetts 02116

Harcus Krakow Gallery
7 Newbury Street
Boston, Massachusetts 02116

Michigan

Donald Morris Gallery, Inc.
105 Townsend
Birmingham, Michigan 48011

Minnesota

John C. Stoller & Company
400 Marquette Avenue
Minneapolis, Minnesota 55402

Missouri

The Greenberg Gallery
44 Maryland Plaza
St. Louis, Missouri 63108

New York

Acquavella Galleries, Inc.
18 East 79th Street
New York, New York 10021

Brooke Alexander, Inc.
20 West 57th Street
New York, New York 10019

Blum-Helman Gallery
20 West 57th Street
New York, New York 10019

Grace Borgenicht Gallery
724 Fifth Avenue
New York, New York 10019

Susan Caldwell Gallery Inc.
383 West Broadway
New York, New York 10012

Leo Castelli Gallery
420 West Broadway
(and 142 Greene Street)
New York, New York 10012

Castelli Graphics, Inc.
4 East 77th Street
New York, New York 10021

Paula Cooper
155 Wooster Street
New York, New York 10012

Robert Elkon Gallery
1063 Madison Avenue
New York, New York 10028

André Emmerich Gallery, Inc.
41 East 57th Street
New York, New York 10022

Richard L. Feigen & Co., Inc.
900 Park Avenue
New York, New York 10021

Ronald Feldman Fine Arts
   Gallery, Inc.
33 East 74th Street
New York, New York 10021

Fischbach Gallery
29 West 57th Street
New York, New York 10019

Xavier Fourcade, Inc.
36 East 75th Street
New York, New York 10021

Getler/Pall Gallery
50 West 57th Street
New York, New York 10019

James Goodman Gallery
1020 Madison Avenue
New York, New York 10021

Graham Gallery
1014 Madison Avenue
New York, New York 10021

Nancy Hoffman Gallery
429 West Broadway
New York, New York 10012

Holly Solomon Gallery Inc.
392 West Broadway
New York, New York 10012

Sidney Janis Gallery
110 West 57th Street
New York, New York 10019

M. Knoedler & Co.
19 East 70th Street
New York, New York 10021

Metro Pictures
169 Mercer Street
New York, New York 10012

Robert Miller Gallery, Inc.
724 Fifth Avenue
New York, New York 10019

David McKee Gallery
41 East 57th Street
New York, New York 10022

O. K. Harris Works of Art
383 West Broadway
New York, New York 10012

Pace Editions, Inc.
32 East 57th Street
New York, New York 10022

The Pace Gallery of New York,
   Inc.
32 East 57th Street
New York, New York 10022

Betty Parsons Gallery
24 West 57th Street
New York, New York 10019

Max Protetch Gallery
37 West 57th Street
New York, New York 10019

Sonnabend Gallery
420 West Broadway
New York, New York 10012

Sperone Westwater Fischer
142 Greene Street
New York, New York 10012

Allan Stone Gallery
48 East 86th Street
New York, New York 10028

John Weber Gallery
420 West Broadway
New York, New York 10012

Alexander Willard, Inc.
660 Madison Avenue
New York, New York 10021

Zabriskie Gallery
29 West 57th Street
(and 521 West 57th Street)
New York, New York 10019

Pennsylvania

Makler Gallery
1716 Locust Street
Philadelphia, Pennsylvania 19103

Texas

Janie C. Lee Gallery
2304 Bissonet
Houston, Texas 77005

Watson/de Nagy & Company
1106 Berthea
Houston, Texas 77006

For More Information

Lucy Lippard, *Pop Art* (New York: Frederick A. Praeger, 1966).
Barbara Rose, *American Art Since 1900,* revised edition (New York: Praeger Publishers, 1975).
Irving Sandler, *The Triumph of American Painting: A History of Abstract Expressionism* (New York: Praeger Publishers, 1970).
Irving Sandler, *The New York School: The Painters and Sculptors of the Fifties* (New York: Harper & Row, 1978).

The best way to keep up with more recent developments in contemporary art is to review on a regular basis the following art journals: *Art in America, Art News, Artforum,* and *Arts Magazine.*

If you want to see the most important articles from the past twenty years, you don't need to hunt through the stacks of a library for them: The articles have been anthologized in a series of volumes by Gregory Battcock, published inexpensively in paperback by E. P. Dutton & Co. The series includes *The New Art, Minimal Art*, and *Idea Art.*

AMERICAN ART

For centuries, American artists were the stepchildren of the art world. Our greatest talents studied in Europe under European masters and sometimes didn't bother to return. The roster of expatriate masters is impressive: Gilbert Stuart, John Singleton Copley, Benjamin West, James Abbott McNeill Whistler, John Singer Sargent, Mary Cassatt, and Marsden Hartley, among others. Although some returned, they continued to feel unrecognized or even rejected by their countrymen.

Throughout the years, the art market has reflected this low esteem. Little more than a decade ago, the record price for an American painting was only $75,000—the price paid for a *trompe l'oeil* oil by William Harnett. Only a few figures, such as Lawrence Fleischman of the Kennedy Galleries in New York, remained optimistic about the market for American art. "Mark my words," he said, "the time is not far off when we will see an American painting sell for $500,000."

Market Turnaround.   Fleischman proved prophetic. In 1980, Frederic Edwin Church's masterpiece, *Icebergs,* arrived on the auction block at Sotheby's in New York. When the last gavel fell, the work had been purchased by Lamar Hunt for the Dallas Museum of Art. The price: an astounding $2,500,000. Even European collectors were impressed. They had been collecting *contemporary* American art since the 1960s, but now they began to look further into the American past. American art, slighted for so long, had finally arrived.

The Revolution in American Art.   What started the revolution in the American art market? Although collectors continued to prefer old masters and Impressionists, the available works were too few and too expensive. As a result, the large and growing population of buyers began to cast around for new schools of art to fill the void. Not surprisingly, their attention soon fixed on early American art, which offered old-master quality without the old-master prices.

American art also benefited from several developments unrelated to market forces: first, a general reappraisal of nineteenth-century art that swept the art world in the 1960s and '70s; and, second, a specific reawakening of interest in America's past. This new-found appreciation—even nostalgia—for preindustrial American society, culminating in the 1976 Bicentennial celebration, helped "prime" the market for art of the same period. David Riesman, the eminent sociologist, takes the argument one step further and attributes the new interest in American art to an ethnic revival of "the smallest minority in America, the white Protestant."

When, in 1980, the Metropolitan Museum opened its spacious new

American wing, it was clear beyond mistake that American art had finally come of age.

It's Still Cheaper to Buy American

Although American art is now more expensive than it has ever been, it's still often cheaper than its European counterpart. For example, the auction record price for an American Impressionist painting, Childe Hassam's *October Sundown Newport* (1901), is $205,000. Not cheap, certainly, but considerably cheaper than the million-dollar-plus prices routinely commanded by the leading French Impressionists.

It bears repeating that the $205,000 was the *record* price. In the same sale at Sotheby's in 1980, a large watercolor and gouache by Hassam, *Hutchinson House, Easthampton,* sold for only $4,750. An oil painting by Marsden Hartley, the American Cubist, *Still Life with Calla* (1928–1929), went for a paltry $7,500. Of course, these were not among either artist's most important works. But it is still remarkable that any competent work by artists of their stature could have sold for so little.

Howard L. Katzander, an expert on the art market, says, "Collectors who read only about the big records in the million dollar range, and fear they have missed the boat when it comes to American paintings, are missing a bet. The field is still wide open, and those with a cultivated, as well as an educated, eye can begin collecting American art on their own terms."

A Road Map of American Art

To date, only a small group of American artists has achieved old-master status. This favored fraternity includes Colonial artists such as John Singleton Copley, Gilbert Stuart, and Benjamin West; a few great nineteenth-century masters such as Frederic Edwin Church, Thomas Eakins, Winslow Homer, and Albert Pinkham Ryder; some turn-of-the-century painters such as John Singer Sargent and James Abbott McNeill Whistler; and the "Eight"—Arthur B. Davies, William Glackens, Robert Henri, Ernest Lawson, George Luks, Maurice Prendergast, Everett Shinn, and John Sloan.

Until recently, these were the only names inaccessible to the beginning collector. Unfortunately, the list has continued to grow and now includes all of the leading artists in the following movements. For your convenience, the artists are divided into several categories based on style, but only with the caution that most artists really belong in more than one. "A lot of artists evolved from one movement to another," says Roger Howlett of Childs Gallery in Boston.

Childe Hassam. *Une Averse, Rue Bonaparte.* 1887. Oil on canvas. 40¼" x 77¼". Courtesy Hirschl & Adler Galleries, Inc., New York.

Buy the Best.   The first rule of art collecting is to buy only the best. If you can't afford a first-rate work by a first-tier American Impressionist, don't settle for a second-rate work by the same artist. Instead, look for a first-rate work by a second-tier Impressionist. Don't buy a mediocre work by Childe Hassam when you can buy a great work by Charles H. Davis. As the prices for first-tier American artists have continued to rise, they have pulled the prices for secondary artists with them. The difference, however, remains dramatic. Works by the first-tier artists now sell for $100,000 or more, sometimes much more, while the best works of the second-tier artists still sell for around $10,000. But the price curve for both is definitely upward, and, in a few years, $10,000 will seem like a bargain.

Instead of buying a work by a second-tier artist from a popular movement, consider buying a work by a first-tier artist from a less popular (and less expensive) movement: a Barbizon landscape by Alexander Wyant, for example. Not all American art movements have appreciated at the same rapid rate. Obviously, you should look for movements as well as artists still on the way up.

Nineteenth-Century Still-Life Painters

Still life was a favorite genre in America during the nineteenth century and it attracted some of our best painters. Although the prices vary significantly from one artist to another, they are often within reach of the beginning collector. Artists to look for include William Mason Brown,

Robert Speare Dunning. *Still Life: Grapes, Pear, Peach, and Plum.* 1896. Oil on canvas. 7⅛" x 11¼". Courtesy Hirschl & Adler Galleries, Inc., New York.

John Francis, Paul Lacroix, George Henry Hall, Martin Johnson Heade, and Severen Roesen.

Somewhat better-known are the *trompe-l'oeil* paintings of William Michael Harnett and John Frederick Peto. For excellent *trompe-l'oeil* paintings at lower prices, look at the work of George Cope and Richard Labarre Goodwin.

The Luminists and the Hudson River School

The American Luminist and Hudson River School painters celebrated the American wilderness in dramatic, light-filled landscapes. A work by their leading light, Frederic Edwin Church, has already fetched the record price for an American painting. Works by other members of this group, including Albert Bierstadt, Thomas Cole, Jasper F. Cropsey, Asher B. Durand, Sanford Gifford, and J. F. Kensett are also expensive today.

Works can still be purchased for prices ranging between $2,000 and $12,000, however, by artists such as James Renwick Brevoort, Alfred T. Bricher, John Casilear, Samuel Colman, Regis Gignoux, David Johnson, Jervis McEntee, James David Smillie, and John Williamson.

American Academic Artists

Like their counterparts in Europe, the American academicians painted melodramatic subjects with almost photographic clarity. Also like their

Top, James Renwick Brevoort. *Half Moon Cove, Gloucester Bay.* 1871. Oil on artist's board. 8¾" x 14½". Private collection. Courtesy Adams Davidson Galleries, Washington, D.C.

Bottom, John Williamson. *Scouting Party in the Catskills.* 1873. Oil on canvas. 15" x 23". Private collection. Courtesy Adams Davidson Galleries, Washington, D.C.

S. S. Carr. *Hide and Seek*. 1876. Oil on canvas. 20¼″ x 16¼″. Courtesy Hirschl & Adler Galleries, Inc., New York.

European counterparts, they are regaining their long-lost popularity. The best of these artists, such as Eastman Johnson, managed to display great artistic energy even within the constraints of nineteenth-century academic conventions. Among the less expensive artists to consider: J. G. Brown, S. S. Carr, Will Low, A. Wordsworth Thomson, and John Tracy.

The Tonalists and American Barbizons

George Inness is the best-known of the American Tonalists, a group of landscape painters in the best of the American Luminist tradition. As the Luminist school begins to attract a larger following, it's only a matter of time before other Tonalists, such as Henry Pember Smith, come into favor as well.

Alexander Wyant. *Summer Landscape*. c. 1885. Oil on canvas. 19½" x 22½". Private collection. Courtesy Adams Davidson Galleries, Inc., Washington, D.C.

The American Barbizons were a group of landscape painters so closely related to the European Barbizons that they adopted the same name. The best of their paintings—dark, brooding forests, varied only by the occasional addition of an animal—transcend the restrictions of the genre. William Morris Hunt, Hugh Bolton Jones, Homer Dodge Martin, Francis Murphy, Dwight Tryon, and Alexander Wyant are among the best known of the American Barbizons. Many American Barbizon works are still available in prices ranging from $2,000 to $10,000.

The American Impressionists

The American Impressionists are now almost as popular as their French counterparts—and not just Mary Cassatt, the one American painter who really *is* a French Impressionist. Especially popular—and expensive—are the works of Childe Hassam, William Merritt Chase, John Henry Twachtman, and the other members of the "Boston Ten," a group that broke away from the Society of American Artists much the way Monet, Renoir, and Sisley left the Parisian Salon years before. One of the Boston Ten, Theodore Robinson, went to France to work with Monet and eventually married his stepdaughter.

John J. Enneking. *Blue Hill*. 1877. Oil on canvas. 15¾" x 24". Photograph by Herbert P. Vose. Courtesy Vose Galleries of Boston, Inc.

Works by lesser American Impressionists, such as Cecilia Beaux, John F. Carlson, Charles H. Davis, J. J. Enneking, Walter Griffin, Edward Redfield, Edmund Tarbell, Ross Turner, Theodore Wendel, and Charles Woodbury, can still be purchased for $10,000 or less. Works by American Post-Impressionists, such as Dodge Macknight and Gardner Symons, are also available for that amount.

The American Cubists

The American followers of French Cubism have gained considerable favor in recent years: partly because they bask in the light of Picasso and Braque, and partly because their best works are independent, vigorous, and thoroughly American variations on the French model. The best American cubists were Stuart Davis, Marsden Hartley, and John Marin. Patrick Henry Bruce, Gerald Murphy, Max Weber, and Stanton Mac-Donald Wright are also on the list of inaccessible American masters.

Less expensive, but also very desirable, are works by Herbert Barnett and Carl Knaths.

The Precisionists and Art-Deco Artists

The Precisionist artists, notably Charles Sheeler and Charles Demuth, painted objects with machine-like precision. The smooth, rounded forms

Marsden Hartley. *Musical Theme*. 1912–1913. Oil on canvas. 25½" x 21". Courtesy Hirschl & Adler Galleries, Inc., New York.

Louis Lozowick. *Newark Waterfront 1929*. 1929. Oil on canvas. 20½″ x 14⅛″. Courtesy Hirschl & Adler Galleries, Inc., New York.

of Guy Pène du Bois's Art-Deco paintings are also highly appealing to us now that we have begun to look at Art-Deco objects with more understanding and appreciative eyes.

Related works can be purchased more cheaply by artists such as George Ault, Ralston Crawford, Elsie Driggs, Mabel Ducasse, Stefan Hirsch, Louis Lozowick, and Niles Spencer.

American-Scene Painters

Most of the American-Scene painters grew up in the Midwest. Their works, which feature rural scenes and small-town vignettes, illustrated the hardy, traditional American values typical of the region. The most famous artists of the American Scene are Thomas Hart Benton, John Steuart Curry, Reginald Marsh, and Grant Wood.

Somewhat less famous—and more affordable—are Isabel Bishop, Paul Cadmus, Adolf Dehn, Alexander Hogue, Peter Hurd, Joe Jones, Fletcher Martin, and Paul Sample.

Independent Realists

While painters like Marsden Hartley and John Marin were importing the French revolution in art, a large group of less adventurous American artists were painting conventionally realistic—yet spirited—landscapes, still lifes, and portraits. Long forgotten in the rush toward more avant-garde work, these truly independent artists are finally receiving the attention they deserve. The greatest artist in this group was Edward Hopper.

The market for works by less famous independent realists, notably the artists who painted in Boston and Rockport, Massachusetts, offers some of the best prices currently available in American art. Among the artists to consider: Frank W. Benson, Jay Conaway, Joseph DeCamp, I. M. Gaugengigl, Aldro Hibbard, H. Dudley Murphy, Robert Emmett Owen, William M. Paxton, Aiden Lasell Ripley, Paul Sample, George Sloane, William Lester Stevens, Anthony Thieme, and John Whorf.

Folk Artists

American folk art comes in an endless variety: weather vanes, duck decoys, tavern signs, hooked rugs, and quilts. While the prices of folk paintings are often high (Edward Hicks's famous versions of *The Peaceable Kingdom* sell for as much as $200,000), folk objects are still relatively inexpensive. Even the finest quilts, for example, sell for little more than $10,000. With luck, good ones can be purchased for less than $100. Just be aware that folk art is easy to fake. Expert Dorothy Kaufman cautions that buying folk art at auction "can be as risky as betting at Aqueduct."

Edward Hopper. *The Evening Wind*. 1921. Etching. 7" x 8⅜". Courtesy Hirschl & Adler Galleries, Inc., New York.

Getting In on the Ground Floor

If $10,000 is still too much, you can find excellent American paintings and sculptures for less, sometimes much less. You simply have to look at works by third-tier artists—artists who have only recently surfaced in the scholarly literature. Such artists were often well-known in their times but have fallen into obscurity since. The clever collector tries to identify those artists whose talents are on the verge of being rediscovered.

High Risks Bring High Returns. Ted Cooper of the Adams Davidson Gallery in Washington, D.C., suggests that new collectors think first of third-tier artists. "Scholars are finally catching up, trying to shed light on these forgotten Americans." Cooper believes works by these little-recognized artists offer collectors not only first-rate works at relatively low cost, but also the best investment opportunities. "If I had $50,000 and I wanted to turn it into $250,000 in three years, I'd buy top-quality drawings and watercolors by American masters or else I'd buy several top-quality pictures by little-known painters. I have a lot of faith in the market."

Finding Third-Tier American Artists. How do you find the work of third-tier artists with the best investment potential? One way is to develop a good relationship with a dealer. Good dealers are experts in locating artists with potential; if you trust your dealer, you can let him do the searching for you.

Trust a Dealer's Eye. An interesting example of an artist who has recently moved from the third tier to the second is Molly Luce, an American-Scene painter. Like her more famous colleagues in the movement—Benton, Wood, and Curry—Luce painted rural and small-town America. Her painting took her to such "inartistic" sites as Glen Ridge, New Jersey, and Kingsville, Ohio. Luce exhibited regularly during the 1920s and 1930s at such prominent institutions as the Chicago Art Institute and the Corcoran Gallery. The Metropolitan even purchased two of her paintings in the thirties and forties.

After this early success, however, Luce disappeared from the public eye for almost four decades. She was "rediscovered" in Little Compton, Rhode Island, still painting at the age of eighty-one. At that time, a friend

Molly Luce. *Pennsylvania Coal Country.* 1927. Oil on canvas. 22" x 28". Museum of Art, Carnegie Institute, Pittsburgh. Gift of the H. J. Heinz, II Charitable and Family Trust. Courtesy of Childs Gallery, Boston.

brought her work to the attention of Roger Howlett, owner of Childs Gallery in Boston, who acquired her exclusive representation.

Before Luce's rediscovery, you could have purchased any of her works for less than $500. Howlett put her finest works on sale at $1,500, then doubled the prices two months later. After the opening of Luce's retrospective exhibition in the fall of 1980, her prices rose again to the $10,000 level. In January 1981, *Pennsylvania Coal Country* (1927), was acquired by the Carnegie Institute of Art. In three years, Luce's prices had jumped from $500 to $10,000—a remarkable rise by anyone's standards.

Trust Your Own Eye. Not surprisingly, many collectors don't leave the job of finding good artists to their dealers. After all, half the fun of collecting is deciding what to collect. If you're among the adventurous, and want to explore the frontier of American art on your own, I recommend that you read the relevant literature, visit museum collections regularly, attend major exhibitions, and frequent galleries and auction houses listed below that specialize in American art.

Where to Buy American Art

Arizona

Elaine Horwitch
4200 Marshall Way
Scottsdale, Arizona 85251

California

Terry De Lapp
P. O. Box 69175
Los Angeles, California 90069

Maxwell Galleries Ltd.
551 Sutter
San Francisco, California 94102

Hunter Gallery
278 Post
San Francisco, California 94108

Connecticut

Tillou Gallery, Inc.
Prospect Street
Litchfield, Connecticut 06759

Thomas Colville
58 Trumbull Street
New Haven, Connecticut 06511

District of Columbia

Adams Davidson Galleries Inc.
3233 P Street N.W.
Washington, D.C. 20007

Illinois

Campanile Galleries, Inc.
200 South Michigan
Chicago, Illinois 60604

R. H. Love Galleries
100 East Ohio Street
Chicago, Illinois 60611

Massachusetts

Childs Gallery
169 Newbury Street
Boston, Massachusetts 02116

Vose Galleries of Boston Inc.
238 Newbury Street
Boston, Massachusetts 02116

New Mexico

Fenn Galleries, Ltd.
1075 Paseo de Peralta
Santa Fe, New Mexico 87501

New York

Alexander Gallery
117 East 39th Street
New York, New York 10016

Hirschl & Adler Galleries, Inc.
21 East 70th Street
New York, New York 10021

H. V. Allison & Co.
11 East 57th Street
New York, New York 10022

Kennedy Galleries, Inc.
40 West 57th Street
New York, New York 10019

America Hurrah Antiques
316 East 70th Street
New York, New York 10021

Coe Kerr Gallery
49 East 82nd Street
New York, New York 10028

Berry-Hill Galleries, Inc.
743 Fifth Avenue
New York, New York 10022

M. Knoedler & Co.
19 East 70th Street
New York, New York 10021

Chapellier Galleries
22 East 80th Street
New York, New York 10021

Gerald Kornblau
250 East 58th Street
New York, New York 10022

Davis & Long Co.
746 Madison Avenue
New York, New York 10021

Kenneth Lux Gallery
1021 Madison Avenue
New York, New York 10021

Graham Gallery
1014 Madison Avenue
New York, New York 10021

James Maroney incorporated
129a East 74th Street
New York, New York 10021

Frank Rehn Gallery, Inc.
655 Madison Avenue
New York, New York 10021

George E. Schoellkopf Gallery
1065 Madison Avenue
New York, New York 10028

Pennsylvania

David David Inc.
260 South 18th Street
Philadelphia, Pennsylvania
19103

Frank S. Schwartz & Son
1806 Chestnut Street
Philadelphia, Pennsylvania
19103

For More Information

The first step in a good reading program is an historical survey. I recommend:

Barbara Novak, *American Painting of the Nineteenth Century: Idealism and the American Experience* (New York: Harper & Row, 1969).

Theodore E. Stebbins, Jr., *American Master Drawings and Watercolors,* (New York: Harper & Row, 1976).

Whitney Museum of American Art, *The Flowering of American Folk Art 1776–1876,* text by Jean Lipman and Alice Winchester (New York: The Viking Press, 1974).

Whitney Museum of American Art, *200 Years of American Sculpture,* (Boston: David R. Godine, 1976).

John Wilmerding, *American Art,* Pelican History of Art (New York: Penguin Books, 1976).

If you want more information on first- and second-tier artists, consult the bibliographies at the back of these books. If you want an introduction to the less well-known, third-tier artists, consult one of the following dictionaries and guides:

Boston Museum of Fine Arts, *M. and M. Karolik Collection of American Water Colors and Drawings: 1800–1875,* 2 Volumes (Boston: Museum of Fine Arts, 1962).

Boston Museum of Fine Arts, *American Paintings in the Museum of Fine Arts, Boston,* 2 volumes (Boston: Museum of Fine Arts, 1969).

James F. Carr, ed., *James F. Carr: Mantle Fielding's Dictionary of American Painters, Sculptors, and Engravers* (New York: James F. Carr Publisher, 1965).

George C. Grace and H. Wallace, *The New York Historical Society's Dictionary of Artists in America 1564–1860* (New Haven: Yale University Press, 1957).

National Collection of Fine Arts, *Dictionary to the Bicentennial Inventory of American Paintings Executed before 1914* (Washington, D.C.: National Collection of Fine Arts, Smithsonian Institution, 1976).

FURNITURE

The highest prices in the art market today are paid for the "fine arts": paintings, sculptures, drawings, and prints—works without practical value created solely for esthetic contemplation. This is a recent development. Three decades ago, the "decorative arts"—furniture, carpets, porcelain, glass, and pottery—were valued at least as highly as the fine arts. Germain Seligman, one of the leading art dealers at the turn of the century summarized the current wisdom: "Quality has no bounds," he said; "it is a universal property which unites all great works of art, be they manuscripts, armor, paintings, or sculpture." When newspapers headlined record auction prices in the twenties, it was not for paintings or sculptures—even old masters. It was for pottery—probably *majolica,* a richly decorated form of Renaissance ware.

Today, a first-rate piece of majolica would cost you as little as $2,000 or $3,000. Other examples of decorative art might cost you more—perhaps much more. In fact, the record price for a piece of furniture was paid by the Getty Museum in Malibu, California, in 1980. The piece: an eighteenth-century French corner cabinet. The price: $1,779,000. That's a considerable amount of money, but the record price for a painting is about eight times higher. The point is unmistakable: Objects are no longer the prize in the art market.

When quality is high but prices low, wise collectors take note. Wise collectors are very active in the market for furniture and the other decorative arts.

French, English, American

The $1,779,000 record auction price for a lot of furniture was paid for a piece of French furniture. Until recently, the record price for a lot of English furniture was paid for eight George II side chairs, crafted in England for a Spanish duke. The chairs were sold at Christie's in New York in 1980 for $290,000. The record price for American furniture was set at Sotheby's the same year. The piece was a Chippendale mahogany Goddard-Townsend chest of drawers and the price was $360,000.

French. The price differences are not surprising. It's generally acknowledged that the richest European furniture ever made is French furniture from the reigns of Louis XIV, Louis XV, and Louis XVI. For

Tilliard. Pair of Louis XV giltwood fauteuils. Mid-18th century. Courtesy Christie's, New York.

materials, craftsmanship, and design, you have to go out of the Western world, to Ming China, perhaps, to find comparable quality.

Although French furniture dominated the auction block for decades, all but the richest collectors are finally being discouraged by the high prices. Gerald Stiebel, of Rosenberg Stiebel in New York, the finest American dealers in French furniture, admits that "in the next one to five years there will be a drop. Fifty to 60 percent will be unsold at auctions." Stiebel hedges a bit, however: "The newspapers will say the bottom has fallen out, but it won't be true. As in the depression, there will be a market for the top things, and because people will be selling their heirlooms, there will be a lot to buy." Given the high prices and the depressed investment prospects, however, the beginning collector should avoid the best French furniture.

Look for Less Expensive Items. If you still wish to collect French furniture, Colin Streeter, a New York-based consultant, suggests that you concentrate on "museum condition" pieces rather than "museum quality" pieces. In other words, says Streeter, you should be willing to compromise on the artistic quality of a piece but not on its condition.

The investment market in French furniture has traditionally centered on elaborate court furniture. As a result, prices are significantly lower for relatively plain *chateau* furniture. Chairs are also generally plainer, and therefore cheaper, than commodes, desks, and other case pieces. This is *real* French provincial furniture and it's especially cheap outside France.

Thierry Millerand, furniture expert at Sotheby's, suggests that you consider two kinds of French furniture. On the one hand, he recommends less sought-after items from the eighteenth century: "A very simple but stylish Louis XV chair with no carving, special provenance, or history, but with very nice proportions, can cost $500 to $600. A pair for $1,000 to $1,500. (Pairs carry a premium.) A very smart Louis XVI mahogany commode can go for as little as $3,000."

On the other hand, Millerand recommends furniture from the less sought-after nineteenth century: "In French nineteenth-century furniture, Napoleon III and Victorian *papier-mâché* furniture are still quite inexpensive. Look for the things that are very strong in design without being fussy. An Empire console can go for as little as $800 to $1,200. During the Charles X period, the second quarter of the century, furniture had very pure lines, and it is still quite cheap for what it is. There's not much of it, but it's not in demand either. A chest of drawers in light wood can be $2,000."

Charles X walnut arm-chairs. c. 1820. Courtesy Christie's East, New York.

If you still crave high-style French eighteenth-century furniture, Colin Streeter suggests that "the savvy individual meets far less competition for outstanding Dutch, German, and Italian furniture influenced by French styles than he does for even second-rate French pieces of the same period."

Streeter also recommends later French adaptations of eighteenth-century French styles: "During the 1970s, the highest percentage gains in European furniture, aside from the skyrocketing French and English 18th century aristocratic pieces, have been in top quality furniture in the classic eighteenth-century French court styles made after 1850 and signed by firms such as Dasson, Linke, and Sormani."

English. English furniture continues to be a favorite among collectors. It is unimpeachably conservative and unquestionably elegant, yet simple enough to accommodate contemporary lifestyles. And, of course, even at its best, English furniture is also much cheaper than French furniture; it's even cheaper than English-influenced American furniture. Robert C. Woolley, senior vice president of Sotheby's, argues that eighteenth-

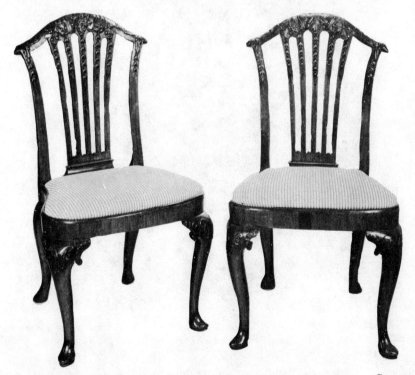

Set of twelve George I walnut dining chairs. Early 18th century. Courtesy Christie's, New York.

Chippendale mahogany serpentine front secretary, Salem, Massachusetts, c. 1760–1780. Courtesy Israel Sack, Inc., New York.

century English furniture is cheaper than its counterparts from France or America and will appreciate more quickly. But beware: The gap is closing quickly, especially for the best Chippendale and Queen Anne eighteenth-century pieces. In 1946, a Queen Anne walnut bookcase sold for $2,100. In 1980, the same piece sold at Christie's for $125,000.

For the best bargains, Streeter recommends English Provincial furniture from between 1650 and 1825. "English country craft traditions," he says, "were coarse by contemporary Newport or Philadelphia standards, but the condition of surviving pieces should be judged by the same fastidious standards collectors expect of American furniture. Plain Irish furniture of circa 1720–1770 is also undervalued. Later Irish neo-classic furniture passes for English and still commands English prices."

American.   In the 1970s, American furniture, long considered inferior to comparable furniture from England, finally came into its own. Collectors prize especially the rich designs and subtle charms of the best Boston, Philadelphia, and Newport eighteenth-century manufacturers. The market for American furniture reached some sort of milestone at the Edgar William and Bernice Chrysler Garbisch sale in 1980. Proceeds from the sale amounted to almost $4,000,000. With prices at that level, even European collectors have taken note. Their active competition for the best American pieces is proof that American furniture has finally come of age.

Federal mahogany candlestand, New York or Connecticut. c. 1790–1815. Courtesy Christie's, New York.

In American furniture as in English, pieces from the eighteenth century command the highest prices. Chippendale and Queen Anne are particularly expensive. Hepplewhite, Sheraton, and Federal are somewhat cheaper.

American Federal. American Federal pieces made by informally trained craftsmen outside the major furniture centers are especially reasonable today. Dean Failey of Christie's notes: "Recently we sold a simple but handsome, tall Federal mahogany wardrobe that still has its finials, opens up to three sliding shelves and three long drawers below. It fetched $1,900. If it had eagles inlaid on the doors, it would suddenly have been a $5,000 to $8,000 piece of furniture." At the same sale, a Federal mahogany window seat sold for $600 and a pair of Federal carved mahogany side chairs sold for $400 each.

English Regency. English Regency is a good eighteenth-century buy at the moment. Collectors who want eighteenth-century English furniture at bargain prices should also take some advice from the market for French furniture: Look for relatively plain pieces in relatively plain materials; or else, look for first-rate nineteenth-century reproductions of eighteenth-century styles (these are known as Centennial furniture).

Pilgrim oak and pine chest-on-frame or dower chest, Massachusetts area. c. 1680–1700. Courtesy Israel Sack, Inc., New York.

Seventeenth Century

As always, the prices are lower in the less popular periods and styles. Therefore, even better bargains can be found in furniture from before the eighteenth century. Try seventeenth-century furniture: English Renaissance, Elizabethan, Jacobean, or Baroque furniture on the one hand, American Pilgrim on the other. Many collectors find these styles too large, too heavy, too elaborate, or too plain. American Pilgrim furniture, for example, has been out of fashion since the 1920s. With prices prohibitive elsewhere in the market, however, it will probably soon return to favor. According to Gerald Bland of Sotheby's, seventeenth-century furniture pieces "are mostly the work of local craftsmen in small regional workshops. They're not high-style, but can be very comfortable for rustic houses. A nice seventeenth-century armchair sells for between $300 and $1,500."

Colin Streeter recommends that you also consider Italian Renaissance furniture: "Italian and Renaissance furniture of the sixteenth and seventeenth centuries crashed with the stock market in 1929, and scarcely anything useful has been written since then on this once-fashionable subject. Collectors who dare to buy at auction and can find their way through the maze of tarted-up pieces, pieces made out of authentic bits, and the outright fakes of circa 1850 to 1930, get great value. However, these outscale chairs, chests or *cassoni,* and chest-benches or *cassapanche* are not well-suited to cramped modern habitats."

Nineteenth and Twentieth Centuries

Bargains can also be found in furniture from *after* the eighteenth century. Empire furniture from the early nineteenth century is rapidly becoming more popular, which means that it's rapidly becoming more expensive. Sales were brisk in 1980, often at prices of $25,000 or more for individual pieces; but good American Empire sofas are still available for about $1,000. According to Streeter, even better bargains are to be found in late classical American furniture made in Baltimore, Boston, New York, and Philadelphia from 1820 to 1845.

Higher prices are gradually making their way toward the present. Collectors are beginning to favor styles as recent as Rococo Revival (high established), Renaissance Revival (now higher), Arts and Crafts (coming up), Art Nouveau (peaking off), and Art Deco (coming up).

Art Deco.   Art-Deco furniture, for example, did not begin to attract serious collectors until a decade ago. But it soon made up for lost time. In 1980, Sotheby's auctioned the great Art-Deco collection from Manik Bagh, the palace of the Maharajah of Indore, India. A chrome and

French Renaissance carved
oak choir stall. Courtesy
Christie's East, New York.

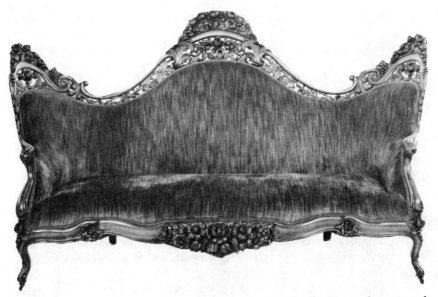

Attributed to John Henry Belter. Victorian Rococo Revival carved rosewood sofa, New York. c. 1850–1860. Courtesy Christie's, New York.

aluminum bed, the work of Louis Segnot, was sold for an astonishing $136,000.

Victorian. For many years, Victorian furniture was regularly sent not to the auction house but to Goodwill. People found it heavy, elaborate, too richly colored, and hopelessly old-fashioned. That attitude is changing. Indeed, a Rococo Revival rosewood center table by the fine American Victorian furniture designer, John Henry Belter, sold in 1980 for $60,000. Nevertheless, most prices for Victorian furniture fall far below that level and bargains are still readily available. J. Brian Cole of Christie's says, "There are only three or four people in the whole United States who collect Belter so far. If they aren't interested in a Belter lot because it doesn't conform to some specification of their collecting, you may get a buy." In fact, good pieces by Belter (and by other major manufacturers of the period such as John and Joseph Meeks and Herter Brothers) can still regularly be purchased for under $3,000.

Arts and Crafts. At the other end of the spectrum, collectors have not yet cultivated a taste for the plain, solid furniture of the Arts and Crafts movement. You can still buy almost any piece by the leading American practitioner, Gustav Stickley, for less than $10,000. A good secretary by Stickley should sell for between $2,000 and $3,000. But remember, that's three times what the same piece was worth in 1975, and the price shows no sign of leveling off. Arts and Crafts furniture may still be available at relatively low prices, but not for long.

Authenticity

Colin Streeter notes that "authenticity is a more perplexing problem in furniture than in many other fields of collecting because wood is so adaptable. Besides the innocent re-interpretations and literal reproductions that still pass for genuine, 'fakes' consist of (1) genuine pieces that have been 'tarted up' with additional carving, metal mounts, or other additions, (2) rebuilt furniture made of genuine elements, (3) 'married' pieces, or (4) pieces refinished with gilding or paint.

"No furniture that is stained up, tarted up, gilded up, married, enriched with carving, repainted, or rebuilt has dependable value, beyond its decorative assets. Half the highly touted English lacquer furniture that currently brings top prices will 'crash' in the next twenty years. Buyers who are fastidious about 'museum' condition rather than 'museum' quality will find increasing competition for the cleanest pieces during the 1980s."

How to Detect Faked and Forged Furniture. With enough practice, you, like most experts, can distinguish a revival piece or a reproduction from a genuine antique on the basis of condition, materials, color, quality, or style. For example, certain kinds of wood are found in furniture made at different times in different countries. The wood used in concealed places—backs, supports, drawer linings—is especially revealing. Signs of use and aging are also helpful in distinguishing genuine pieces from reproductions or recent revivals. With time and use, wood furniture acquires a *patina* that is nearly impossible to simulate. Even the most carefully tended pieces eventually show signs of use. Therefore, in assessing the authenticity of a piece, you should always look first at those areas that receive the most wear. In a chair, for example, look at the feet, the arms, the seat, and the back. If the patina is uniform or the piece doesn't show areas of heavy wear, it may not be a genuine antique.

Where to Buy Furniture

California

Stair & Co., Inc.
10900 Wilshire Boulevard
Los Angeles, California 90024

Richard Gould Antiques, Ltd.
216 26th Street
Santa Monica, California 90402

Connecticut

John Walton Inc.
Box 307
Jewett City, Connecticut 06351

Delaware

David Stockwell Inc.
3701 Kennett Pike
P. O. Box 3840
Wilmington, Delaware 19807

Illinois

Malcolm Franklin, Inc.
126 East Delaware Place
Chicago, Illinois 60611

Kentucky

The Strassel Company
1000 Hamilton Avenue
Louisville, Kentucky 40204

New York

A La Vieille Russie, Inc.
781 Fifth Avenue
New York, New York 10022

Didier Aaron, Inc.
32 East 67th Street
New York, New York 10022

Arthur Ackermann & Son, Inc.
50 East 57th Street
New York, New York 10022

Philip Colleck of London, Ltd.
122 East 57th Street
New York, New York 10022

Dalva Brothers, Inc.
44 East 57th Street
New York, New York 10022

Devenish & Company Inc.
929 Madison Avenue
New York, New York 10021

Benjamin Ginsburg Antiquary
Inc.
815 Madison Avenue
New York, New York 10021

The Incurable Collector, Inc.
42 East 57th Street
New York, New York 10022

Jordan/Volpe
457 West Broadway
New York, New York 10012

Bernard & S. Dean Levy Inc.
981 Madison Avenue
New York, New York 10021

Rosenberg & Stiebel, Inc.
32 East 57th Street
New York, New York 10022

Israel Sack, Inc.
15 East 57th Street
New York, New York 10022

Garrick C. Stephenson
50 East 57th Street
New York, New York 10022

Stair & Co., Inc.
59 East 57th Street
New York, New York 10022

Vernay & Jussell, Inc.
825 Madison Avenue
New York, New York 10021

Pennsylvania

Herbert Schiffer Antiques
Box E
Eaton, Pennsylvania 19341

Alfred Bullard, Inc.
1604 Pine Street
Philadelphia, Pennsylvania
19103

Virginia

Glenn C. Randall
229 North Royal Street
Alexandria, Virginia 22314

Ricks Wilson, Ltd.
Merchants Square
P. O. Box 504
Williamsburg, Virginia 23185

For More Information

General

Robert Bishop and Patricia Coblenz, *Furniture 1: Prehistoric through Rococo* (New York: Cooper-Hewitt Museum, 1979).

Helena Hayward, ed., *World Furniture* (New York: McGraw-Hill Book Co., 1965).

Marvin Schwartz and Betsy Wade, *The New York Times Book of Antiques* (New York: Times Books, 1972).

Peter Thornton, *Seventeenth-Century Interior Decoration in France, England, and Holland in the Seventeenth Century* (New Haven: Yale University Press, 1978).

American

Robert J. Clark, ed., *The Arts and Crafts Movement in America* (Princeton, N.J.: Princeton University Press, 1972).

Helen Comstock, ed., *The Concise Encyclopedia of American Antiques* (New York: Hawthorn Books, 1958).

Joseph Downs, *American Furniture, Queen Anne and Chippendale Periods, in the Henry Francis du Pont Winterthur Museum* (New York: Macmillan Co., 1952).

Jonathan Fairbanks, *American Furniture: 1620 to the Present* (New York: Richard Marek, 1981).

William McPherson Horner, Jr., *Blue Book, Philadelphia Furniture, William Penn to George Washington, with special reference to the Philadelphia-Chippendale School,* reprint (Washington, D.C.: Highland House Publishers, 1977).

John Kassay, *The Book of Shaker Furniture* (Amherst, Mass.: University of Massachusetts Press, 1980).

Charles F. Montgomery, *American Furniture of the Federal Period (1788–1825)* (New York: Viking Press, 1966).

Wallace Nutting, *Furniture Treasury,* 3 volumes (New York: Macmillan Publishing Co., n.d.).

Wallace Nutting, *Furniture of the Pilgrim Century 1620–1720,* 2 volumes (New York: Dover Publications, 1965).

Marvin D. Schwartz and others, *The Furniture of John Henry Belter and the Rococo Revival* (New York: E. P. Dutton, 1981).

Berry Bryson Tracy, *Classical America* (Newark, N.J.: The Newark Museum, 1963).

Berry Bryson Tracy, *Nineteenth-Century America* (New York: Metropolitan Museum of Art, 1970).

English

J. Munro Bell, ed., *The Furniture Designs of Chippendale, Hepplewhite and Sheraton* (New York: Robert M. McBride and Co., 1938).

Ralph Edwards, *The Shorter Dictionary of English Furniture* (New York: Hamlyn/American, 1976).

John Fowler and John Cornforth, *English Decoration in the Eighteenth Century* (New York: Barrie & Jenkins, 1978).

Christopher Gilbert, *The Life and Work of Thomas Chippendale,* 2 volumes (New York: Macmillan Publishing Co., 1979).

Mark Girouard, *Life in the English Country House: A Social and Architectural History* (New Haven: Yale University Press, 1978).

John Gloag, *A Short Dictionary of Furniture* (Winchester, Mass.: Allan Unwin, 1976).

Eileen Harris, *The Furniture of Robert Adam* (New York: St. Martin's Press, 1973).

Helena Hayward and Patricia Kirkham, *William and John Linnell: Eighteenth-Century London Furniture-Makers,* 2 volumes (New York: Rizzoli International Publications, 1980).

Peter Ward-Jackson, *English Furniture Designs of the Eighteenth Century* (London: Victoria and Albert Museum, 1958).

French

Geoffrey de Bellaigue, *The Rothschild Collection at Waddesdon Manor, Furniture, Clocks and Gilt Bronzes,* 2 volumes (Fribourg: The National Trust, 1974).

Svend Eriksen, *Early Neo-Classicism in France* (Salem, N.H.: Faber and Faber, 1974).

Serge Grandjean, *Empire Furniture: 1800 to 1825* (New York: Taplinger Publishing Co., 1966).

Pierre Verlet, *French Furniture and Interior Decoration of the 18th Century,* translated by George Savage (London: Barrie & Rockliffe, 1967).

Francis J. B. Watson, *Wallace Collection Catalogue: Furniture* (London: Wallace Collection, 1956).

Francis J. B. Watson, *The Wrightsman Collection,* first 2 volumes (New York: Metropolitan Museum of Art, 1966).

CARPETS

It is not often that political events affect the art market, but it happened in 1979 when the Ayatollah Khomeini unseated the Shah of Iran from the Peacock Throne.

The effect on the market for antique carpets was cataclysmic. According to Michael Grogan, a carpet specialist at Sotheby's, "High class, commercial 'city' rugs went down in price because the big buyers had been wealthy Iranians who no longer had money. There was very little buying—but a lot of selling."

If politics has distorted the market for oriental carpets, so has economics—and with more far-reaching results. Even before the Iranian political upheaval, the supply of recent carpets from Iran had already begun to dry up. The flow of oil was responsible for that: "With oil revenues of $75 million per day," said Abdi Parvizian, a carpet dealer in Washington, D.C., "people are not going to weave rugs."

America Is the Best Source.   Ironically, the best source for antique orientals has for some time been the United States, not the Orient. Since colonial times, wealthy American merchants have been importing carpets to decorate their homes and offices. As a result, the United States is currently the world's primary source of antique Oriental carpets. Rug merchants from Europe, the Middle East, even Iran, must come to New York to replenish their stocks.

History, Craft, Art.   Oriental carpets are exciting to collect for several reasons. They are remarkable social documents (tribal carpets, in particular, document the lives of the people who made them); astounding feats of craftsmanship (some have as many as two thousand knots per square inch), and art objects of often dazzling beauty.

Iran. Serape carpet. Early 20th century. 11'3" x 9'. Courtesy John C. Edelmann Galleries, Inc., New York.

Techniques, Styles, and Designs

The world of Oriental carpets is both vast and diverse—a diversity made confusing by the lack of a commonly accepted set of categories or vocabulary. If you wish to explore the world of Oriental carpets, you'll need to know the many techniques used to weave them: from *pile* rugs, generally knotted with Turkish (also called *Gördes)* and Persian (or *Sehna*) knots, to *brocaded* rugs, such as the *sumak,* and the pileless, slit-tapestry weave rugs known as *kilims.*

You also need to know the four major areas of the Middle East where most Oriental carpet designs originated: the Anatolian, Caucasian, Iranian, and Turkoman regions. Finally, you'll need to be able to distinguish the various designs, which generally take their names from the cities where they were first developed, such as the Hamadan, Kashan, and Kerman designs, all named after cities in Iran.

Grades

If you decide to collect carpets seriously, you will also need to know the differences between carpets made for the court (usually of very high quality and based on unique designs created by the best of the court artists); commercial carpets (made from standard designs by trained weavers in large urban workshops or by villagers in a sort of Middle Eastern cottage industry); and finally, village and nomadic carpets, generally designed and made by a single weaver for personal use. These rarely are as sophisticated as court or commercial carpets but often of equal—if different—beauty.

Periods

Finally, you will even need to learn a little about carpet history. You'll learn about the great classical age of carpets, roughly from 1500 to 1700, in which the Oriental carpet as we know it developed. You'll discover how the many designs invented during that classical age were replicated, combined, and further developed during the second golden age of weaving from 1850 to 1925. You'll also learn how to distinguish the finest carpets of the recent past.

The Older the Better. Carpets are among the few works of art that actually *improve* with age. Their rich colors become more and more beautiful as they mellow with time and wear. This is fortunate, since collectors generally *prefer* earlier carpets to later ones—not just because the earlier ones are rarer, and therefore more valuable, but also because they are better carpets. Whereas most of the early carpets were designed

Caucasus. Star Kazak rug. Late 19th century. 7'8" x 5'3". Courtesy John C. Edelmann Galleries, Inc., New York.

Turkey. Mudjar prayer rug. Mid-19th century. 6′ × 4′4″. Courtesy John C. Edelmann Galleries, Inc., New York.

and woven individually by craftsmen who spent years on a single piece, most of the recent ones were made according to standard patterns in large workshops. Such mass production has resulted in lower standards: In some modern carpets, cheap commercial dyes have gradually replaced natural dyes, synthetic materials have supplemented wool and silk, attention to detail has given way to assembly-line indifference.

However, the rule that older carpets are better carpets is not inflexible: Excellent carpets have been made throughout the past half century. The point is simply to beware the superficial charms of new carpets. Their plush piles are better suited to wall-to-wall. Above all, avoid the touristy red "Bukharas" manufactured by the thousands in Pakistan and India. These have approximately the same artistic value (and investment value) as machine-made "orientals" broadloomed in Belgium or Japan.

How to Evaluate an Oriental Carpet

Experts evaluate an Oriental carpet according to several criteria. First, how appealing is the design? (This is largely a matter of taste, but Western collectors' tastes usually run toward geometric patterns and bold colors.) How tight is the weave? (Experts have traditionally evaluated carpets within each geographical grouping partly by the number of knots per square inch.) How fine is the quality of the materials? (The best carpets are generally made from the best wools, sometimes interlaced with strands of silk and even threads of precious metals.) Walter Denny, a leading carpet expert, suggests that "budget-conscious collectors sidestep categories of rugs made popular by publications and exhibitions in favor of lesser-known groups of rugs which haven't attained 'star' quality yet."

Condition. The budget-conscious collector should also be prepared to show some flexibility in applying the final criterion of quality in the rug market: condition. Since carpets are made to be walked on, condition is often a major problem. The standards by which you should judge condition are different for carpets than for other works of art. "Good" condition does not mean that the carpet is or looks brand new. "Poor" condition means that it is filled with gaping holes or has been heavily and obviously restored.

Within these limits, condition is largely a matter of individual taste. If your first priority is beauty rather than investment value, I recommend that you look for carpets that are a little worn or slightly repaired. Just make sure that the rugs haven't been cut down or spliced together; that the dyes haven't run significantly, faded beyond distinction, or been "painted" back in; that the fibers are still strong and rot free; and that the restoration work, if any, is not too extensive. If the rugs need additional repair work, be sure to factor the extra cost into the purchase price.

Recommended Styles

All the experts seem to agree that carpets will increase dramatically in value during the 1980s. But what particular periods and styles should you look for? Walter Denny suggests that "very few people can still afford fine old classical carpets. The competition today centers on the best new commercial Iranian carpets (such as Nayyins and Sarouks) and on older tribal and nomadic carpets from all regions: Anatolian, Caucasian, Iranian, and Turkoman. Whereas collectors pay high prices for the best recent commercial carpets, they generally prefer tribal and nomadic carpets made before 1920."

Both kinds of carpets can be good investments. Once overheated, the market for commercial Iranian carpets has stabilized with the departure of Iranian buyers. Remember, however, that with a recent commercial carpet you get a rug designed by one person and manufactured by another; with a tribal or nomadic carpet, you get a work of art designed and executed by a single person who takes pride in his creation.

Older Iranian carpets fall into three categories. "Top-of-the-line" carpets include Bijar, Isfahan, Kashan, Nayyin, Senneh, Serabi, Tabriz, and Qum; "middle-of-the-line" carpets include Heriz, Joshagan, Kerman, Sarouk, and Sultanabad; "lower echelon" carpets include Gorevan, Hamadan, Karaja, Meshed, and Meshkin. Good small carpets in the middle and lower categories are available for less than $2,000. Even the best village and nomadic rugs are generally available for between $6,000 and $10,000.

Kilims. Denny and other experts recommend that new collectors begin their search with flat-weave kilim carpets. Until recently, these pileless, tapestry-weave rugs were spurned as too crude to be collectable. Collectors were also afraid that the rugs were too thin to wear well, forgetting that they didn't have to be placed on the floor—that they could be hung on the wall instead. Now that older and finer rugs are so expensive, however, collectors have begun to "discover" the unusual colors and simple, strong geometric designs of kilims. Collectors are particularly attracted to the rich colors and fine patterns of Caucasian kilims.

Of course, this fledgling interest in kilims has already pushed prices higher. John C. Edelmann, the New York auctioneer, notes that a good eighteenth-century carpet that would have brought $1,200 a decade ago would now bring $12,000 or more. Despite the rising demand, however, very good kilim rugs still sell for as little as $1,000 to $4,000.

True Oriental Carpets. Finally, don't forget that some of the best Oriental carpets come from the Orient. According to Grogan, "Chinese

Caucasus. Shirvan Kilim. Late 19th century. 9'9" x 5'. Courtesy John C. Edelmann Galleries, Inc., New York.

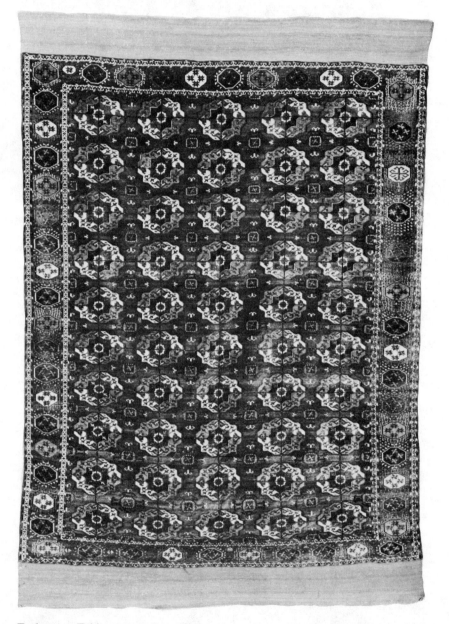

Turkestan. Tekke carpet. Late 19th century. 7'4" x 6'. Courtesy John C. Edelmann Galleries, Inc., New York.

carpets have never really paralleled the appreciation of Persian ones, but they're starting to take off. They were most commonly made from 1870 to 1920 in colors made from vegetable dyes. They come in beautiful blues, ivories, peaches. Although wool, they look like Chinese blue-and-white porcelain. Small ones, four by seven feet, go for between $800 and $1,200. Room-size ones cost between $3,000 and $5,000.''

Where to Learn More

The best way to learn more about carpets in a short time is to join both the Textile Museum in Washington, D.C. (2320 S Street N.W., Washington, D.C. 20009) and one of the regional rug societies around the country (the New York Rug Society or the Pittsburgh Rug Society, for example). These organizations publish helpful newsletters, sponsor lectures and seminars, and conduct tours of galleries and museums.

Where to Buy Carpets

California

Baktiari
2843 Clay Street
San Francisco, California 94115

Illinois

Maury Bynum Oriental Rugs
500 North Michigan Avenue
Chicago, Illinois 60611

Joseph Fell, Ltd.
3221 North Clark Street
Chicago, Illinois 60657

Maryland

Michael's Rug Gallery, Inc.
415 East 33rd Street
Baltimore, Maryland 21218

Mark Keshishian & Sons, Inc.
6930 Wisconsin Avenue
Bethesda, Maryland 20015

Massachusetts

The Fine Arts Rug Company
1475 Beacon Street
Brookline, Massachusetts
    02146

Koko Boodakian & Son, Inc.
1026 Main Street
Winchester, Massachusetts
    01890

New York

Berdj Abadjian
1015 Madison Avenue
New York, New York 10021

Berji Andonian
245 Fifth Avenue
New York, New York 10016

A. Beshar & Company, Inc.
49 East 53rd Street
New York, New York 10022

Doris Leslie Blau, Inc.
15 East 57th Street
New York, New York 10022

Vojtech Blau Inc.
800B Fifth Avenue
New York, New York 10021

Dildarian, Inc.
595 Madison Avenue
New York, New York 10022

John C. Edelmann
   Galleries, Inc.
123 East 77th Street
New York, New York 10028

Marvin Kagan, Inc.
991 Madison Avenue
New York, New York 10021

Ohio

Richard Markarian
101 West 4th Street
Cincinnati, Ohio 45202

Pennsylvania

Maqam
2815 Queen Lane
Philadelphia, Pennsylvania
   19129

For More Information

Siawosch Azadi, *Turkoman Carpets,* translated by Robert Pinner (Fishguard, Wales: Crosby, 1975).

Walter B. Denny, *Oriental Rugs* (New York: Cooper-Hewitt Museum, 1979).

M. L. Eiland, *Oriental Rugs,* revised and expanded edition (Boston: New York Graphic Society, 1976).

Kurt Erdmann, *Oriental Carpets: An Account of their History,* translated by Charles Grant Ellis, 2nd edition (New York: Universe Books, 1962).

Anthony N. Landreau, ed., *Yorük: The Nomadic Weaving Tradition of the Near East* (Pittsburgh: Museum of Art, Carnegie Institute, 1978).

Anthony N. Landreau and W. R. Pickering, *From the Bosphorus to Samarkand: Flat-Woven Rugs* (Washington, D.C.: Textile Museum, 1969).

Yanni Petsopoulos, *Kilims: Flat-woven Tapestry Rugs* (New York: Rizzoli International Publications, 1979).
Ulrich Schürmann, *Caucasian Rugs* (London: Allen and Unwin, 1967).

In addition, the novice collector is advised to subscribe to one or both of the following magazines: *HALI,* a German publication, and *Rug News.* Also extremely useful are the hardback catalogues published occasionally by several European dealers, notably, Bausback in Mannheim (N 39 6800) and Lefevre & Partners in London (152 Brompton Road, London SW3 1HX).

EUROPEAN PORCELAIN

The market for European porcelain remains small. In fact, most porcelain buyers are dealers—which suggests just how specialized the field is. Perhaps because it's so small, the European porcelain market is unusually

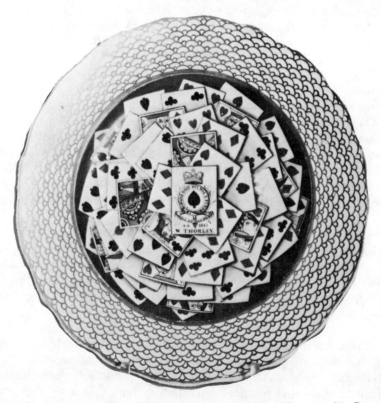

English Coalport Factory. Card Plate. c. 1743. Porcelain. Diameter: 9″. Courtesy Earle D. Vandekar of Knightsbridge Incorporated, Los Angeles.

steady. Leland La Ganke, the New York dealer, says, "The business seems unflappable. It moves along in its own slow steady way."

Prices for European porcelain move steadily too—steadily upward. "Except for Chinese porcelain," says La Ganke, "no category of art has appreciated at such a high rate during the past decade." In 1968, a large Meissen dish from the service of Empress Elizabeth of Russia sold for $3,840. The same dish sold in 1980 for $14,000. Because collectors today generally prefer fine arts to decorative arts, small decorative figurines currently bring the highest prices. The record price for European porcelain is $130,000 for two Meissen swans set on elaborate ormolu bases from the Nelson Rockefeller collection.

Prices Remain Low. Although porcelain prices have risen steeply in recent years, they remain *relatively* low. "European porcelain is one of the few areas in which a new collector can start a collection and hope to see it become comprehensive," says Paul Vandekar, a dealer in Los Angeles and New York. "Even some of the finest pieces of English porcelain, for example, regularly sell for less than $5,000. That same amount won't buy you very much in the market for old masters."

An International Market

Contrary to popular opinion, the market for porcelain is *not* chauvinistic. Only a few collectors prefer the products of their own countries. English collectors have traditionally preferred the finest English items: Bow, Chelsea, and Derby, among others. Some English collectors even prefer the products of their own particular counties: Inhabitants of Staffordshire buy Staffordshire porcelain; inhabitants of Yorkshire buy Yorkshire. Yet Sèvres, the finest French porcelain, sells better—and at higher prices—in the United States than in France.

The most highly valued European porcelain, with a strong international market, is German, especially pieces from the famous Meissen factory; and Belgian, especially Tournai. By contrast, the least appreciated and understood porcelain is Italian. For that very reason, it's also the best bargain.

Large Services

Because fewer people today have any use for large, elaborate dinner services, they are often broken up and auctioned as separate items. Breaking up a service of porcelain is a crime. It's also senseless. Items are considerably cheaper per item when they're bought in a set than when they're bought individually. A sixty-piece Chelsea service was sold at the Garbisch auction in 1980 for $16,000. That works out to about $250 per

Derby. Chestnut basket, cover and stand. c. 1765. Porcelain. Height: 7″, length 10″. Courtesy Earle D. Vandekar of Knightsbridge Incorporated, New York.

piece, or *half* what the items would have brought if they had been sold separately.

If you have little practical use for a sixty-piece service, buy it anyway. Large services were always intended primarily to be displayed, not used.

Where to Buy European Porcelain

California

Earle D. Vandekar of Knightsbridge, Inc.
8485 Melrose Place
Los Angeles, California 90069

New York

À La Vieille Russie, Inc.
781 Fifth Avenue
New York, New York 10022

The Antique Porcelain
  Company
48 East 57th Street
New York, New York 10022

La Ganke & Co.
1093 Second Avenue
New York, New York 10022

D. M. & P. Manheim Antiques Corp.
c/o Miss Milicent Manheim
20 East 68th Street
New York, New York 10021

Philip Suval, Inc.
17 East 64th Street
New York, New York 10021

Earle D. Vandekar of
  Knightsbridge, Inc.
1166 Second Avenue
New York, New York 10021

Pennsylvania

Mathew & Elisabeth Sharpe
The Spring Mill Antique Shop
Spring Mill
Conshohocken, Pennsylvania
19428

For More Information

Rollo Charles Ernest Benn Ltd., *Continental Porcelain of the 18th Century* (Toronto: University of Toronto Press, 1964).

Warren E. Cox, *The Book of Pottery and Porcelain,* 2 volumes, revised edition (New York: Crown Publishers, 1970).

H. D. Eberlein and R. W. Ramsdell, *The Practical Book of Chinaware,* revised edition (Philadelphia: J. B. Lippincott, 1948).

Geoffrey A. Goddens, *Goddens Guide to English Porcelain* (New York: Granada Publishing, 1978).

William B. Honey, *Dresden China: An Introduction to the Study of Meissen Porcelain* (New York: Tudor Publishing Co., 1946).

W. B. Honey, *Old English Porcelain: A Handbook for Collectors* (New York: Whittlesley House, n.d.).

Maria Penkola, *European Porcelain* (Rutland, Vt.: Charles E. Tuttle, 1968).

Henry Sandon, *The Illustrated Guide to Worcester Porcelain: 1751–1793* (New York: Praeger Publishers, 1969).

George Savage, *18th-Century German Porcelain* (London: Spring Books, 1958).

For more specialized books on English porcelains, the reader is encouraged to look at the other books of Geoffrey A. Goddens as well as the books of John Twitchett.

GLASS AND POTTERY

The recent renaissance of Art Nouveau and Art Deco has had a dramatic effect on two art forms favored by Art-Nouveau and Art-Deco artists: glass and pottery. In a recent eighteen-month period, similar leaded-glass lamps by Louis Comfort Tiffany, the American Art-Nouveau master, sold for $60,000, then $150,000, and finally $360,000—a phenomenal rise even by art-world standards.

If you still want to collect Tiffany glass, it should come as a relief that other examples sell for considerably less. The prices quoted above were

Louis Comfort Tiffany. Spiderweb leaded glass, mosaic, and bronze table lamp.
Height: 33″, diameter of shade: 20″. Courtesy Christie's, New York.

paid for relatively rare works by Tiffany: "Spider Web" table lamps made of leaded glass, mosaic, and bronze. By contrast, a floor lamp with an iridescent yellow glass shade might sell for as little as $1,500.

European Glass Masters

Among the greatest Art-Deco masters in Europe was René Lalique, known for his work in pressed glass and *cire-perdu*. Not long ago, a cire-perdu cougar made by Lalique about 1910 sold for the record price of $39,000. You should be aware, however, that during the past year the record prices coaxed a wave of Lalique works onto the market, creating a glut that actually lowered their prices by about 20 percent.

If European Art-Nouveau and Art-Deco glass interests you, you'll want to examine Cameo glass by Émile Gallé, Daum, and Muller Frères and pâte-de-verre glass by Francis Décorchemont, Georges Despret, Gabriel

René Lalique. *Tulipes*. Luminaire made of clear and frosted glass set in an electrified, chrome-plated base. Length: 18½″. Courtesy Christie's, New York.

Argy-Rousseau, and Almaric V. Walter. Although a major piece by Gallé fetched $275,000 at Christie's in 1980, excellent works by these masters can be purchased for between $1,000 and $25,000.

American Art Glass

If the prices of glass by Tiffany and the other Art-Nouveau and Art-Deco masters are about to scare you away, don't let them. With a relatively small investment, a beginning collector can assemble a fine collection of American art glass. Fashioned after early nineteenth-century British models, the finest examples of this highly decorated ornamental glass work were created in the United States between 1880 and 1900—not just by Tiffany, but by a wide range of manufacturers. Art glass is extremely varied and beautiful—ranging from incised Cameo glass and multilayered Cased glass to painted and gilded glass.

Recommended Manufacturers. Here are the major manufacturers to look for:

Boston & Sandwich Glass Company
   Established in 1825, Sandwich, Massachusetts

Durand Art Glass
   Established in 1924, Vineland, New Jersey

Hobbs, Brockunier & Company
   Established in 1820, Wheeling, West Virginia

Libbey Glass Company
   Established in 1888, Toledo, Ohio

Mt. Washington Glass Works
   Established in 1837, New Bedford, Massachusetts

New England Glass Company
   Established in 1814, East Cambridge, Massachusetts

Quezal Art Glass and Decorating Company
   Established in 1901, Maspeth, New York

Smith Brothers
   Established in 1876, New Bedford, Massachusetts

Steuben Glass Works
   Established in 1903, Corning, New York

Louis Comfort Tiffany
   Established in 1848, New York, New York

Edward T. Hurvey, Rookwood Pottery, Cincinnatti, Ohio. Earthenware vase with vellum glaze. Height: 12½″, diameter: 6⅜″. Photograph by Scott Hyde. Courtesy Jordan-Volpe Gallery, New York.

Union Glass Company
 Established in 1854, Somerville, Massachusetts

American Art Pottery

American art pottery also remains a good bargain even though some of the finest pieces, especially works from the Rookwood Pottery in Cincinnati, bring prices in the tens of thousands. Like American art glass, American art pottery is based on British models. The early examples were generally created by amateurs, most of them women. Many of these amateur pottery groups turned into professional businesses. Between 1870 and 1920, there were 118 potteries operating throughout the United States but clustered in California, Massachusetts, New York, and Ohio. Some of these potteries continued to operate after 1920, and although the later pieces are not as good as the earlier ones, they're much less expensive.

Soaring Pottery Prices. Like the prices of glass, pottery prices have risen at an astonishing rate. A decade ago, you could have purchased the finest examples of American pottery for several hundred dollars. Not long ago, an earthenware vase decorated with the bust of a Sioux Indian made at the famous Rookwood Pottery of Cincinnati sold for $32,000. (Todd Volpe of Jordan/Volpe in New York calls Rookwood the Rolls-Royce of American art pottery.) But, once again, the major price increases have affected only the showiest pieces. Many examples of American pottery, even Rookwood, are still available for between $250 and $700.

Recommended Manufacturers. If Rookwood is generally too expensive, which other American art potteries should you look for? Todd Volpe offers the following suggestions: "With Grueby, pay attention to the form and design. If it's a cucumber- or squash-like piece, make sure it really achieves the texture and color of the vegetable. Weller is another name that comes up at sales—it was a commercial art-pottery factory, the designs mass-produced and copied from other potters. Sicard, one of the Weller potters, is very well-known for his iridescent glazes." Other American art potteries to note: Dedham, Newcomb, and Van Briggle.

American Stoneware

American decorated stoneware, made from about 1720 through 1895, is also a good buy. These strong, simple vessels are of two kinds: the first and earlier style is decorated with incised designs; the second is decorated with painted designs. The record price for a stoneware vessel is $2,500, paid for a very early piece, signed and dated 1806. According to Boston

Grueby Pottery, Boston, Massachusetts. Earthenware vase with matte glaze. c. 1899. Height: 15½", diameter 8". Courtesy Jordan-Volpe Gallery, New York.

dealer and collector Terry Vose, other excellent pieces continue to be available for between $250 and $300. These works could have been purchased a few decades ago for $2 or $3. But don't let that discourage you. The prices can only go up.

Where to Buy Glass and Pottery

Florida

Grover Antiques
744 21st Avenue, South
Naples, Florida 33940

Indiana

Opal Sallee
11208 Crestview Boulevard
Kokomo, Indiana 46901

New York

Gem Antiques
1088 Madison Avenue
New York, New York 10028

Jordan/Volpe
457 West Broadway
New York, New York 10012

Leo Kaplan Antiques
910 Madison Avenue
New York, New York 10021

Simon Lieberman Ltd.
985 Madison Avenue
New York, New York 10021

Macklowe Gallery
982 Madison Avenue
New York, New York 10021

Lillian Nassau Ltd.
220 East 57th Street
New York, New York 10022

Minna Rosenblatt Ltd.
816 Madison Avenue
New York, New York 10021

Pascoe & Solomon, Inc.
1122 Madison Avenue
New York, New York 10028

George E. Schoellkopf
1065 Madison Avenue
New York, New York 10028

D. Leonard & Gerry Trent
950 Madison Avenue
New York, New York 10021

West Virginia

Newcomer/Westreich
1200 Washington Street
Harper's Ferry, West Virginia
25425

For More Information

Victor Arwas, *Glass: Art Nouveau to Art Deco* (New York: Rizzoli International Publications, 1977).

Henry Blount and Berenice Blount, *French Cameo Glass* (Des Moines, Iowa: Wallace-Homestead Book Co., n.d.).

Robert J. Clark, ed., *The Arts and Crafts Movement in America* (Princeton, N.J.: Princeton University Art Museum, 1972).

Egon Neustadt, *The Lamps of Tiffany* (New York: Fairfield Press, 1980).

Paul Evans, *Art Pottery of the United States* (New York: Charles Scribner's Sons, 1974).

Ray and Lee Grover, *Art Glass Nouveau* (Rutland, Vt.: Charles E. Tuttle, 1967).

Ray and Lee Grover, *Carved and Decorated European Glass* (Rutland, Vt.: Charles E. Tuttle, 1970).

Robert Koch, *Louis C. Tiffany: Rebel in Glass,* revised edition (New York: Crown Publishers, 1964).

Ralph and Terry Kovel, *Kovel's Collector's Guide to American Art Pottery* (New York: Crown Publishers, 1974).

Herbert Peck, *The Book of Rookwood Pottery* (Sparks, Nev.: Bonanza, 1968).

Albert Christian Revi, *American Art Nouveau Glass* (Nashville, Tenn.: Thomas Nelson, Inc., 1968).

ANTIQUITIES

Antiquities are exciting to own not only for their beauty but also for their age. They are windows on distant times and places. And best of all, they are surprisingly inexpensive. The prices for antiquities are, by and large, lower than for more recent works of comparable quality. A Roman glass bowl brought $1,900,000 in 1974. That was a large sum, of course, but small by comparison to prices paid for the best paintings by the old masters and Impressionists. The very finest ancient fabric currently available on the market—a large Peruvian Chimu piece in superb condition—is priced at only $65,000, much less, for example, than the amounts regularly charged for works by the contemporary Photorealist artist, Richard Estes.

The World at Your Hands. The range of antiquities is as wide as the world is large. There are ancient Greek pottery, Roman sculptures, and Peruvian textiles, all underpriced at present. You can buy a first-rate Peruvian textile for $3,000. A good small Egyptian figurine might go for as

Roman. Figure of Venus of
Anadyonene. c. 2nd century A.D.
Bronze. Height: 5½". Courtesy
Christie's, New York.

little as $1,000. A Greek terra cotta statuette from the fourth century B.C. might run between $500 and $1,000. A good small Roman bronze might be purchased for as little as $2,000. Hellenistic Greek vases from the south of Italy are frequently available for much less. None of these is a small sum. But just imagine what you get for your money: not just the joy of looking at beautiful objects, but also the joy of looking at objects that have been looked at for two millennia or more.

Fabrics and Fragments

Of course, the wise collector only wants to collect objects of the very finest quality. Edward H. Merrin, the New York dealer, suggests that the budget-conscious collector in search of museum-caliber antiquities investigate two areas: fabrics and fragments. "Fabrics," Merrin says, "are among the great bargains. You can find objects of a 1,000 years' age and of great artistic merit with relatively little investment. Excellent examples can be purchased for between $3,000 and $5,000." Merrin also recommends that the collector consider sculpture fragments: "For example, you could buy a fragment of a Ptolemaic relief, with almost the entire head, for less than $3,500. And the amount would buy you an object of great quality."

Where to Buy Antiquities

California

Stendahl Galleries
7055-65 Hillside Avenue
Los Angeles, California 90068

New York

André Emmerich Gallery Inc.
41 East 57th Street
New York, New York 10022

Edward H. Merrin Gallery, Inc.
724 Fifth Avenue
New York, New York 10019

Mathias Komor
19 East 71st Street
New York, New York 10021

John Wise Ltd.
15 East 69th Street
New York, New York 10021

For More Information

Ranuccio Bianchi-Bandinelli, *Rome: The Center of Power* (New York: Braziller, 1970).

Left, Egyptian, Middle Kingdom, 11th or 12th Dynasty. Relief fragment. c. 2133–1786 B.C. Limestone. 11½ x 12½". Courtesy Christie's, New York.

Below, Chavin culture, Peru. c. 1000-600 B.C. Textile. 37½ x 23½". Courtesy Edward H. Merrin Gallery, New York.

Yuan Dynasty. Wine ewer. Early 14th century. Porcelain. Height: 13¼″. Courtesy Christie's, New York.

Ranuccio Bianchi-Bandinelli, *Rome: The Late Empire*, A.D. *200–400* (New York: Braziller, 1971).

Miguel Covarrubias, *Indian Art of Mexico and Central America* (New York: Alfred A. Knopf, 1957).

Elizabeth Kennedy Easby and John F. Scott, *Before Cortes,* introduction by Thomas P. F. Hoving (New York: Metropolitan Museum of Art, 1970).

André Emmerich with Lee Bolton, *Art before Columbus* (New York: Simon and Schuster, 1970).

George M. A. Hanfmann, *Roman Art* (Greenwich, Conn.: New York Graphic Society, 1964).

William C. Hayes, *The Scepter of Egypt,* 2 volumes (New York: Harper & Row, 1953–1959).

Alan Lapiner, *Pre-Columbian Art of South America* (New York: Harry N. Abrams Publishing Co., 1976).

Gisela M. A. Richter, *A Handbook of Greek Art,* 6th edition, redesigned (London: Phaidon, 1969).

ORIENTAL ART

Americans are not the only collectors who have shown renewed interest in their own culture. Consider the market for Oriental art. The vast price increases of recent years can be attributed almost entirely to the appearance of rich, patriotic collectors from the East—first the Japanese, then the Chinese. Today, at any important sale of Oriental art, you're certain to see collectors from Tokyo, Taipei, Singapore, and Hong Kong. A dealer in Oriental art was recently quoted as saying, "Nowadays, it all depends on who's got the yen."

Crafts Come First

The market for Oriental art differs from the market for Western art in one significant way: The prizes in Oriental art are "decorative" rather than "fine" arts. Almost as a rule, the highest prices are paid for ceramics, especially ceramics made in China and Japan for imperial use. In 1980, for example, a dealer from Japan and a collector from Singapore bid against each other at Christie's for an early Ming underglaze copper-red dish. The final bid: $423,000. That kind of price is not at all unusual for fine early ceramics, or for early jades and bronzes.

Other Categories.   As these prices have risen beyond the means or even the comprehension of most collectors, other categories of Oriental art have attracted collectors' attention. More recent works—works from the seventeenth through the nineteenth centuries—are now avidly sought after. Twentieth-century works, however, especially recent works from the People's Republic of China, are still viewed with skepticism by dealers and collectors.

Prices are also rising rapidly in the market for other, less fashionable crafts: Chinese lacquer; cloisonné; and objects carved from ivory, wood, bamboo, and stone. Indeed, there is a consensus among dealers that the best bargains in Oriental art can be found in these "secondary" art forms. As in the West, prices are also better in the market for folk art than in the market for the products of more sophisticated urban ateliers. A Chinese woodcarving is generally cheaper than a Chinese porcelain, and a folk woodcarving is cheaper still.

Oriental Painting.   There is a long and fine tradition of painting in the Orient. In fact, even though the prices don't reflect it, painting was considered the highest form of art in the East long before it achieved that status in the West. Paula Gasparello, an expert on Chinese painting at Sotheby's, told *The Collector-Investor* in 1980, "The market is sorting itself out. It is a question of educating people, of establishing prices. In China, painting is a fine art with a long tradition. For the Chinese themselves the painting is the most important art, ceramics are a craft."

Until recently, it was difficult to generate enthusiasm for Oriental painting because good examples came on the market so rarely. According to Derek Gillman, Gasparello's counterpart at Christie's, rarity is becoming less of a problem. Another problem has yet to be resolved, however: the art itself. Oriental painting is both extremely subtle and radically different from Western painting. It is also very difficult to attribute specific Oriental paintings to specific artists. "It's an area distinctly Chinese, not like porcelain," says Dean Schwaab, the Chinese expert at Phillips Auctioneers. "It is very much of Chinese taste. Americans have never had an appetite for it. But certainly the Chinese and Japanese do. It is an area to look into, but it takes more knowledge and more taste to do it wisely."

The Art of Japan

Japanese art has traditionally been less popular than Chinese (although *Shōgun* may change all that). Not only are there fewer examples of Japanese art, that art was made available to Westerners comparatively late. As a result, Western collectors have had less time to develop a taste for it.

One thing the Chinese market and the Japanese market have in common is that the bargains in both can be found in the "secondary" art forms. Richard Wold, an expert at Samuel T. Freeman in Philadelphia, says, "The early, serious Japanese wares are hard to find. But the collector with a sensitive eye can find later ceramics, carvings and cloisonné that are desirable."

Wood-Block Prints. Although fine Chinese and Japanese paintings are relatively esoteric and require considerable amounts of money and expertise, Japanese wood-block prints are surprisingly accessible. These prints were favorites of the Impressionists and Post-Impressionists, who borrowed many of their design principles such as flat areas of color and "snapshot" cropping. For that reason, they're easy on the Western eye. They're also easy on the Western pocketbook. Although a few of the best Japanese wood-block prints cost well over $10,000, many are available for a few hundred. David Bathurst of Christie's is especially enthusiastic about Japanese wood blocks: "At about $1,000 today, many of them aren't overpriced, and an investor might do well."

Chinese Export

Not all Chinese art was made for domestic use; much of it, especially porcelain from the eighteenth and nineteenth centuries, was made exclusively for export to the West. This *export ware* is another favorite among collectors. Chinese export that resembles a work made for domestic use is commonly said to be in the "Chinese taste." An object that emulates European designs is said to be in the European or Western taste. Because there is practically no market for export ware among Eastern collectors, and because so many items have traditionally been available to American collectors, prices for the best pieces are generally lower than for the best pieces of domestic ware. In fact, the cheapest items of Chinese export are very cheap indeed. Colin Sheaf of Christie's notes that "blue-and-white Chinese export patterns are always popular, and there are still lots around for" relatively modest prices.

Lower Cost and *Lower Quality?* Before you go out and invest in a collection of export ware, however, you should know that many people believe there are differences of quality as well as destination. "The pieces intended for Western consumption are called 'decadent' by many collectors," says James Lally, Sotheby's Oriental expert in New York. "The Chinese artisans who made these Export pieces, while they may have produced exquisite works of great beauty, did not care for the elaborate motifs and variety of colors they used with such skill."

Other experts disagree. Horace Gordon of Elinor Gordon in Villanova,

Hokusai. *Travellers Crossing the Fukui Bridge in Echizen Province*. Woodblock print. *Oban yoko-e*. Courtesy Christie's, New York.

Chinese export. Figures holding vases. c. 1765. Porcelain. Height: 11½". Courtesy Earle D. Vandekar of Knightsbridge Incorporated, Los Angeles.

Chinese export. Soup plate with Arms of Baker. c. 1740. Porcelain. Diameter: 9″. Photograph by Barry Korn. Courtesy Earle D. Vandekar of Knightsbridge Incorporated, Los Angeles.

Pennsylvania, recently told *The Collector-Investor:* "Export porcelain was made side-by-side with many of the fine imperial pieces in the same kilns with the same workmen. There are beautiful examples of both and, believe me, there are some very mediocre examples of both." Paul Vandekar, with galleries in Los Angeles and New York, says that it is wrong to compare Chinese export porcelains with porcelains made for the Chinese market: "The export ware has very little to do with Oriental art. The shapes, the designs, and everything else were influenced by western taste. Only the manufacture was Oriental. Whether you prefer one to the other is essentially a matter of taste."

Robert Woolley of Sotheby's says that, given the low prices of export ware, it's a definite bargain: "Chinese export porcelain is going to take off more than it has. In spite of some isolated high prices, you're still buying most things in hundreds of dollars."

Condition

The beginning collector looking for bargains in Oriental art should be aware that, contrary to general principles, pieces in less than optimum condition can sometimes still be good buys. "It is safe to say that the perfect pieces in all areas of Chinese porcelains—both export and imperial—are getting more and more difficult to find," says Allan S. Chait of the Ralph M. Chait Galleries in New York. "As time passes, pieces get broken, fall out of circulation into the hands of museums or simply disappear. There is not room today to be so particular and pristine about cracks and flaws. If you want a rare piece that has great beauty, you may not be able to turn your nose up because of a crack or minor repair."

Where to Buy Oriental Art

California

Stair & Co., Inc.
10900 Wilshire Boulevard
Los Angeles, California 90024

Earle D. Vandekar of
   Knightsbridge, Inc.
8485 Melrose Place
Los Angeles, California 90069

New York

Frank Caro Co.
41 East 57th Street
New York, New York 10022

Ralph M. Chait Galleries, Inc.
12 East 56th Street
New York, New York 10022

R. H. Ellsworth, Ltd.
960 Fifth Avenue
New York, New York 10021

Hartman Rare Art
978 Madison Avenue
New York, New York 10021

Fred B. Nadler Antiques, Inc.
31 East 64th Street
New York, New York 10021

Stair & Co., Inc.
59 East 57th Street
New York, New York 10022

J. T. Tai & Co., Inc.
810 Madison Avenue
New York, New York 10021

Earle D. Vandekar of
   Knightsbridge, Inc.
1166 Second Avenue
New York, New York 10021

Doris Weiner Gallery
41 East 57th Street
New York, New York 10022

Weisbrod & Dy, Ltd.
906 Madison Avenue
New York, New York 10021

William H. Wolff, Inc.
22 East 76th Street
New York, New York 10021

Pennsylvania

Mathew and Elisabeth Sharpe
The Spring Mill Antique Shop
Spring Mill
Conshohocken, Pennsylvania
19428

Elinor Gordon
P. O. Box 211
Villanova, Pennsylvania 19085

For More Information

Carl L. Crossman, *The China Trade* (Princeton, N.J.: Pyne Press, 1972).

Geoffrey A. Goddens, *Oriental Export Market and its Influence on European Wares* (New York: Granada Publishing, 1979).

David S. Howard, *Chinese Armorial Porcelain* (Salem, N.H.: Faber and Faber, 1974).

David Howard and John Ayers, *China for the West,* 2 volumes (London: Sotheby Parke Bernet, 1978).

Sherman E. Lee, *A History of Far Eastern Art,* revised edition (Englewood Cliffs, N.J.: Prentice-Hall, Inc., n.d.)

Daisy Lion-Goldschmidt and Jean-Claude Moreau-Gobard, *Chinese Art, Vol. I* (New York: Rizzoli International Publications, 1980).

R. Soame Jenyns and William Watson, *Chinese Art, Vol. II* (New York: Rizzoli International Publications, 1980).

Robert T. Paine and Alexander Soper, *The Art and Architecture of Japan,* Pelican History of Art, 2nd edition (Baltimore: Penguin Books, 1974).

Benjamin Rowland, *The Art and Architecture of India: Buddhist, Hindu, Jain,* Pelican History of Art, 3rd edition (Baltimore: Penguin Books, 1967).

Lawrence Sickman and Alexander Soper, *The Art and Architecture of China,* Pelican History of Art, 3rd edition (Baltimore: Penguin Books, 1968).

New Guinea. Sepik. Human skull. 19th century. Human skull with mud, paint, and cowrie shells. Courtesy Merton Simpson Gallery, Inc., New York.

PRIMITIVE ART

"Primitive Art" is, in fact, not primitive at all. There's nothing primitive about the emotional impact of an African mask, the sophisticated design of a North American Indian basket, or the careful crafting of a bowl from Micronesia. For many years, experts have wanted to change the name "primitive" to something less derogatory—and more accurate. The trouble is, the alternatives are not much better: "Third World" is too unspecific; "ethnic," too vague. So we're stuck with "primitive."

Modern artists were among the first Westerners to help us appreciate the artistic value of "primitive" art. Since the beginning of the twentieth century, modern masters such as Braque, Brancusi, Matisse, Modigliani, and Picasso have admired African art, collected it enthusiastically, and even incorporated its elements into their own work. Picasso praised one African sculpture as "more beautiful than the Venus de Milo."

The Market for Primitive Art

During the past decade, the prices for first-rate works of primitive art have soared. In 1979, for example, a fifteen-inch figure made by a master carver of the Tshowke people of Angola was sold at auction for the astounding price of $506,000. Soon thereafter, a Dutch collector sold twenty-four pieces from the kingdom of Benin, which once ruled a large part of present-day Nigeria, for $1,750,000. One of the objects, a fifteenth-century bronze head of an *oba,* or king, which the collector had bought twenty-five years earlier for $900, brought $470,000.

Exceptional examples of oceanic art also fetch high prices today. An Island drum supposedly used during ritual human sacrifices recently sold for $446,500. American Indian art is also gaining ground in the art market, although it has not yet caught up with African or Oceanic work. The auction record is still held by a copper and sheep's-horn dagger made by the Tlingit Indians of the Pacific Northwest region which sold for $72,000.

Difficult to Predict. If these prices are about to scare you away, don't let them. For one thing, the market for primitive art is even harder to predict than the market for Western art. It has been generally strong over the last few years. Nevertheless, at a recent auction, 189 out of 276 lots failed to sell. Even the objects that sold went for unexpectedly low prices.

Despite the occasional high prices, most primitive objects remain underpriced. That Tshowke ancestry figure may have sold for more than $500,000, but you can still buy a superb African mask for between $5,000 and $10,000. You can even buy a moderately good mask for less than

Northwest Coast. Tlingit. Raven mask. 19th century. Wood with copper strips. 6½" x 8". Courtesy Merton Simpson Gallery, Inc., New York.

$2,500: less, that is, than a moderately good *print* by a contemporary master. Indeed, one of the advantages of collecting primitive art is that the finest examples can be acquired for much less than comparable examples of Western art.

Good, Right, and Old

What factors should you consider in collecting primitive art? Most dealers agree that there are three basic questions: Is it good? Is it right? And is it old?

First, Is It Good?   As with any kind of art, it takes time to learn the subtle distinctions between one work and another. At first, it may seem as if they all look more or less alike. If you look more carefully, however, you'll soon see that some pieces are far better proportioned, designed, and crafted than others. Some pieces will stand out immediately as bland, hackneyed, or clumsy. Perhaps the object was made by an apprentice

Zuni Pueblo, New Mexico. Water jar. c. late 19th century. Pottery. Height: 12″.
Courtesy Pueblo One Indian Arts, Scottsdale, Arizona.

Gabon. Fang. Reliquary figure. Late 19th century. Wood. Height: 17″. Private collection. Photograph by Malcolm Varon. Courtesy The Pace Gallery of New York, Inc.

craftsman rather than by a master. Perhaps it was made by a master on a bad day. Whatever the case, in primitive art, as in all art, quality is the first consideration.

Second, Is It **Right?**   With few exceptions, there was no "art for art's sake" in Third-World cultures. Art was made to serve a purpose, whether it was religious, political, or military. Although many objects, like African masks, no longer serve a purpose, craftsmen have continued to make them for sale to Western collectors. These objects are considered "artificial" because they weren't created to serve the purpose they *appear* to serve: masks never worn, sacrificial figures never used in a religious ceremony, weapons never taken to war. Collectors are particularly suspicious of objects that have been adapted to Western purposes such as Eskimo ivory cribbage boards. The only notable exceptions are Navajo rugs that were never used to cover Navajo floors.

Finally, Is It **Old?**   What really matters isn't the chronological age of a piece but whether or not the piece is "pre-contact." Was the object made before the "primitive" society was contaminated by contact with other cultures? "What you look for," says Norman Hurst of Te Paske & Hurst in Cambridge, Massachusetts, "is pre-contact, but that is relative. It depends on how much the contact shocked the culture out of its primitive ways." Oceanic art is generally pre-contact if it was made before 1880. African art remained pre-contact until the first decades of this century.

Tourist Carvings.   In collecting primitive art, the most important things to avoid are recent carvings made for the tourist trade. Occasionally, these objects are sent briefly to a village to serve in a dance and acquire some patina of authenticity. More often, they travel directly from the carver to the merchant to you. You see them—bland, stiff, empty, often ridiculously ugly—at airports, hotel shops, and street carts in Third-World countries and at curio stores in the West. Some examples of tourist art are better than others—the carved-wood antelope headdresses from Mali, for example—but all of it should be avoided by the serious collector.

Fakes.   Much more difficult to detect than tourist art is an outright fake. As the supply of primitive works has dwindled and the demand has risen, skilled craftsmen have begun to copy primitive works of museum quality. They bury the objects in mud or rub them with sand to simulate age and wear, then market them—convincingly—as authentic pieces. Despite the special problem of fakes, however, I encourage you to consider collecting primitive art. Simply take a few precautions: Stay out of curio shops, deal only with responsible dealers, and work to educate your own eye.

Where to Buy Primitive Art

Arizona

Pueblo One
3815 North Brown Avenue
Scottsdale, Arizona 85251

California

Harry A. Franklin Gallery
9601 Wilshire Boulevard
Beverly Hills, California 90210

James Willis Gallery
109 Geary at Grant
San Francisco, California 94108

Illinois

Linda Einfeld
620 North Michigan Avenue
Chicago, Illinois 60611

The Indian Tree
223 East Ontario Street
Suite 201
Chicago, Illinois 60611

Michigan

Donald Morris Gallery, Inc.
105 Townsend
Birmingham, Michigan 48011

Missouri

Alexander-Suggs Gallery, Inc.
6330 South Rosebury
St. Louis, Missouri 63105

New Mexico

Dewey/Kofron Gallery
112 East Palace Avenue
Santa Fe, New Mexico 87501

New York

Alan Brandt, Inc.
44 West 77th Street
New York, New York 10024

J. Camp Associates, Ltd.
380 West Broadway
New York, New York 10012

Ben Heller Inc.
121 East 72nd Street
New York, New York 10021

L. Kahan Gallery Inc.
48 East 57th Street
New York, New York 10022

Michael Oliver, Inc.
22 East 72nd Street
New York, New York 10021

Merton D. Simpson Gallery
Inc.
1063 Madison Avenue
New York, New York 10028

Pace Primitive
32 East 57th Street
New York, New York 10022

F. Rolin & Co. Inc.
1000 Madison Avenue
New York, New York 10021

George Terasaki
10 East 67th Street
New York, New York 10021

Texas

Shango Gallery
2606 Fairmount Street
Dallas, Texas 75201

For More Information

Ferdinand Anton, Frederick J. Dockstader, Margaret Trowell, and Hans Nevermann, *Primitive Art: Pre-Columbian/North American Indian/African/Oceanic* (New York: Harry N. Abrams, Inc., Publishers, 1979).

Ralph T. Coe, *Sacred Circles: Two Thousand Years of North American Indian Art* (London: Arts Council of Great Britain, 1976).

William Fagg, *African Tribal Images* (Cleveland: Cleveland Museum of Art, 1968).

William Fagg and Margaret Plass, *African Sculpture: An Anthology* (New York: E. P. Dutton, 1966).

Peter Gathercole, Adrienne L. Kaeppler, and Douglas Newton, *The Art of the Pacific Islands* (Washington, D.C.: National Gallery of Art, 1979).

Werner Gillon, *Collecting African Art,* introduction by William Fagg (New York: Rizzoli International Publications, 1979).

Evan Maurer, *The Native American Heritage: A Survey of North American Indian Art* (Chicago: Art Institute of Chicago, 1977).

Robert Farris Thompson, *African Art in Motion: Icon and Act,* introduc-

tion by Katherine Coryton White (Los Angeles: University of California, 1974).

Margaret Trowell, *Classical African Sculpture* (New York: Praeger Publishers, 1970).

Susan Vogel, ed., *For Spirits and Kings,* translated by Kate Ezra (New
York: Metropolitan Museum of Art, 1981).

Whitney Museum of American Art, *Two Hundred Years of North American Indian Art,* text by Norman Feder (New York: Praeger Publishers,
1971).

Frank Willett, *African Art: An Introduction* (New York: Praeger Publishers, 1971).

What Not to Collect

Now that you know what to buy, here is some advice on what *not* to buy. Because a complete listing of things to avoid would fill several books, this chapter focuses on the three main culprits: reproductions, limited-edition art, and schlock art. Most of this so-called "art" isn't worthy of the name. And, like all bad art, it's also a bad investment.

REPRODUCTIONS

If you can't afford to buy a real museum masterpiece (and who can?), why not buy a photographic reproduction of a museum masterpiece?

Until recently, no true "collector" would have considered substituting a reproduction, no matter how great the work, for an original, no matter how modest. During the past decade, however, some of the nation's most prominent museums and collectors began to market high-class art reproductions to would-be collectors, arguing that they were performing a valuable service in making great art available to the public at low prices. Suddenly, reproductions were respectable.

Not for long. Rising sales of reproductions were greeted throughout the art world with cries of outrage. The copies, they said, were rip-offs: bad art, bad investments, even bad copies. Where does the truth lie? Do reproductions serve a noble purpose, making great art available at modest prices? Or, as their critics claim, do they trick the ignorant into paying too much money for too little art? Should you ever consider buying a reproduction for your own collection?

The Met Becomes a Market

When eminent art institutions such as the Metropolitan Museum of Art in New York began selling reproductions, it was for one simple reason: money. With rising expenses and dwindling stock revenues, museum directors had to turn *somewhere* for more income. Trend setters like Thomas Hoving, former director at the Met, decided that reproductions were the answer. In a sense, they were: The Met now derives much of its annual revenues from its salesroom. If reproductions make great art available to the masses, it's only by helping museums make enough money to keep their doors open.

The row over reproductions came to a head some time after Hoving left the director's office at the Metropolitan. He was so successful at making money for the museum, he decided to make some for himself. In 1978, Hoving exploited his credibility as director emeritus of the nation's largest museum to promote the sale of a "limited edition" reproduction of Andrew Wyeth's *The Quaker*. Hoving asked prospective buyers to become "original owners" of the Wyeth reproduction, implying to the careless or the naïve that they would become owners of an original Wyeth.

Hoving soon entered into even muddier waters. At $155 for the framed picture, he said he found it "impossible to imagine" that the Wyeth reproduction "will not prove to be a sensible investment." Anyone who markets a reproduction hopes that the investment mystique of original works of art will somehow rub off on the reproductions themselves—that customers will assume reproductions, like original works, will appreciate. Hoving all but promised it.

The Nelson Rockefeller Collection

In 1978, Nelson Rockefeller also got into the reproduction racket. The former Vice President demonstrated the family entrepreneurial touch by making the Nelson Rockefeller Collection, Inc., big business. He invested $4,000,000 in the project, selecting 118 of his own works to be reproduced. The objects ranged in price from $35 to $7,500 and were to be sold both through a fancy showroom on Fifty-seventh Street in New York and by mail, through an elegant catalogue.

Rockefeller spared no effort or expense in locating the best craftsmen and most advanced technology to reproduce objects such as Picasso's *Girl with Mandolin,* a medieval bronze sculpture from Benin, and a set of Meissen porcelain. He also showed admirable discretion in reproducing works only with the express permission of the artists or their estates, as well as generosity in paying a royalty of 5 percent on all sales.

In addition, Rockefeller made it perfectly clear that he was dealing in reproductions, not in original works of art. When Albert Elsen, the Rodin expert, complained that the identification marks on the Rodin reproductions were "too small, not readily visible, and easily eradicable," Rockefeller offered to explore ways to identify the works more clearly. From the beginning, he made no claims whatsoever about the investment value of his merchandise. Still, when critics of the new high-class reproductions mounted their attack, Rockefeller stood in the line of fire.

The Attack on Reproductions

Robert Hughes rebuked Rockefeller with devastating eloquence on the pages of *Time* magazine. Hughes noted that the former governor claimed to have started the Nelson Rockefeller Collection because "Happy and I decided to share with others our joy in living with these beautiful objects and the thrills we have experienced collecting them." Hughes didn't buy this for a moment. "It's frankly a business proposition," Hughes wrote. "We share our art with you; you share your money with us."

The Art Dealers Association issued a more formal statement attacking all those who sold reproductions as works of art, making Rockefeller the main butt of its attack. The ADA argued that "knowledgeable art buyers" wouldn't be taken in by the sham. Instead, "the sale targets are those unsophisticated about art and so unlikely to know that the Rockefeller reproductions are not works of fine art, have no intrinsic esthetic worth and have little or no resale value."

Reproductions are obviously good for the museums and dealers who sell them. But are they good for you?

Reproductions (Almost) Never Look Like the Real Thing

Some reproductions *are* better than others. The Nelson Rockefeller Collection takes more care—and charges more money—than most of its competitors. In reproducing paintings, for example, the collection starts with photographs made using the most technically advanced Cibachrome process. Scottish craftsmen then "texturize" the surfaces of the photographs to give them the look and feel of brushstrokes. Texturizing surfaces is nothing new, of course. In the past, however, it always meant covering photographic reproductions of paintings with a random layer of fake, see-through plastic brushstrokes. The Rockefeller innovation has been to make the transparent plastic overlay conform generally to the contours of the brushstrokes in the original painting.

All this effort has gone very much to waste. When you pay $850 for a reproduction of Picasso's *Girl with Mandolin* in the Nelson Rockefeller Collection, you still get only a photograph of a painting, one that is little more convincing than the run-of-the-mill photographic reproductions that you bought to decorate your college dormitory room at a fraction of the cost.

Paintings, Drawings, Prints. Some art forms reproduce better than others. For obvious reasons, large paintings with rich colors and complicated brushwork reproduce the worst. Small black-and-white-drawings or prints on paper reproduce much better. In fact, photomechanical reproductions of etchings and engravings made during the nineteenth century can fool all but the most educated eye.

Sculptures. Sculptures, too, can be reproduced more successfully than paintings. But the degree of success depends on the kind of sculpture involved. Wood carvings are either carved by hand, in which case they don't look like the original, or else they are molded in plastic, in which case they don't look *or* feel like the original. Some sculptures are supposed to be touched, something you should avoid when you visit a museum but should feel free to do when you own the sculpture yourself. Touch the polymer resin copy of a Japanese wood carving in the Rockefeller Collection and you'll discover it has none of the surface quality— none of the "feel"—of the original.

By contrast, reproduction bronze casts can be extremely close to the original; after all, they're made from the original bronze material using the original casting process. Nevertheless, reproduction bronzes are often cast from an original bronze, rather than from the plaster or wax model that the sculptor used to cast the original.

What difference does it make? Art historians and connoisseurs call these casts from other casts *surmoulages.* The surest way to tell a surmoulage from an original cast is to compare the size: A surmoulage is always slightly larger than the original sculpture. But an expert doesn't have to go to the trouble of taking measurements. He can distinguish the true from the false by quality alone: No surmoulage can achieve the delicacy or detail of the original. Although the difference is generally more subtle, experts can even identify a reproduction bronze that's been cast from the sculptor's own model. The *patina,* or color, of the bronze is never the same as the original.

Objects. The most successful reproductions are reproductions of ceramics, silver, crystal, and other objects *intended* to be produced in large numbers by careful craftsmen. Rockefeller's *Girl with Mandolin* looks nothing like a real painting; but his Meissen plates are very close to the real thing.

Even when reproductions are at their best, however, even when they're all but indistinguishable from the original, there are still compelling reasons to avoid them.

Reproductions Are Expensive

The alleged justification behind reproductions is that they make great art available at low prices. As we've seen, reproductions are *not* great art. They're not cheap, either. Reproductions may be cheaper than originals, but the difference in price is never great enough to warrant the loss of quality and authenticity. The Rockefeller reproductions cost as much as $7,500—the price for his copy of Rodin's *Age of Bronze*. That's not cheap by anyone's standard, even a Rockefeller's.

Why Not Buy an Original Instead?

For $7,500, you can buy the reproduction of Rodin's *Age of Bronze,* or you can buy several unique works by young sculptors: a collection of originals for the price of one reproduction. John Tancock, an officer of Sotheby Parke Bernet and a Rodin expert, points out that for $7,500 you can purchase an *original* Rodin. It won't be the *Age of Bronze,* but it will be a work cast under the artist's supervision from the artist's own wax or plaster model and not from another cast.

Reproductions Have Little or No Investment Value

The high price of a good reproduction would be *somewhat* justified if it had investment value, which it doesn't. Spend $7,500 for a Rodin reproduction and a decade from now it may not even be worth what you paid for it.

The Whole Enterprise Is Wrongheaded

What if you can't tell the difference between a good reproduction and an original? What if you don't *care* what the reproduction costs, or what a poor investment it is? Buying a reproduction is still wrongheaded. It's simply wasteful to put that much time, energy, talent, and money into reproducing works of art that already exist when the same resources could be invested in creating new ones.

LIMITED-EDITION ART

In recent years, several manufacturers have capitalized on the collecting craze by issuing "limited" editions of art objects: porcelain birds and figurines, Christmas plates, religious and commemorative medals, presidential plaques, coins in silver and gold, and anything else collectors can be persuaded to buy. The limited-edition art market has grown so vast it now overshadows the market for serious art. Hundreds of thousands of these objects are manufactured and marketed each year, promoted by full-color advertisements touting their high esthetic quality and investment potential.

Beware. Most limited-edition art is not art and has little investment potential.

Sentimental Curiosities, Not True Art. Limited-edition art is just plain bad art: both in subject and in form.

The subjects are often ludicrous. For example, Franklin Mint, the General Motors of limited-edition art, markets a series of porcelain bells commemorating the official flowers of all fifty states. The tiny bells come in a "complimentary" wooden display box you can mount on your wall that looks even worse than the bells themselves.

Limited edition artists are also particularly fond of "adorable" subjects: teary-eyed clowns, cherubic children, cavorting lovers, and, of course, animals and birds—especially birds. In addition, there are coins commemorating presidential inaugurations that will never be traded and leather-bound books that will never be read.

But subject matter isn't the only problem. Most limited-edition art objects are ugly. Carefully shaped to the tastes and whims of a mass market, most of them have less spontaneity and genuine esthetic merit than a television commercial. And they certainly lack the latter's entertainment value and redeeming cleverness.

Reese Palley and Edward Marshall Boehm: Merchants of Limited-Edition Art

In their more candid moments, even some of the people who make and sell limited edition art admit how bad most of it is.

Reese Palley. The most aggressive and successful salesman of limited-edition art is undoubtedly Reese Palley, who markets it from showrooms in Atlantic City, San Francisco, and Paris. Palley once tried to make a go of selling serious art but found that he didn't have the knack. He once bought and sold a portrait only to discover afterwards that it was by Raphael. You can't make mistakes like that and remain in the serious art business for long. Palley eventually liquidated his stock of paintings and sculptures and started trading in limited editions instead. He's candid about his fall from grace: "If I had any sensibility or good taste," he once told reporters, "I'd be embarrassed. To hell with that."

Edward Marshall Boehm. If Reese Palley is limited edition art's most accomplished merchant, Edward Marshall Boehm is its most accomplished manufacturer. Boehm (pronounced "Beem") is known primarily for his porcelain birds, referred to in the trade as Boehm Birds.

Boehm, who opened his firm in Trenton, New Jersey, in 1949, got his start with shamelessly sentimental subjects: angels, madonnas, and Beau Brummel figurines. But his real interests lay elsewhere. As soon as his business got under way, Boehm indulged his passion for animals by breeding an assortment of tropical fish, insects, race horses, chimpanzees, otters, schnauzers, and prize Holsteins. He also built an aviary for the starlings, bluebirds, greenbuls, magpies, and birds of paradise that he collected during his extensive travels. Gradually, Boehm restricted his porcelain designs to the animals and birds he loved so much. His products range from a tiny titmouse to the enormous pair of swans that Richard Nixon presented to the People's Republic of China.

It's not difficult to see why Boehm birds have inspired such a large and loyal following. Boehm (who designs all the figurines himself), and the hundreds of artisans who cast, fire, and paint the objects are unquestionably skilled at their various crafts. Boehm birds are well-made, educational, and, occasionally, pleasing to the eye. But they are not great art. A Noah's contingent of birds and animals have found their way into porcelain immortality under Boehm's careful supervision. But the figurines have too little vitality or formal variation to sustain a serious collector's interest. They capture the variety of the animal kingdom, perhaps, but not the expressive potential of art.

Little or No Investment Potential

In most cases, the investment potential of limited-edition art is nil. The problem is that the word "limited," like the word "art," is often used very loosely. The editions are limited, all right—to the number of people who *want* them.

Not Really Limited. For example, Franklin Porcelain recently issued a "firmly limited edition" of *The American Goldfinch* by "artist" Peter Barrett. (The yellow-winged bird in the figurine rests on a bell, which means that the people at the Franklin Mint must have sold a lot of official state flowers.) The edition was limited first to one per customer. Second, "the total edition" was "limited forever to the exact number of individuals who order the songbird bells by the closing of the issuing year." In other words, the company sent out the publicity, counted the orders, *then* set the limit. It could have been fifty—or fifty thousand. In cases like this, the numbers can be so high that the word "limited" loses all real meaning.

There are, of course, two main reasons to limit an edition. First, it allows the objects in the edition to be checked more carefully for quality. Second, it ensures sufficient rarity to preserve artistic uniqueness and investment value.

Limited-edition manufacturers may check for quality more carefully than Ford Motors, but they generally provide about the same level of artistic uniqueness. The investment value of limited editions is based on the notion that there are people who *want* the objects but can't get them because they are so rare. Obviously, if an item is "limited" to everybody who wants it, its investment value is zero. In short, buying limited-edition art makes no artistic sense and less financial sense.

Some Exceptions.   Some limited editions *are* limited. The molds are broken *before* the manufacturers know how many customers to count on. Of course, they often produce enough examples in the first place to satisfy any conceivable demand. Occasionally, however, the limits do ensure meaningful rarity. For example, Boehm made only fifty copies of the *Fondo Marino,* a 291-part sculpture with coral reed, sea horses, hermit crabs, shells, sea anemones, and several kinds of fish.

When interest in a limited-edition art object is keen (as it generally is with Boehm products), and when the size of the edition is small (as it sometimes is with Boehm products), there may be some investment potential. For example, Boehm sold its first meadowlarks in 1957 at $350 apiece. In 1971, they were selling for $3,200, although price dropped somewhat thereafter.

Still, there is a definite limit to the investment potential of Boehm birds. It bears repeating that the highest prices are paid only for art of the highest quality. In other words, the highest prices will *never* be paid for limited-edition art objects.

SCHLOCK ART

Most of the art galleries in this country don't deal in art at all; they market schlock. Members of the art world refer to them not as art galleries but as art "stores."

What is schlock art? The best way to recognize it is by the subject:

waifs with large eyes; sailboats drifting off into a scarlet sunset; young lovers swooning under a full moon; anything that's cloying or clichéd, sensationalist or sentimental. It's not just the subject matter, however, that makes schlock art schlock. It's also the technique. In fact, much schlock art doesn't even have a subject. But with or without a subject, its colors are either garish or saccharine, its brushwork either splashy or precious.

A Growing Menace

Schlock art is not hard to find. It's in the home departments of most large department stores, in theater and hotel lobbies, in malls and shopping centers, and, more and more often, in special stores devoted to the works of single schlock artists.

Some schlock art is unabashedly commercial. It's made by moonlighting commercial artists, or even worse, factories of destitute art students who employ assembly-line techniques: One "artist" paints the sky, another the waves, and a third the sailboat. The result: truckloads of practically identical works polluting the world at the rate of $60 for a "sofa-sized" picture.

This kind of schlock is offensive to almost everyone and easy to detect. Sometimes, however, schlock art takes subtler, more expensive, more subversive forms. Big-eyed Keene children are schlock, of course. But so are some paintings by the greatest painters who ever held a brush. Be on the lookout for insipid subjects and lazy technique in works of even the best artists. Keep these basic points in mind:

1. *It's Sometimes Hard to Tell Schlock Art from Serious Art.* Peter Paul Rubens could be mistaken for a schlock artist, especially when he painted religious or mythological subjects. The hallmarks of his style are the danger signals of schlock: exaggerated emotions, theatrical brushwork, and bright colors. With a little time and a lot of experience, any collector can make the sometimes subtle distinction between sentiment and sentimentality.

2. *Any Artist Can Have a Bad Day.* At the Fogg Art Museum of Harvard University, two paintings by Claude Monet hang side by side. One, the *Gare St. Lazare,* is among Monet's great masterpieces. The other, a portrait of an old lady with her pet dog, is sentimental enough to serve on the lid of a chocolate sampler. It's hard to believe the painter of the powerful *Gare St. Lazare* created this canine kitsch, but he did.

Consider also the example of Joan Miró, another major artist who had both good and bad days. Miró made great works throughout his career, but he also turned out hundreds of weak ones along the way. His recent prints—especially appealing to uneducated collectors—are of dubious quality. Unless you know what you're doing, it's probably wise to avoid Miró prints altogether.

3. *Some Artists Go Downhill.*   It is common wisdom that money and success tend to undermine an artist's integrity. Supposedly, the successful artist stops painting for himself and starts painting for the market. The result is high-class schlock.

In fact, few artists are hurt by success. Henri Matisse, for example, who achieved critical recognition and financial security early in his long life, painted some of his greatest works literally on his death bed. The fact remains, however, that success *did* destroy several prominent twentieth-century artists. The most important examples—and the saddest—are Marc Chagall, Giorgio de Chirico, Salvador Dali, and Victor Vasarely. Each artist, after an important early career, failed to fulfill the promise of his youth. Each began to rework earlier ideas in increasingly boring works.

4. *Schlock Art Doesn't Have to Be New.*   Schlock art is as old as the entrepreneurial spirit. According to the British art historian Herbert Read, the first artist to cultivate a mass market—and the first to pay the price of popularity—was William Hogarth, the eighteenth-century British satirist. Read says that all of Hogarth's work is "vigorous, lively, mordant and full of wit." But there are times when "the satire is apt to be too obvious, the symbolism quite commonplace, the moral without wit or subtlety."

5. *The Artist Himself Doesn't Always Know It's Schlock.*   There is little doubt that Salvador Dali knows that his recent works are schlock. It was recently revealed that Dali routinely signed huge quantities of blank paper which were later filled in by a business colleague with "Dali" works. Not all schlock artists, however, are aware of their status. Hogarth may have preferred his subtlest works, or he may have been so close to his audience that he too preferred the more obvious ones. In other words, not all schlock artists are guilty of *intentional* schlock.

Artists to Avoid

There are some artists the serious collector should *always* avoid. They are incapable of a genuine sentiment, a heartfelt color, or spontaneous brushstroke. They are the masters of schlock:

Bernard Buffet.   During the 1950s and 1960s, Buffet rose to the top of the contemporary art market. His "spare" paintings, recognizable by their slashing, bold, black lines, impressed connoisseur and casual collector alike. Fortunately, about 1970, time caught up with the Paris-based artist. He painted a few too many maudlin clowns and quaint Parisian tourist traps for his own good. People finally recognized his "spare" style for what it was—simplistic rather than simple. Buffet's prices plummeted as collectors rushed to unload their erstwhile prizes.

Frank Gallo.   Gallo's sculptures of nubile young girls fashioned from plastic resin looked interesting when they first appeared on the art market in the 1960s. More than a few museum curators added one to their collections. But the prepubescent bodies and young faces with bored, wistful looks have failed to pass the test of time—the ultimate arbiter of schlock. One by one, all of those museum purchases have gone into basement hiding.

Peter Max.   Several decades from now, Peter Max's poster art will still have historical interest. He managed to capture—notably in his famous portraits of the Beatles—the essence of pop culture in the sixties. But the future's interest in Peter Max will be *strictly* historical.

LeRoy Neiman.   The King of Schlock. Illustrating the 1976 Summer Olympics for ABC made Neiman a household name. His trick is to choose subjects so patently popular that no one cares what the art actually looks like: athletics primarily, but not exclusively. It's hard to think ill of an "artist" clever enough to devote a series to the great golf courses of the Western world. But Neiman did not become the king of schlock by subject matter alone; his guilt extends to shamelessly garish colors and splashy, inept brushwork.

Norman Rockwell.   Painter *par excellence* of Mom, apple pie, and the Fourth of July, Rockwell traffics in clichés. The subjects are not as bad as the way they're painted. His illustrator's style tended to embalm everything it portrayed. That's why his quickly brushed oil sketches are considerably more appealing than his finished works. In fact, many of these sketches rise above their clichéd subject matter and achieve the level of genuine art.

Fritz Scholder.   Scholder updates the nostalgic western subject matter of Remington and Russell with a few avant-garde touches: flat, "bold" areas of color and a few "honest" drips of paint. The combination of sentimental subjects and pseudo-sophisticated techniques has seduced a number of otherwise discerning collectors.

Simbari. Ignore both the alluring European name and the alluring European subjects: resorts on the Côte d'Azur, Parisian cafés, racecourses, and the like. Schlock is schlock, in any language.

These are the grand masters of schlock. There are a number of other artists, however, who have tarnished their reputations by creating schlock at some point in their careers. These artists should also be avoided by any collector who is not confident of his ability to distinguish the good from the bad:

Alexander Calder. Calder was unquestionably a great sculptor. But you have to be an uncritical Calder fan to hold his paintings and especially his prints in the same high regard. The thick black lines and red, yellow, and blue forms are childish, not childlike. In fact, Calder himself rarely made his prints; craftsmen transferred the images from gouache to silk screen.

Marc Chagall. At the beginning of the century, Chagall painted great, visionary paintings, based on Russian folk art. But how often can you repeat the same vision before it loses its power to surprise and mystify? Unfortunately, after much repetition, Chagall's works did lose that power, and, along with it, their artistic quality.

Salvador Dali. Dali is the premier example of a good artist gone bad. A pioneering master of the Surrealist movement during the 1920s and 1930s, he created riveting works like the famous *Persistence of Memory,* the landscape with melting watches. After about 1933, however, Dali's output grew increasingly commercial. The best that can be said for it is that it's *exuberantly* commercial. In fact, Dali's late works are little better than autographs: The signature, not the image, commands the high price. Richard H. Solomon of Pace Editions in New York recently delivered Dali's eulogy as an artist. "Originally, Dali was a very legitimate and brilliant Surrealist," Solomon said, "but somewhere along the line—and it's hard to put a finger on where—he became a merchandising phenomenon."

Giorgio de Chirico. De Chirico established a group of artists in Italy between 1915 and 1930 known as the Scuola Metafisica, the Metaphysical School. His paintings from that period are key works of twentieth-century art. After 1930, however, De Chirico abandoned this early, innovative style for a series of tedious academic paintings. Unable to market these new works, he spent the rest of his career making copies of his own earlier works.

Joan Miró.   Miró's work ranges in quality from very good to very bad. This is particularly true of his prints, the very works a beginning collector is most likely to buy. While his early prints are considered masterly, most of the later ones—the ones found in most galleries—are far from it. There are a few exceptions, of course, even among his latest prints, especially his post-1966 aquatints.

Victor Vasarely.   During the 1940s and 1950s, Vasarely painted a number of elegant black-and-white abstractions which created, almost incidentally, a sensation of optical movement. Since then, his paintings have been little more than optical tricks. Besides, he made the fatal mistake of adding color to his formula without first developing a talent for it.

Bad Art Is a Bad Investment

Since schlock art appeals to such a large public, some people believe the demand for it will always outstrip the supply—a formula for an attractive investment. Jack Solomon, President of the Circle Fine Art Corporation, predicts that "the future of the market lies [in those] artists who relate to the broadest number of people." Norman Rockwell will last longer, goes the argument, than Robert Rauschenberg.

The argument has two major flaws. First, even though the demand for schlock art is heavy, so is the supply. Whereas the supply of serious art is limited by the constraints of creative inspiration, the supply of schlock is limited only by the constraints of the marketplace.

Second, even though a large public might someday pay $5,000 for a LeRoy Neiman sports print, it will never pay $50,000. Record prices are generated by competition between a few passionately committed collectors, not by the curiosity of many casual fans. Thousands of people spending $5,000 may make a LeRoy Neiman rich; they may even make a Jack Solomon rich. But they won't make each other rich.

The Care and Preservation of Art

Henry Kissinger has said that Americans are better at wanting than at having. The same could be said about art collectors: They bring energy and diligence to the search for new objects, but ignore the need to care for those objects once acquired. "It's amazing," says Christian Jussel of Vernay & Jussel, the New York furniture dealer, "the same people who take perfect care of the possessions they use every day like a car, will buy a painting or rug or piece of furniture, and that's the last they want to hear about it."

Unless a collector is going to care properly for a work of art, he shouldn't buy it. Caring for a work means having it restored if it's in poor condition. It means treating the work properly so that no new problems develop. Finally, caring means protecting and insuring the work against fire and theft.

There are two reasons to care for a work of art. The first is selfish. Proper care will maintain both the beauty and the investment value of your collection. You'll enjoy the objects more while you own them and they'll be worth more if you decide to sell them. The second reason is selfless. Regardless of his legal rights, a collector is really just a trustee of the art he acquires. It's his to keep and enjoy for a time, then pass on for others to enjoy after him. In this fundamental sense, a collector acquires duties as well as rights when he purchases a work of art. Prime among these duties is the obligation to care for his collection.

SECURITY

Art theft has become a major national and international crime. In the United States alone, reported thefts (many thefts go unreported) now number more than fifty thousand annually, and that number is doubling every two years. According to Thomas McShane, senior arts thefts investigator for the Federal Bureau of Investigation, "Art thefts are now second only to narcotics activity."

Many thefts are the work of organized crime and employ sophisticated art experts. One group, McShane notes, is capable of stealing antiques in Europe and flying them to Los Angeles within twenty-four hours. By working so quickly, the group can have the antiques sold by the time they're reported missing. "Disposal of even well-known art items can be easier than might be otherwise supposed," says McShane. "International fencing operations are growing rapidly." In fact, some works are stolen "to order." A client decides he wants a Rembrandt, locates a poorly guarded one in a public or private collection, then commissions a professional thief to steal it for him.

Fortunately, organized crime leaves most art collections alone. Art thefts on a more modest level are committed by "unorganized," common thieves who generally prefer works in which the materials are intrinsically valuable, especially silver and jewelry. Even a small-time thief can fence a Georgian silver service or a rare Indian Mughal necklace. Although art thefts are relatively rare among typical collections, however, you never know when a thief who came in for your stereo will walk out with your Rembrandt. Regardless of the odds, it pays to take adequate precautions.

Security Starts at Home

Start by making your home more secure. The effort is certainly worth it: The steps you take to protect your art collection will help protect everything else in your home.

Doors and Locks. Exterior doors should be solid. If they aren't solid wood, they should be covered with metal. The lock—or locks—should be tamperproof. You will want at least two. One should be a multiple-point locking device such as those manufactured by Fishet, Mul-T-Lock, and Spider Lock of America. At least one of the locks should have a pick-resistant cylinder (leading brands include Abloy, Emhart, Keso, Medeco, and Sargent). This lock should have several nonremovable bolts and should be protected by a guard plate so that the thief can't simply remove the lock instead of picking it. Finally, both a peephole and a chain lock are essential.

Windows. There are two ways to protect a regular sash window. First, you can drill holes through the sides of the frames where the two sections overlap. When the window is closed, you simply insert a five-sixteenths-inch bolt through the hole. A second method is to prop a piece of wood between the top of the bottom section and the window casing. This method is simpler but also more unsightly. Similar arrangements can be used to protect sliding glass doors and windows.

All these arrangements prevent a thief only from breaking a lock and entering; they don't prevent him from breaking the *window* and entering. Only bars can prevent that.

Noise Alarms. For $50 or less, you can buy a burglar alarm that can be attached to a door or window and that will emit a piercing wail if anyone tries to force it. These alarms operate very much like the more common battery-powered fire alarms which you should also install. You can even get a system that connects several windows and doors to a single alarm for less than $100.

Of course these noise alarms are useful when you're in the vicinity. But they can also be useful if you're away. A thief is looking for an easy house to rob. A piercing sound is likely to send him searching for easier prey. In fact, if you have a decal on your window indicating that the house is protected by an alarm, the thief may just move on. "You don't ever stop crime," says an FBI official, "you just force it to go somewhere else."

Central-Station and Direct-Connect Alarms. "A local alarm system is good for an ordinary home," says Robert Volpe, New York City's chief art-theft investigator. "But if the home has an expensive collection, something a burglar really wants, he's liable to try again, only the next time he will be prepared to defeat the system." For more certain protection, at much higher cost, you can purchase an alarm system that not only scares burglars away but also alerts the police and the fire department. *Direct-connect* systems send the message directly to the police. Although desirable, such systems are discouraged by police departments who complain of too many false alarms. If you can't secure a direct-connect alarm, try a *central-station* alarm. This will send a message to a command center which in turn alerts the police or fire department, sometimes after running an independent check.

A Variety to Choose From. Alarm systems come in a wide variety of makes, models, and price ranges. Some are extremely sophisticated, capable of detecting someone walking through a room, as well as someone forcing a window or door. There are motion detectors, microwave systems, and infrared systems. The primary drawback of these more sophisticated systems (aside from expense) is the ease with which they can be accidentally triggered—by a child, a pet, or even the owner during a momentary lapse of concentration. An official of ADT, one of the leading alarm manufacturers, has said, "The best system in the world is no good if it isn't turned on or if the door isn't locked."

How to Find an Alarm Company. You should take care in selecting the company to install your system. Although comparison shopping is appropriate, price should not be your main consideration. Efficiency and solvency are the key factors. You want a company that will get the police or the fire department to you when you need them. Since one company's alarm system can rarely be adapted, you also want a company that won't go out of business any time in the foreseeable future, leaving you with an elaborate, expensive, and useless alarm system. Among the major national alarm companies are ADT, Holmes, Honeywell, and Wells Fargo. If you want to use a local firm, ask your local police department for recommendations.

Operation Identification. Finally, you should be aware of Operation I. D. This is a program, offered by many police departments throughout the country, in which you can have your objects permanently marked with your Social Security number and location code making them easier to trace and more difficult to fence. To put the thief on notice that your goods are marked, the police will supply you with Operation I. D. decals. The identification numbers are etched in an inconspicuous place with an electric tool. Even porcelains and glass objects can be marked, though this is a delicate job. A more sensible method is to mark the bottoms with a code in fluorescent paint. The police recommend that you inscribe works on paper with the same codes using invisible but indelible ink. The primary disadvantage of Operation I.D. is that by permanently marking your works you risk lowering their value.

Other Suggestions

There are several other steps you can and should take to protect your collection:

      1. When you go on vacations, have a friend pick up your mail and newspapers.

2. Leave an outside light shining when you're home and when you're away.

3. Don't mention how long you'll be away in a telephone answering machine message.

4. Don't talk about travel schedules or your collection in public places.

5. If you lend your works to a museum for exhibition, lend them anonymously.

6. Avoid articles about your collection. They tend to ennumerate the finest items and clever thieves have been known to use them as shopping lists.

Notify the Authorities. If, despite your precautions, a work of art *is* stolen, call the police immediately. The FBI can be contacted if the work or works stolen are worth more than $50,000, or if you have reason to believe that the works have crossed state lines. You'll also want to notify one of the organizations that records thefts: The Art Dealers Association of America (575 Madison Avenue, New York, N.Y. 10021) or the International Foundation for Art Research, commonly called IFAR (654 Madison Avenue, New York, N.Y. 10021). IFAR publishes a monthly newsletter, *Stolen Art Alert,* that lists and illustrates stolen objects. It's also a good idea to notify newspapers and to place advertisements in art publications. Unfortunately, even if you take all these steps, your chances of recovering a stolen work remain slim.

INSURANCE

You must insure your collection. Insuring your collection may not enable you to replace lost objects; nothing can do that. But adequate insurance does allow you to minimize your financial loss.

Homeowners' and Tenant Homeowners' Policies

If you have a homeowners' policy or a tenant homeowners' policy, your collection is already insured against fire, theft, smoke, vandalism, hail, ice, sleet, falling trees, falling airplanes, and a host of other occurrences, both plausible and implausible. It's *not* insured against gradual deterioration, wear and tear, rust, mold, rot, moths, vermin, inherent defects, war, nuclear damage, and damage from improper efforts at restoration or repair. It also is not insured against your own carelessness. If you accidentally damage the object or lose it, your insurance will not cover the loss.

The main limitation of a typical policy is the amount the insurance company will pay if a covered loss occurs. Your policy protects both your dwelling and the personal property located in it. The personal property, however, is protected only up to a certain percentage of the value of the dwelling—generally 50 percent. If your collection is worth more, the remainder is unprotected.

Fine-Arts Policies

The best way to insure your art collection is to purchase a special fine-arts policy. This is either a "personal articles floater" or a "scheduled personal property endorsement" attached to your primary policy. (The policy is "scheduled" because the protected items are listed individually.) The primary additional protection of a fine-arts floater is against accidental loss. In addition, you can insure every work in your collection at its full appraised value.

Rates. Fortunately, fine-arts floaters are inexpensive. (Policies on silver and jewelry are the major exceptions.) A floater on a collection worth $25,000 might cost only $25 a year. Rates will vary, however, depending on several factors including location, building construction, proximity to police and fire departments, and security arrangements.

Requirements. The money you put into a central alarm system will be recouped over the years in lower insurance charges. In fact, a company probably won't issue a fine-arts floater for a collection worth more than $100,000 unless it is protected by a central alarm system. Under no circumstances will an insurance company issue a fine-arts floater without a recent bill of sale or professional appraisal. In order to maintain the policy, you must then have the appraisal updated periodically, usually every three years.

Additional Coverage. If you add a new work to your collection, most floaters will provide additional coverage for a period of up to three months and an amount up to 25 percent of the policy. This provision gives you time to arrange permanent additional coverage for the new acquisition.

There are several clauses or "endorsements" you may want to add to your fine-arts policy. One is an inflation-guard provision which automatically adjusts the appraised value of your collection to account for inflation. You may also wish to arrange special coverage for periods when objects are not under your physical control: loaned to a museum, displayed in a gallery, or awaiting auction.

Doing Without.   Despite the relatively low cost of fine-arts insurance, some collectors still do without it. They prefer to leave their objects uninsured, which means that they assume the risk of loss themselves. Part of that risk, however, is shared by the United States government in the form of a tax deduction. You can't take a deduction if you lose money when a work is sold unless the IRS considers you a "dealer" or an "art investor" instead of a simple "collector." But regardless of your status, you can take a full deduction when a work is either lost or destroyed.

CONSERVATION

If a work is in poor condition when you buy it, or is damaged while in your possession, you will need the services of a skilled conservator. Note that the preferred term is now "conservator," not "restorer": a change in terminology that reflects changing attitudes toward the care and preservation of art.

Yesterday: Restoration.   Throughout history, severe damage has been done to works of art in the effort to "restore" them. Before 1600, few artists considered their creations immortal; they assumed that time and wear would take their toll. A wornout work would simply be replaced. Works were occasionally salvaged for economic reasons, but the owner's objective was to make them look new again, not to return them to their original state. The artist called upon to do the work felt free to repaint whole areas or, if the canvas was in particularly bad condition, repaint it entirely. No attempt was made to recapture the style of the original; in fact, the restoration was considered an "improvement" if it conformed to more recent fashions.

Today: Conservation.   Today, collectors and conservators alike believe that a work is the expression of the artist's individuality, and should be respected as such. "The concept of restoring has changed as much as the technique," says Professor Giancarlo Colalucci, the conservator charged with cleaning Michelangelo's frescoes in the Sistine Chapel. "We are much more respectful of the masters than the early restorers. We don't try to improve, but to conserve an artistic record."

Conservators devote themselves not to making an object look new but to repairing any major damage that threatens to cause further deterioration. Only after a conservator has corrected these "structural" problems will he attempt to clean the work and reconstruct lost areas. In doing so, he uses materials that have been carefully tested for harmful side effect and that can be easily removed by future conservators.

Collectors and Connoisseurs

A good collector is a ''connoisseur'': He has a thorough understanding of a work's physical properties, as well as its history and quality. You don't have to earn a degree in art conservation, for example, to learn how an oil painting on canvas is constructed.

The artist first builds a *canvas stretcher,* usually of wood, and places wedges or *keys* in the corners to tighten a loose canvas. The canvas is usually made from linen, cotton, or hemp. To keep the oils from eating into and weakening the fibers, the artist coats the canvas with a *sizing,* creating a smooth, absorbent surface to receive the oil paints. These are *pigments* or colored particles suspended in a binding *medium.* The artist builds up the surface with several layers of paint and covers the complete work with *varnish* to protect the finish and reflect light evenly.

Each step in this elaborate procedure can lead to problems of conservation: If stretched too thin or stored in heat or humidity, a canvas can loosen on the frame; if left on a loose canvas, the sizing and paint can crack and flake; if untreated for twenty to fifty years or exposed to harsh sunlight, varnish can begin to discolor.

Conservators: Calling in the Experts

No amateur should attempt to cure any of these common ills. If you tried to reline a loose canvas or reattach flaking paint, you'd only do more damage. If you tried to clean discolored varnish or grime from a picture, you might remove the grime, but you'd probably remove most of the original painting along with it. Although you should never attempt serious conservation work on your own, you should at least know enough about conservation to recognize the need for a conservator's help.

Cost.   Conservation work is extraordinarily expensive. A conservator is a skilled professional with extensive training in both laboratory chemistry and studio art. Like the training, the work itself is long and laborious. Reattaching tiny flakes of paint on a damaged canvas is both time-consuming and boring. The monumental task of cleaning the Sistine Chapel frescoes of Michelangelo will take chief Vatican conservator Colalucci and a team of assistants twelve years and three million dollars. Even for conservation on much more modest works, you should be prepared to pay hundreds or even thousands of dollars.

Before hiring a conservator, be sure to get an estimate. Consider how much the object is worth, then decide whether the contemplated conservation work is structural or merely cosmetic. Larry Shar, a conservator in New York, told *The Collector-Investor,* ''More important than cleaning is structure—the canvas or panel. The esthetic part you can really take care of anytime, but if the painting is starting to flake, or if it is not adhering, it must be fixed at all costs.''

How to Find a Conservator.   Conservators, like doctors, are available at varying levels of expertise and with a wide range of specialities. You want a conservator who is highly skilled in the field appropriate to your needs. The best way to find a good conservator is to ask a museum curator or dealer. The better conservators are also generally fellows of The American Institute for Conservation of Historic and Artistic Works. You can write for a list of fellows to 1511 K Street N.W., Suite 725, Washington, D.C. 20005.

MAINTENANCE

If you're not trained as a conservator, you should never attempt sophisticated conservation work on your own. There is much you *can* do, however, to ensure that a work will not require conservation work. Maintenance is simply a matter of knowing what can hurt a work of art and how to prevent it:

Human Error

Most damage is caused by human error. Collectors cut paintings down to fit a particular wall, destroy drawings by hanging them in direct sunlight, or splinter valuable furniture by careless moving or improper use.

Temperature and Relative Humidity

High temperatures and humidity levels are dangerous, particularly if they fluctuate radically from day to day or from season to season. Chemical deterioration almost never takes place without water. Humidity causes metals to oxidize, textiles to discolor, and woods to warp. It also encourages mold and other forms of microbiological infestation. Humidity is particularly dangerous on pastels.

For most art materials, the optimum temperature is 62 to 68 degrees Fahrenheit and the optimum relative humidity is 45 to 55 percent. These conditions should be maintained throughout the year. That usually means careful air-conditioning and dehumidification during the summer, heating and humidification during the winter. In addition, works should be kept away from heating and air-conditioning ducts, window air-conditioners, and fireplaces.

To protect wood from drying out and cracking, it should be periodically waxed. Many dealers recommend Butcher's wax or Simoniz wax, among other brands.

Sunlight

Sunlight can wreak havoc, especially on works of art on paper. It bleaches the colors and dries the paper, weakening and yellowing it. Harsh light can also discolor or even crack varnish, and can cause bitumen, a dark pigment used in many nineteenth-century paintings, to soften and wrinkle. Harsh light can also foster the growth of small rust-colored mold spores, or *foxing* as it is called. Although natural sunlight is the primary danger, exposure to any high-intensity light, such as that of a fluorescent lamp, can also be damaging. Incandescent lights are preferable, but still harmful.

Avoid hanging paintings directly across from a window. If you insist on displaying a work on paper, it should be relegated to a wall that receives little or no sunlight. In addition, the windows of the room or the Plexiglas used in the frame should be coated to screen harsh ultraviolet rays. Experienced collectors, however, avoid hanging works on paper for long periods anywhere, no matter how dark.

Insects and Vermin

Unfortunately, some of the greatest art lovers are insects and vermin. Silverfish delight in the sizing on fine paper. The lowly cockroach is a connoisseur of watercolor pigments. Termites are as easily satisfied by the legs of a Louis XV commode as by the foundation of your house. Moths and rats refuse to distinguish between a blanket and a Bukhara.

Microbiological infestation is more difficult to detect than insects and vermin, but ultimately just as dangerous. Fungi and mold spores travel on dust particles. If it's hot and humid, they're likely to make a pleasant home in your works of art.

Keep your home free of vermin and insects. Fumigate regularly. Spray-can insecticides are not enough; it's a job for professional exterminators, although you should instruct them to use insecticides that won't harm works of art. Fungicides are also available, but only an expert conservator knows how to use them on works of art. To prevent microbiological infestation in the first place, keep your environment cool and dry. You might also try placing containers of paradichlorobenzene crystals (mothballs) near your works, although caution must be used with nineteenth- and twentieth-century works that may include synthetic dyes.

Dirt and Pollution

Never hang anything over a working fireplace; both the heat and the soot can damage it. Accumulated soot on a painting is expensive to remove and can cause permanent damage. Soot *can't* be removed from works on paper, however, and *always* causes permanent damage. Automobile and industrial pollution is harmful, especially to paper, textiles, stone, and metal.

Matting and Framing Works on Paper

In framing works of art on paper, the mat is the key element. The mat, not the frame, touches the work and therefore is capable of doing the most damage. Mats are made from one of two materials: wood pulp or cotton rag. Whenever you have a work matted, be sure to ask for 100 percent rag matting. You have to *ask* for it. It's more expensive than the other kind, so if you don't ask for it, the framer will almost always give you a mat made from wood pulp. Don't settle for matting that has rag sheets on either side of a wood pulp filler. It's got to be *all* rag—both the masking board *and* the backboard.

The Worries of Wood Pulp.   Why is the material so critical? Unpurified wood pulp is acidic and acid destroys paper; the higher the raw wood-pulp content, the more acid. That's why newsprint—which is 100 percent wood pulp—self-destructs in a few months. Mats with even the slightest raw wood-pulp content will begin to self-destruct after a few years. That's only the beginning of the trouble. The acid will eventually seep into the work of art and destroy it, too.

Check the Mats You Already Have.   It is important to ask for all-rag matting when you have a new work matted. But if this is the first you've heard about the dangers of wood pulp, you should also check every mat already in your collection for the telltale signs. If the mat is foxed or discolored, it was clearly made from poor quality board. Unfortunately, the danger signs are often more subtle. Most bad mats are made from wood pulp faced with rag. If the beveled edge of the mat looks darker or dirtier than the front, it's probably because the cut edge, which reveals the acidic core, has already begun to self-destruct. Check to make sure that no foxing or other serious damage has affected the work, then have it rematted immediately.

Hinges.   There are several methods of attaching a work to the backboard. The best is to use hinges which permit the paper to move freely and can be easily removed. The number of hinges depends on the size of the work (two for a small work, three or more for a large one). The placement depends on the format. The hinges, like the mat itself, must be nonacidic, preferably a thin, strong Japanese paper. The hinges should be attached not with glue or synthetic adhesives but with library paste or, better yet, the nonacidic starch paste that museums use. Don't use masking tape, Scotch tape, or dry mounting.

Make Sure the Mat Is Thick Enough.   You should also make sure the mat is thick enough to separate the surface of the work from the glass. If there's not enough separation, moisture may condense under the glass and transfer to the paper. The paper might even stick to the glass and be seriously damaged. Most collectors prefer four-ply matting, though two-ply is acceptable on small works. If you frame a work of art on paper without matting it, you should ask the framer to recess it by inserting wedges along the insides of the frame.

Glass.   Glass prevents dust and grease from accumulating. Whether you use glass or Plexiglas is a matter of choice, though museum curators generally prefer Plexiglas, especially for large works, because it is lighter and less fragile. Plexiglas can also be easily coated to screen out harmful ultraviolet rays. (Be sure to ask for U.F. 3 or 4 Plexiglas.) Plexiglas also has some drawbacks: it costs more, scratches easily, and attracts static electricity. You should never use Plexiglas in framing pastels, even if it has been sprayed with an antistatic coating, since the slightest residual charge might dislodge particles of the delicate pastel chalk.

Framing Oil Paintings

Although framing a painting on canvas presents fewer problems than framing a work on paper, certain precautions should be taken. First, the canvas stretcher should fit somewhat loosely in the frame to accommodate their different rates of expansion and contraction. Instead of nailing the stretcher to the frame, use metal clip fasteners.

Protecting the Front.   There is no need to put glass over an oil painting. It not only creates a glare, it also traps moisture. The only time to consider *glazing*—or putting glass on a painting—is when the surface is in such disrepair that glass is needed to prevent the loss of flaking paint. If you have a painting that has deteriorated to this extent, you should be thinking about conservation, not glazing.

Protecting the Back.   Although you needn't cover the front of an oil painting, you should cover the back. A sheet of thick cardboard will keep out the dust and protect the canvas. You shouldn't seal the back off entirely, however, or else you'll restrict air circulation. One possibility is to leave a small hole covered with gauze in the cardboard backing.

Finding a Framer

If you use a good framer, you shouldn't have to teach him his trade. A good framer, for example, would never use anything but rag matting. A good framer may also be able to help you decide which frame *looks* best, since he will have considerable experience framing similar items for dealers, curators, and major collectors.

Bad framers have a remarkable capacity to destroy a work of art. They have been known to cut prints down to a "manageable" size: erase "unsightly" signatures; even "touch up" a faded spot or two. Although framers are legally responsible for these acts of negligence, it may be impossible to repair the damage and it's difficult to recover the financial loss. Moreover, framers are responsible for damage that occurs to a work in their shops only if the damage results from their negligence. If a painting is scratched, scuffed, or damaged by "mere" careless handling or improper storage, the loss is yours.

How do you find a good framer? The answer will sound familiar by now: Ask a good dealer or museum curator. There is often only one competent framer in any locale, and the dealer or curator can tell you which one that is. Take the name and check it out for yourself. Inspect the framer's materials and methods to ensure that they conform to the standards listed above.

Doing It Yourself. The services of a good framer are expensive. If you collect works on paper and mat them instead of framing them, you may want to lower your costs by matting them yourself. All it takes is mat board, hinging tape, and a mat knife (all of which can be purchased cheaply at an art-supply store). To cut a mat properly requires considerable dexterity with the knife. It is no easy matter to maintain a beveled edge at a consistent angle along a straight line. So practice on scraps before cutting your first mat.

You may want to take advantage of the more sophisticated machinery and the patient instruction available at do-it-yourself framing establishments like Frameworks. These shops are also helpful if you want to make your own frame. They will sell you the molding and provide you with the necessary tools.

Placing a Work

Never hang a painting in oils on canvas from the stretcher. Hang it from a wire stranded and strong enough to hold somewhat more than the weight of the work. The wire should be attached to ring-eye screws inserted in the frame: an arrangement that permits a more even distribution of the weight.

The nail should be strong enough to hold the work and anchored firmly into the wall. If you can't find a stud, you may have to use a different kind of nail: masonry nails for masonry walls, butterfly screws for plaster walls. If you have any questions about hanging a work (especially a large one), consult a carpenter.

Dust. All pictures should tilt slightly forward from the wall. This will help keep dust from accumulating on the front and permit air to circulate freely around the back. Oil paintings should be dusted only with a feather duster or a very soft brush. They should not be dusted often, and if there's any sign of flaking or other weakening of the pigment, they shouldn't be dusted at all. If you clean a picture covered with glass, don't use a spray-on glass cleaner unless you spray it on the cloth *before* wiping the surface. Because Plexiglas is easily scratched, it should be treated with particular care.

Objects. As you can imagine, objects—like paintings—should be securely positioned. Ask an expert for advice if the object is particularly fragile.

Storage and Shipping

If you decide to store a work, you should be especially careful. First, make sure the storage area meets the same standards set for display areas: stable, cool temperatures; clean, dry air; no insects and vermin; relative darkness. Don't seal the objects in plastic since this will restrict the free flow of air and encourage condensation.

Paintings. Store paintings vertically, unless they're in bad condition, in which case they should be stored horizontally. Stored paintings should be separated by sheets of corrugated cardboard to keep the frame or screw eyes of one painting from scratching the surface of another. To protect the surface of the painting from dust, fasten a clean piece of cloth or brown paper horizontally across the back of the work, then drape it loosely over the front.

Works on Paper. Prints and other works on paper should be matted and stored in specially prepared *solander boxes*. These are sturdy, dust-free boxes that hold between seventeen and twenty matted works. They have hinged backs that open to permit easy removal. For added protection, a sheet of glassine paper should be placed between the surface of the work and the mat frame. Hold mats with both hands to avoid unnecessary strain, and open them by lifting from the outer edge. Do *not* open them by lifting from the opening or "window," a common practice that often results in serious damage.

Shipment. Most damage to works of art happens during shipment. If you need to move a work, whether to a museum for exhibition, to an auction house for sale, or simply from one room to another, there are certain precautions you should be aware of.

Avoid Unnecessary Moving. Any time you move a work of art, you risk damaging it. Therefore, move your collection as seldom as possible. This is especially important if a work is unusually fragile. Many collectors, for example, make it a rule never to loan a pastel to a museum.

Know the Object. It is important to know the condition of an object before you consider moving it. You may wish to check with a conservator before any move.

Wash Your Hands. You should always wash your hands before handling works of art, especially works of art on paper. Perspiration, not dirt, is the real problem. Your hands leave a film of grease that attracts dust and dirt. Metal sculptures with delicate patinas are so badly damaged by finger marks that conservators wear thin white gloves when handling them. If you think *this* is precious, they wash their hands before putting the gloves on and they wash the gloves frequently.

Hold Works with Two Hands. You want to avoid putting any additional stress on one part of the work and the possibility of dropping it. You should hold pictures with the surface facing towards you, so that, if you accidentally bump into something, the image will not be damaged. When carrying pieces of furniture, hold them by a structural element: a chair by the seat, for example, not by the back or arms. If a work is heavy, don't try to carry it yourself.

Watch Out for the Frame. Frames are often as fragile—and as valuable—as the works themselves. Be as careful with the surface of a gold-leaf frame as with the painting itself. Don't lean a frame against a wall without first placing a protective pad (a small carpet sample is ideal) underneath it.

Professional Movers.   If you plan to ship a work a long distance, you probably should use a professional packing and moving company. Be sure to use one that specializes—or at least has experience—in transporting works of art. A dealer or museum curator can recommend the leading specialist in your area.

Doing It Yourself.   If you do move a work of art yourself, you should wrap and crate it carefully. The crate should be equipped with handles. It should also be large enough to accommodate the work without touching it at any point. The work should be wrapped in waterproof paper, then surrounded with plenty of resilient packing material. Although the crate itself can be nailed together, after the object is in place the top should be fastened with screws to avoid jarring. *Fragile, This Side Up,* and *Keep Dry* labels are essential. When you unwrap the work, check for any dislodged pieces.

If you place more than one painting in a single crate, remove the screw eyes and wires so they won't damage the surface of the adjacent work. You should also separate them with sheets of cardboard. If you wrap a work that's framed with glass, place strips of tape over the entire glass surface. If the glass should break en route, the tape will prevent the loose glass from damaging the work. Do *not,* however, tape a Plexiglas frame. The corners of gilt plaster frames should be specially protected by folded newspaper or corrugated cardboard.

For More Information

Cincinnati Art Museum, *Art Conservation: The Race Against Destruction* (Cincinnati, Ohio: Cincinnati Art Museum, 1978).

Francis W. Dollos and Ross L. Perkinson, *How to Care for Works of Art on Paper,* 3rd edition (Boston: Museum of Fine Arts, 1973).

Frieda Kay Fall, *Art Objects: Their Care and Preservation: A Handbook for Museums and Collectors* (La Jolla, Calif.: Laurence McGilvery, 1973).

Scott Hodes, *What Every Artist and Collector Should Know about the Law,* foreword by Harold Haydon, A Dutton Visual Book (New York: E. P. Dutton & Co., Inc., 1974).

George L. Stout, *The Care of Pictures* (New York: Dover, 1948).

Robert Weinstein and Larry Booth, *Collection, Use and Care of Historical Photographs* (Nashville, Tenn.: American Association for State and Local History, 1977).

Carl Zigrosser and Christa M. Gaehde, *A Guide to the Collecting and Care of Original Prints* (New York: Crown Publishers, Inc., 1965).

INDEX